T0010702

Expand Your
Magnificent
MIND

Expand Your Magnificent MIND

More Insights on Success from José Silva

José Silva

with José Silva Jr. and Ed Bernd Jr.

MEDIA

Published 2023 by Gildan Media LLC
aka G&D Media
www.GandDmedia.com

EXPAND YOUR MAGNIFICENT MIND. Copyright © 1969–2023 by José Silva and José Silva Royalties Inc. All rights reserved.

No part of this book may be used, reproduced or transmitted in any manner whatsoever, by any means (electronic, photocopying, recording, or otherwise), without the prior written permission of the author, except in the case of brief quotations embodied in critical articles and reviews. No liability is assumed with respect to the use of the information contained within. Although every precaution has been taken, the author and publisher assume no liability for errors or omissions. Neither is any liability assumed for damages resulting from the use of the information contained herein.

Front Cover design by David Rheinhardt of Pyrographx

Interior design by Meghan Day Healey of Story Horse, LLC

Library of Congress Cataloging-in-Publication Data is available upon request

ISBN: 978-1-7225-0646-9

10 9 8 7 6 5 4 3 2 1

CONTENTS

PART 2
SOME BASIC TECHNIQUES FOR YOU TO USE

PART 3
SOME PERSONAL REFLECTIONS

PART 4
WHAT MOTIVATED MY FATHER

Contents

INTRODUCTION

by Ed Bernd Jr.

An Extraordinary Life

Every now and then somebody comes along whose achievements rise far above the ordinary; rise far above even the great achievements of other notable people.

Those achievements can be in the arts, they can involve fundamental scientific discoveries, perhaps entertainment or sports, maybe government and politics.

In some instances, such a person might directly touch the lives of millions of people. But it is a rare thing indeed for anyone to do what José Silva has done:

José Silva has achieved greatness because other people have become greater as a result of his life.

He has been directly responsible—through personal contact, or through lecturers he has trained—for helping millions of people worldwide take greater control over the events in their own lives, and thus relieve suffering and help make the world a better place to live.

Meet José Silva

Only the barest outline of the sacrifices he has made are known: the hours spent in study rather than with his family, the criticism and ridicule of his friends because he was exploring something new and strange and unknown to them, the obvious cost in money and time and personal effort, the sacrifices of prestige and honor that should have been his for success in other areas.

How long has this gone on?

"He was always reading books," a woman who knew him when they were children recalled recently.

"Usually he would read while he was eating," another friend said. "He was very methodical, very determined."

Another old friend added, "Once he started something, he stayed with it until he completed it."

Speaking of their younger days, one of José Silva's friends explained, "Basically, he was a man of action. He did not discuss his plans ahead of time, and he did not dwell on what he had done afterwards."

The composite picture reveals a man whose entire life was devoted to things that eventually led him to greatness—not the greatness of fame for personal achievement, but greatness because of the achievements of so many other people who have had contact with him.

The José Silva Story

Not many people throughout history can claim to have started with so little, come so far, and achieved so much.

He had lost both of his parents by the time he was six, went to work instead of going to school—he never attended school a day in his life as a student. Yet his scientific discoveries about the mind and human potential have literally changed the consciousness of humanity.

When he was fourteen years old he studied a borrowed correspondence course in radio repair and over the next few years built the biggest electronics repair business in South Texas.

He learned to box in order to defend himself and was good enough that he fought professionally in clubs around South Texas.

He took voice lessons that he had originally purchased for his brother Juan (who wasn't interested) and was so good that the Mexican government offered him a scholarship to study voice in Italy for a year. He was an American citizen, but his father was Mexican and that was enough for the Mexican government.

He was an inventor too, and held three patents including one that was the first patent ever issued that stated "Human concentration turns on an educational program."

Studying the mind

José began to study psychology—the study of human behavior—in 1944, and soon expanded his research to include the brain and mind.

The mind did not reveal its secrets to him easily. He persisted, investing his own time and money, continuing even though critics scorned him.

Today he is recognized as the leading researcher in the world in the field of the mind and human potential. And José Silva's Ultra-Mind ESP System is leading humanity into the beginning of the second phase of human evolution on the planet.

His ultimate achievement was developing a reliable technique to use your ESP to obtain guidance and support from higher intelligence so that you can develop creative solutions to vexing problems in order to improve living conditions on the planet and fulfill your mission in life.

A Feast to Nourish Your Soul

These brief articles are easy to read whenever you have a few minutes for some inspiration and motivation.

Joe Jr.'s commentary at the beginning of each section of the book provides insights into the man and his research that have only been known to his family and a few close friends . . . until now.

To help you take full advantage of José Silva's wisdom and advice, the book includes an appendix with three ways to learn to enter the alpha brainwave level, and many of the problem-solving techniques to help you change your life for the better.

Joe Jr. made sure that the course material presented in this book is exactly the way his father wanted it.

The benefits you will receive by acting on José Silva's insights are far greater than the false promises made by the knock-off copy-cat courses.

Pick José Silva's Magnificent Mind

If you have taken any of the Silva training, then you already know how to use more of your mind. If not, you can take the training for free in the appendix of this book.

Then as you read José Silva's reflections and analysis of how he and others have used their mind to achieve exceptional success, you can do the same with your own Magnificent Mind.

PART 1
DEVELOPING
THE RIGHT MINDSET

1 How to Qualify to Get the Things You Want *(1988)*

We have gotten several requests for help here at the office during the last few days, and I've been thinking about the way some people go about getting things.

A gentleman stopped by to find out what we have to offer.

He has been traveling all over the country, investigating various programs for the last ten years.

He wanted to know if we had a technique to help him select winners at the race track.

"Then," he said, "I would have the money I need to get started on my plans, and to help other people." He assured us that he is considering signing up for the Silva training.

A woman who is a Silva Method graduate called to ask us to help her program to buy a house. "I have found the house we want," she explained, "but the owner wants too much for it. Please send some energy to help us get it." Her husband has been ill and cannot work she told us, and this house would be perfect for them.

A man called from Europe to tell us that he has been programming to make some sales from an advertisement he published, and if he does not make some sales, his business will go bankrupt. He graduated from the Silva Method Basic Lecture Series (BLS) about a month ago he said, and added, "I have not had any big successes yet." He admitted that he has had some small successes, but needs a big success now to avoid bankruptcy.

This is also the time of year when we receive a lot of anonymous "chain letters." I am amazed at how many people go for these impossible get-rich-quick, something-for-nothing schemes.

Do they really believe that everybody in the world can become wealthy simply by mailing a few letters?

Where do they think the money will come from?

Qualifying for Help

There is a fundamental flaw in many of the requests we get. All too often, people put all their energy into programming for what they want to get, rather than what they are willing to give.

The first thing I think about when I hear these requests is about how to qualify for help from higher intelligence.

What I have learned from almost half a century of research and teaching, and almost seventy-five years of living life on this planet, is that the more we do to help correct problems and make our planet a better place to live, the more things we receive.

That makes sense, doesn't it?

Are you employed? If so, does your employer give you a pay check at the beginning of the week, before you do your work?

Or does your employer wait until the end of the work week to pay you?

In life, first we must earn, then we receive compensation.

Why Are We Here?

I think that we were put onto this planet to help perfect the creation.

The Creator got things started. But we are told that we were made in the image of the Creator.

Image is of the mind, so I think that means that we are like the Creator in the way we can use our minds, not in our physical appearance.

How can we help the Creator to perfect the creation?

We can help people regain health and remain healthy.

We can help find ways to eliminate hunger and poverty and homelessness.

We can help bring peace to our planet.

We can stop fighting with one another.

How do we do this?

The best way I know of is to learn to enter the alpha level and function within the subjective dimension.

At beta we *prey on* each other.

At alpha we *pray for* each other.

How to Get Rich

The "secret" of how to get rich is very simple:

If you need a $1 million, just give $10 million worth of service to humanity.

Notice that I did not say to give $10 million worth of your time and your effort. The value is assigned by the recipients of your service.

How can you do that?

First, develop your subjective skills by practicing working health detection and correction cases the way you learned in the Silva ESP training.

Then, when you are proficient in functioning in the subjective dimension, you can enter your level and ask what you should be doing with your life.

You will get an answer.

Finally, use all of your abilities—physical, mental, and spiritual—to fulfill your mission in life.

When you do this, you will be far more than merely rich monetarily, for you will also have spiritual riches as well, and the sense of satisfaction of knowing that you have fulfilled your mission in life.

Note: If you have not taken any of our Courses, you can learn to enter the alpha level with the free training in the appendix.

2 Success Is Not for the Timid
(1984)

Success is not for the timid. It is for those who seek guidance, make decisions, and take decisive action.

Many people learn how to program very effectively, and often they are able to get those things that they program for. Yet they still find their lives limited and unfulfilled.

Other people are very creative, and come up with many excellent ideas, yet never seem to achieve very much, or make money from their ideas, or help anybody with those ideas.

You find all kinds of people. There are those who are excellent at research, at digging out the facts, yet they never determine what to do with those things that they learn.

Some people are so paralyzed by indecision that they literally become nervous wrecks.

To achieve success—and by success I mean whatever you determine success to be for you—you must take appropriate action, for wishing does not make it so. Proper programming, coupled with appropriate action, makes things happen.

How to Proceed

Let's take it step by step.

First, seek guidance.

You do this by entering your level, the alpha level, functioning in the subjective dimension where prayers are effective, where you can make contact with High Intelligence.

Consider your qualifications, what you like, the things you are good at. Then ask what you should do to serve, how you can help the Creator.

Be aware of your strong points, but do not limit yourself; expect creative guidance.

Then clear your mind; expect an answer.

Some people spend all their time asking and talking. You must be a good listener.

Use the MentalVideo Technique that we teach in the new Silva UltraMind ESP System to obtain guidance. The guidance will come. Then you are ready for the second step. If you aren't familiar with the MentalVideo, you can learn it right now in appendix D.

Second, you decide how to fulfill your purpose in life.

This involves both time at level, and action in the physical world. You must program for success, and you must also start doing something.

Some people want to wait until they are perfect before they are ready to fulfill their missions. This is a mistake. If you were perfect, you would not be here in this classroom called Earth. This is our training ground—on-the-job training.

It is very important to learn all you can while you are here. And it is important to love, and to express your love, to other humans on this planet. Learning how to interact better in relationships with other humans is something very important while we are here.

We have a choice about our relationships with others.

We can compete, or we can cooperate.

Throughout the world, many people are competing—often with guns and bombs. It is important that we change this, and help bring peace to our planet.

3 The Secret of the Silva Method's Success *(1988)*

The main factor that produces the beneficial results in the Silva Method is, learning to use the subconscious consciously.

The Silva Method helps people to think and analyze problems at a lower brain frequency.

Normally people think and analyze problems at a higher brain frequency.

Our research indicates that when we do our thinking and analyzing of problems at a lower brain frequency, extra senses appear to come into action, senses that appear not to be activated at higher brain frequencies.

These are senses of the mind.

Since the mind is also known as the psyche, these senses are called psychic senses.

When a person is thinking and analyzing problems at a lower brain frequency, the person is receiving information psychically.

That is, the person is perceiving information with the senses of the mind: the psychic senses.

A person who becomes proficient in the use of the psychic senses is known as a psychic.

The frequency that brings the best results is the ten cycles per second brain frequency.

Previously the ten cycles per second frequency was thought to exist in the subconscious region of human awareness.

Using the ten cycles frequency consciously means that the Silva Method helps people to function with full awareness at the subconscious dimension.

Being able to function consciously within the subconscious dimension is considered as an expansion of awareness.

The perception of information with the senses of the mind is also called intuition.

So the Silva training helps people enhance the intuitive factor.

Intuition is considered to be a survival mechanism that keeps us out of trouble and helps to bring about what we call good luck, because we intuitively happen to do the right thing at the right time.

We should keep in mind that to solve problems, we must have information.

More success or less success in a person's life is directly proportional to the ability to solve problems.

The perception of more information makes it possible to solve more problems, and to achieve greater success.

Why Some People Are So Lucky

Our research indicates that approximately ninety percent of the population functions at twenty cycles per second when awake, while they are thinking and analyzing problems.

That means that ten percent of humanity has learned to function at ten cycles per second by natural means, when they are thinking and analyzing problems.

Ninety percent think and act at twenty cycles per second. Only ten percent of humanity think at ten cycles per second where they have access to information obtained through the senses of the mind, and then act at twenty cycles.

The difference is not where humanity acts, but where humanity thinks.

Intuition appears to function better at ten cycles than at twenty cycles brain frequency.

To be even more successful in your life, practice entering your level every day, and practice using your psychic senses at ten cycles per second.

This is the most important "secret" of success.

Note: If you have not taken any of our Courses, you can learn to enter the alpha level with the free training in the appendix.

4 Easier to Get Information to Correct Big Problems *(1999)*

Problem solving is very important. It seems as though this is the only thing that we are on this planet to do: to solve problems, and nothing else. All kinds of problems.

They say that problem solving makes for success.

In other words, how successful you are depends on how many problems you have solved.

Everything is problem solving.

And now we know that human intelligence can read—or sense or detect—information on other peoples brains, wherever they are, this accumulation of knowledge brings about the enhancement of wisdom. You can also sense other peoples experiences, and this makes you a superior problem solving agent.

You can use your ability to detect information to help you solve all kinds of problems.

Now of course the easiest information detected on any brain cells is information that has been impressed very strongly.

If we have a weak impression, that will be more difficult to detect.

We need to be more proficient in detecting information that is stored on brain neurons.

The stronger the impression on brain cells, the easier it is to detect that information.

Distance is no barrier.

The kind of problem involved is a barrier, because the type of problem determines how strong the impression of the problem will be on brain neurons.

Usually the information that is strongly impressed on brain cells is that information about the most serious kind of problems.

How Strong Impressions Are Made

By stronger we mean:

The more value in the problem.

The more serious the nature of the problem, the stronger the impression will be.

The more enthusiastic the person is about anything, the stronger the impression will be.

So we are saying that an emotional involvement is a factor. It will be a measure of how strong the impression is.

The more emotional the person, the stronger the impression.

People become emotional about problems.

People become emotional about great things.

So everything that is of importance, you can be assured that it has been impressed very strongly because of its emotional involvement.

Minor things, things of very little value, are very faintly impressed, making it more difficult to detect this information.

So we say that information that is of greatest value is information that has been strongly impressed, because of emotional involvement. This is important, of course, for problem solving.

This is the information we need to solve problems. Information that is necessary, that is valuable, either because it was impressed for the survival type of response, the flight or fight type of response, which involves strong emotion, or the enthusiastic type of response that comes when we are doing something very important.

(This is transcribed from a recording of a presentation that José Silva made at an instructor training session in 1969.)

5 You Can Help Bring Peace to the World
(1985)

What Can We Do to Help Stop World Hunger?
We can program, in a concerted effort, of course. And there are many more things we can do to help stop the suffering that we see and hear about.

Financial contributions to the various relief agencies are urgently needed to help deal with the immediate problem, of course.

In addition, program that your contribution will do the most possible good.

How to Program
When programming, remember that we must program specifically.

That is, we must have a specific target area when we program.

When you see pictures of hungry children on television, use that image to help you in your programming.

Of course, whenever you are programming, you do not need to specify the intermediate steps to your goal.

And you can also program for "This or something better."

Programming in this manner allows room for higher intelligence to make adjustments to the plans that we come up with.

But when programming, program that everyone in a certain area be well fed and have an ample supply of nutritious food. Simply programming that everybody in the world be well fed is not adequate.

The more you know about the subject, the more you will be able to help.

If you are really serious about helping, then build your desire to help by observing and learning about the extent of the problem.

Then program for guidance, and program to relieve the problems and bring about the outcome you desire.

A Lasting Solution

When hunger and poverty no longer exist, then perhaps the world can be at peace. If people have what they need, there will be no reason to fight and conquer.

It appears that governments may not be able to bring all this about. Of course, we keep programming for governments to do all that they can in this area.

But our feeling is that it is up to individuals to make the difference.

When you feel that your needs are being met, then you are much more willing to help others.

When you feel peaceful within yourself, then you are more likely to desire a state of peace on our planet.

This is the case with all people, so what we need to do is to help each individual find ways to become peaceful and prosperous.

How You Can Help

The very best method we have found for helping people become prosperous and at peace with themselves is to help them learn to use more of their mind to correct problems.

When you learn to use all of your abilities, to use both sides of your brain to think with, to function in the subjective dimension just as effectively as you function in the physical dimension, then you will attain peace and prosperity.

That does not mean that we will all be millionaires without problems. It means that we will have all the things we need, and we will have the ability to solve problems as we encounter them.

You can help make such a world a reality by practicing and developing your own abilities, and also by sharing with others. Tell others about the Silva ESP training and help them discover for themselves, the potential of their own minds.

You can also help to center other people. Read the Silva Centering Exercise (the Long Relaxation exercise in appendix A) to them for a total of ten hours to center them.

By doing this, you can convert your own portion of the world into a paradise.

When enough people do this, then the entire world will be a paradise.

6 "The Real Thing" for More Success
(1983)

Through the years, many people seem to have been guided and directed to discover the inner abilities they have, their ability to function clairvoyantly, to function in the subjective dimension.

In fact, we have seen so much of this during the last forty or fifty years, that it appears that High Intelligence was trying to get a message through to us.

Why is it then that we are the only ones who have developed a method to train everyone to use this clairvoyant ability?

Maybe the right formula was found because we looked into things, and accepted things, in a different way. Maybe this is why we got onto this, and started pulling a string that led to bigger things.

Correct Use of Knowledge
Regardless of who you are, what race or religion, or where you come from, it is what you have been able to do to help the Creator with creation, to help humanity in solving human problems that counts.

One man spent most of his life at a university simply proving that clairvoyance exists. He used tests that had nothing to do with correcting problems. And after all that time and all that money, all he could demonstrate was that some people have clairvoyant ability.

Even worse, he found that these people would eventually lose their ability to function clairvoyantly after being tested over and over in his laboratory.

There have been other people who have used their clairvoyant ability in business, to amass great fortunes, but often they suffer tragedies in their lives.

Some people have sold their clairvoyant abilities, but they too, have achieved limited success.

Not one of these people was guided to develop a method to train others, reliably and repeatedly, to function as clairvoyants.

Why were we allowed to do so?

My own feeling is that we were allowed to develop this method because we understood the correct use of this ability.

We have been made in the image of our Creator, God, in our ability to use our minds to create, to use our minds to correct problems.

This is what we should do.

Our research produced practical uses for this human ability, and we were guided to develop a program that can help everyone learn to function clairvoyantly.

We were not put here so we can call on God to solve all our problems. We were put here to help the Creator correct problems of creation. Many people, though, seem not to understand this.

We Have the Tools to Help Ourselves

They ask God to save us against wars and things; They should ask God to save us against our own ignorance!

We are suffering because of our own ignorance; it's a tremendous enemy we have here . . . not knowing why you suffer, yet you suffer. Can you solve the problem?

Well, if you can't solve the problem, then you're going to suffer for it. No wonder there are so many incurables. If you want to become God-like, you better learn how to solve problems.

God solves all problems, so if you want to become a God, you better learn how to solve problems.

You will not become God-like by creating problems; if you create problems instead of solving problems, you are going the wrong direction; not siding with God. And I'll guarantee you that you'll get closer to God by solving problems of the Creator's creation than praying day and night.

Now Is the Time for Action

Just know that God did not intend to discriminate; our Creator gave everybody the same faculties, only we ignore that we have them.

And how many of us are going to the tomb, not knowing we have tremendous healing powers, that could help so many people, but we never tried it we didn't know we had this power?

Now we know how to do it.

Spend fifteen minutes a day at ten cycles brain frequency, aware . . . not asleep, but consciously there, through your own efforts, your knowing how to stay there; become attuned.

Obtain your guidance; find out what your mission in life is. Then go forth and fulfill that mission.

Note: If you have not taken any of our Courses, you can learn many of our techniques with the free training in the appendix.

7 The Silva Way to Total Prosperity
(1985)

(Insight from Silva Method Co-Founder Juan Silva, interviewed by Silva Newsletter editor Ed Bernd Jr.)

At Silva International Headquarters, we like to tell people to "Have a prosperous new year."

Some people ask, "Could you give me some specific advice to help me do just that?"

Come into Juan Silva's office, and make yourself comfortable.

Juan is in a talkative mood today. He has been working hard, as usual. It is Friday, almost lunch time, and this afternoon he will make his weekly trip to the golf course with friends he has been competing with for several decades.

But first, he will relax a bit and share with you some of his experiences and ideas regarding total prosperity—not only financially, but also in health, your social life, spiritual life, and all aspects of life.

Juan knows. In his sixty-eight years on this planet, he has been successful in the import-export business, and later, using Silva Method techniques, as an inventor and manufacturer. Since 1968 he has had outstanding success working with his brother José as director of foreign countries for Silva Mind Control International, Inc.

Q: We are given all we need to be prosperous, Juan. What keeps people from being prosperous?
A: (by Juan Silva) Too many people don't use what they know. They wait until an emergency and then try to make miracles.

It is a matter of complacency. When we have a beautiful instrument, but we don't need it, it doesn't occur to us that we should practice it to maintain our effectiveness.

Q: You mean it is like having an electric drill, and drilling holes in a board at random, but if you're not doing something useful, there's no benefit?
A: In this case, the person is not even drilling holes, but just looking at the beautiful drill. It is right by his side, but he is not using it for any purpose.

Q: Why don't people practice more?
A: They don't practice when they don't have any incentive to go to level, to go to graduate meetings, or to practice at home, because they don't have the necessity.

You should not be overcome by the sensation of that nature. You should always set a goal, for you or for somebody else.

If you don't need anything for yourself, I'm sure your brother needs it, your fellow man needs it. Needs your expertise.

If you don't have any knowledge whatsoever of the compensations that you get by helping somebody else, try it one time.

Try it one time, and you will never let go, because it is a beautiful sensation. It is satisfaction you don't get in dollars and cents.

This is what counts in Mind Control. If you take Mind Control for personal interest, material personal interest, you're out.

Q: I've been taught to program for money, change my attitude about money, and make a lot of money. Is this correct?
A: You have to be motivated. You have to have an incentive of some nature, an inner sensation of awareness and insight shall we say, for the need of that money.

Why do you need that money? What are you going to use it on. "To travel, enjoy myself." Perhaps. If you have it coming, perhaps you can do something like that. If you have worked hard enough, if you deserve the money.

Q: How do I become deserving of it?
A: I believe you become deserving of it if you have been a very good serviceable entity in this manner, that you mean well for everybody, try to help everybody. Doing more than you are paid for.

Q: You mean that first I must do more work, then I will earn more? Not the other way around?
A: But to just sit down and program, "I want to become a millionaire, I want to become a millionaire"—I don't see why, I don't see who, and I don't see how you are going to do it.

But if you have a precondition for it, if you precondition yourself for it, if you have an incentive, if you are motivated because you have a necessity for that, I know doggone good and well you can get it. If you need it.

There are a lot of phrases, affirmations, sayings, but look: it is beautiful to come up with a saying, but have you ever wondered how many live that saying?

One from Benjamin Franklin: I wonder how much you'd be worth if you didn't have a penny in your pocket. That's the value of man. But who lives that?

Q: Programming and talk gets us started, but action speaks. And must come first. Is that what you mean? Well, does it help me to use affirmations to change attitudes like "Money is the root of all evil"?
A: Certainly. Why should you associate money with evil? Why should you? If you need money, you should program for money because you need it. Because you have a useful purpose for it.

Q: So there could be blocks and inhibitions that could hurt us even if we are deserving of it?
A: People who make statements of that nature, about money being evil, right there those people are confirming their own attitudes: they have a negative attitude, and they are not going to achieve very much, not only in the way of money, but in anything else.

Forget about the money; with that attitude you can't achieve very much of anything. Because money—the only reason they can say that money is the root of all evil is because they don't have it.

Q: So rather than work on affirmations about changing my attitude towards money, should I do something that would make me feel more deserving? Provide more service, so I don't feel guilty about accepting my rewards?
A: Certainly. That's right. A person with a negative attitude radiates this. When people like that are around other people, they will turn their backs on them.

Q: So how can one change?
A: Going into your level.

A person like this, I'm sure they have not achieved a depth of physical and mental relaxation that will help them. The deeper the better. I don't think he has any part of it. This is what is going to correct that.

Q: If we are actually going to level, won't we begin to intuitively understand these things, and do the right things?
A: Oh, you will understand this and a lot more besides.

The solution you are looking for might not come, but something else will surface and it will solve your problem.

And you will know it is right, so you will do it. You will start providing a service, to make yourself more valuable.

This is what it's all about.

You enter your level, and this is where everything starts working.

Your memory system starts surfacing, all that you've recorded; your intuitive factor becomes activated, and you have the solution, one way or the other. It might not be the one you selected at beta, but you get it.

Q: Looking at it another way, would you say that people who are not prospering because they are not serving, not really helping and doing the job on the planet, that would indicate that those people are not really going to level? They might be going through the motions, but not really getting to level?
A: In all probability, yes, that is true. We have proven that the solution for most problems—and when I say most, it probably is 100 percent—is at this level.

The solution to both subjective and objective problems. This is where you become the most efficient entity there is. This is where you obtain the solutions to your problems, both mental and physical.

See what I'm trying to say? By achieving these levels, you accomplish what you should, because you are a body-mind entity, not just body, not just mind.

You are going back to where you originated from, before you were contaminated. Of course, it takes a little time and a little effort to learn to achieve these deep levels. Not so much time, but it does take the time to do it, because you are going to ventilate a lot of little traumas.

You're going to ventilate a lot of things that make your lips quiver, make you perspire a little, but you will be relieved.

That's why Mind Control is growing throughout the world like it is. Nothing else—nothing else comes up to it. And do you know why?

Because it is the first time in your life that you have ever entered these levels with conscious awareness. The first time in your life that you have reactivated what was dormant for a long period of time.

Q: Thanks for your time and advice Mr. Silva.
A: You're welcome.

8 Proof Found That Mind Can Accelerate Healing *(1996)*

We began our research into the human mind by studying psychology. That led me to the term hypnosis, so I began to study hypnosis.

This produced a lot of valuable information for us.

For instance, I was testing an individual at one time, for positive hallucination. Positive hallucination means that the person would experience more than was actually present in the environment.

Here is how I did it:

Fooling the Body

I took my subject to a deep theta level. Even though he was deeply hypnotized, he had his eyes open and was watching me.

Then I told him that I was going to touch him with a red hot iron. I picked up a piece of stainless steel with a pair of pliers, and touched the back of his hand with it.

Even though the piece of stainless steel was not hot, when I touched him with it, he screamed. He felt the burn. He felt the heat . . . he experienced a positive hallucination . . . he was sensing more than what was there. The piece of stainless steel was still at room temperature.

Not only did he feel the pain, his body responded as if it had been burned.

Ninety percent of the subjects you do this to develop a little red spot, little red dot, as if they were burned with boiling water, or something like that.

Ten percent develop a blister. I was lucky to see that phenomenon. My subject developed a blister.

I asked myself, "What happened here? I didn't burn him. Did I fool the healing process, the natural healing process of the body, to send healing chemistry to a spot that did not need it?"

I realized that that's exactly what happened. My suggestion caused his healing mechanism to build a blister, build new skin under it, and get rid of that burned skin.

But the skin was not actually burned.

Then I wondered, "Could we send in extra healing chemistry to accelerate the healing process?

Of course you can do that. If you can do one, you can do the other. No question there.

Shortcomings of Hypnosis

Many things came through in experimenting with hypnosis.

But there are shortcomings. For instance, I found that the deeper a person went, the more they forgot.

At a certain level, they start forgetting. If you want them to forget everything, then you suggest to them that they forget everything. If you don't want them to forget, then you tell them to remember everything, and they will.

But you leave it alone, the deeper they go, the more they forget, until they forget everything. They remember nothing. If you want them to remember, you have to tell them to remember, then they will. But naturally, they won't.

We kept on working with our subjects hour after hour after hour after hour after hour, until finally they started remembering a little bit, the way they did before, earlier in their training.

Then we continued for even more hours, and they started remembering more, and more, and more. It was as though they had dreamed it. Eventually, they reached the point that they could remember everything that took place while they were at deep levels of hypnosis.

Finding a New Level

We wanted a level where they could remember everything. Not like in hypnosis where the deeper they went, the more they forgot.

As we continued to investigate, we found that what was happening, they were coming up from theta to alpha. Theta is the deepest you can go in hypnosis. They were coming a little bit at a time, until finally they got to alpha, and then they remembered everything. They could even talk to you, like they did before.

A hypnotized subject in theta never asked questions. Their mind functions inductively, like when they were prior to seven years of age. When you take them to five cycles theta, that is comparable to when they were five years old.

Why do they forget? Because now they are fifty. That happened forty-five years ago, brain-wise. How can they remember?

So there at five cycles, in deep hypnosis, their mind functions inductively. They cannot formulate a question. They can answer questions, but they can never ask questions, because they are not able to while they are at that level.

So we found out what level they could become active at. It was at the alpha level that they could activate their mind, that they could analyze information and come up with solutions to problems.

That's how we discovered the alpha dimension and what could be accomplished at alpha.

After that, it was a matter of developing an altered state of consciousness to get a subject to alpha, where they could analyze information, where they could function deductively, where they could ask questions and also answer questions.

This is how we developed the Silva Method.

9 My Thoughts on Our Hypnosis Research   by José Silva Jr.

People sometimes ask about the differences between the Silva Mind Training Systems and hypnosis.

After having observed my father from his earliest research on through the development of the Silva Mind Control Method and the Silva UltraMind ESP Systems, I have seen many, many differences.

Of course, all of the wording is different.

In hypnosis, the hypnotist is always telling you what to do. The hypnotic operator keeps giving you suggestions, commanding you, and telling you what to think and what to do.

For instance, a hypnotist may tell you that you can't open your eyes, and if you accept the suggestion, then sure enough you can't open your eyes.

In very deep hypnosis, the hypnotist will tell you that things are there when they really aren't there, but you will imagine that you see them.

That is called hallucination. You really believe the dog is there.

Or the hypnotist can give you the suggestion that something that *is* there, *is not* there, and you will not see it. You will believe it is *not* there.

When you are under deep hypnosis, when the hypnotist suggests something, you will do it. When the hypnotist gives a command, you will obey it. Of course, you will not obey the command if it is something that goes against your moral or ethical standards.

Strong Rapport With the Hypnotist

Hypnotized subjects are very intuitive.

Hypnotized subjects will do whatever the hypnotist wants, so long as it doesn't violate their moral code.

So if the hypnotist suggests that the subject do something that would be wrong or might hurt someone, but the hypnotist never intends to let the subject actually carry out the instructions, then the subject—who is functioning clairvoyantly at the time—will play the game and pretend they are trying to carry out the instructions, even though they know the hypnotist will stop them.

And the subject will never admit they knew that the hypnotist would stop them, even under hypnosis, because they know the hypnotist doesn't really want them to.

Limitations of Hypnosis

When you first start hypnotizing people, you can ask them questions and they will answer. But they won't ask questions or try to figure things out for themselves.

But after you have hypnotized them so many times, it is like the body develops a mechanism to defend itself:

The subjects begin asking questions themselves.

And they begin using their intuitive ability.

Taking Back Control

When my father first started presenting health cases to my sisters, he had to ask them everything.

He would ask if there was a problem in the head, for instance. He would have to guide them to the areas involved and ask them questions so they could find the problems.

But as you know, with the Silva ESP training, it is just the opposite:

- The orientologist avoids giving any guidance.
- Silva-trained clairvoyants are very active in seeking out the problems:

- Silva-trained psychics do not wait for a body to appear, they visualize one.
- Silva-trained psychics don't wait for something to happen so they can "perceive" what the problem is.
- Silva-trained psychics project right to the problem. They take an active, dynamic role.
- Silva-trained psychics visualize a problem and project it onto the image of the body to see if it fits. If not, they try another problem, and keep on until they find out what the problem is.

Be Sure You're Right and Then Go Ahead

Silva graduates will never be hypnotized, because they are too active, too curious, too interested to ever give up that awareness and involvement.

Things are not done for Silva graduates. Our graduates do things for themselves and for others.

To me, there are a great many differences between hypnosis and the Silva Systems, and the fact that a few superficial aspects appear similar does not mean that the substance of hypnosis and the Silva Systems are anything alike.

It is the difference in meekly doing what somebody else wants, compared with taking charge of your own life, finding out what you need to know to succeed, and then doing it.

A Better, Faster, Superior Method

While my father started with hypnosis, he realized that his subjects were not functioning at normal hypnotic levels.

He thought back to when he was in the Army in 1945 and was assigned to an Army base near Bowling Green, Kentucky, the birthplace of Edgar Cayce, the famous "Sleeping Prophet."

Cayce would enter a state comparable to light sleep, and while at that state he could detect peoples' health problems and advise them of what vitamins and herbs to take to correct their problems.

My father realized that all he needed to do was to guide people to a level comparable to light sleep, so he devised a very simple way to "fool the brain" into thinking that you wanted to go to sleep.

What do you do when you are ready to go to sleep?

- Find a comfortable position, make yourself comfortable.
- Close your eyes.
- Relax physically.
- Calm your mind.

Sound familiar? If you have practiced our Centering Exercise you will recognize those as the steps we take to enter the alpha brainwave level.

That is all it takes. No hypnotic techniques, no need for a hypnotist to take control of your mind and tell you what to do.

We don't take control of your mind. We guide you to enter a level—brain-wise—comparable to light sleep.

Rather than using hypnosis, we might be using a system similar to what Edgar Cayce used.

We are not against hypnosis. There are times when it could be the best and fastest way to get results.

My father always advised to do whatever it takes to solve a problem. Isn't it better to have more tools you can use for problem-solving?

If you haven't yet learned our System, you can get started right now with the free lessons in the appendix.

10 Strengthen Your Immune System to Stay Healthy *(1998)*

The undisciplined mind can make you sick.

It is generally agreed in the medical profession that as much as 90 percent of health problems, or even more, are psychosomatic.

Psychosomatic means that the mind (the psyche) wrongly influences the body (the soma), causing a health problem.

It all starts with fear. Fear is always interpreted by the body as a threat to life. Worrying about anything is a form of fear.

Fear causes the autonomic nervous system to prepare the body for fight of flight. There is wear and tear on the body adjusting to the fight or flight condition.

Wear and tear causes stress, and stress weakens the body's immune system. It is then that health problems begin.

In order to correct this condition, we must learn to place our mind in neutral. When the mind is in neutral, it frees the immune system to do its job, and that is to keep the body healthy by normalizing the abnormal.

Doctors and medicines to not heal; they help the body to heal itself.

For some health problems, the mind needs to be placed in neutral once a day for 15 minutes.

For other health problems, the mind needs to be placed in neutral two or even three times a day, for 15 minutes each time.

Learning to place your mind in neutral helps your doctor accelerate the healing process.

When worry triggers the "fight or flight" response, this activates the body's survival mechanism, causing stress, which in turn causes wear and tear on the body, and the wear and tear causes even more stress.

The autonomic nervous system (a body's survival mechanism) is composed of: the sympathetic nervous system, which accelerates the function of glands, organs, and organ systems; and the parasympathetic nervous system, which decelerates the function of glands, organs, and organ systems.

The autonomic nervous system should function according to body needs, but false fear sends false signals and can cause a gland, organ, or organ system to overwork. This results in stress weakening the immune system, and eventually results in a gland, organ, or organ system breakdown. This causes more stress, and the cycle continues getting worse and worse.

In lay terms, when worry or fear activates the fight or flight response, your heart beats faster, your muscles get tense, and your whole system starts working overtime.

When you put your mind in neutral at alpha, you cannot worry. This allows your parasympathetic nervous system to decelerate the function of your glands, organs, and organ systems, and function only according to the body's real needs.

Some people develop a habit of wrong thinking that eventually develops into what is called a disease.

A chronic health condition can be the cause of a fixed pattern of thinking, holding onto false concepts. This condition causes the glands to deposit into the circulatory system the chemicals that cause the health problem.

When the mind does not interfere with the functioning of the human body, the body knows naturally how to heal itself.

You will accelerate the healing process when you are able to place your mind in neutral from time to time and combine this with any medication that your doctor has prescribed for you.

Learn how to do this with our free lessons the appendix.

11 Silva Graduates and Positive Attitudes *(1980)*

Have you ever wondered where Silva Mind Control graduates fit in the highly complicated, and sometimes irrational, belief systems in the world?

We all know the tremendous personal advantages that the Silva Mind Control Method provides for us, but as a group, what are our contributions in the world's continuous struggle for survival?

I propose that as a group, we are in the vanguard in providing the world with the attitudes and tools necessary for the continued survival of humankind, and that this mission should never be forgotten.

Let me illustrate.

During the last ten years, with the advent of world turmoil and the massive destruction of many institutions and beliefs, there were those who advocated that God is dead.

If God, they argue, is all goodness and God manifests these virtues through human beings, how can God continue to exist as a God of goodness when there is nothing good left in humankind?

Even today there are countless scientists all over the world who are out to prove that nothing really works, and they carry on their work in the name of metaphysics, thus giving the illusion of credibility to their work.

And if things do work, other philosophers say, what good will they do as nothing really matters in this world anyway?

Can you imagine the type of mental attitude these people must possess to continue working on projects that deal with nothing but negativism? And, more important, can we really gauge the tremendous *negative* effects of their work?

Where do graduates of Silva Mind Control fit in this world's belief system?

The answer is very simple, and we learn it during our first encounter with Silva Mind Control: positive mental attitude. This, more than anything, is our contribution to the world, and not only do we talk about it, we also know how to put it into practice with the various techniques at our disposal.

Not only does a positive mental attitude turn weaknesses into strengths, but it also turns destructive forces into beneficial ones. People have a way of becoming what you encourage them to be rather than what you nag them to be.

Being positive is the hallmark of the Silva Mind Control graduate, and sharing this positive attitude should be our mission in life, and we manifest this mission through our beliefs and accomplishments.

We can rest assured that if we want to conform or at least go along with the evolving process of humanity and the evolving process of creation, we need to be on the positive side.

We Must Always Have a Positive Mental Attitude

We don't want to cause pressures, or force or push anything. We want to attract things to enter the proper placement, adjust to the proper grooves, and to move along at the proper rate where everything needs to evolve.

Our job on this planet is to take care of creation.

We are, after all, extensions of our Creator, the highest level of intelligence on the planet.

We need to make sure that the flow of the evolving process continues until peak *perfection* is found, and not peak failure.

It is this attitude and this mission that sets the Silva Mind Control graduate apart, and we need to continue practicing this attitude until perfection is reached.

This is our job, no doubt about it. This is positive thinking and that is why we take it for granted. We never doubt it; it's always positive.

We are not naive enough to think that the world is in a perfect state; there are many things that could be better, but this is why our task is not yet done.

We believe we are on the right side, for thoughts that hinder and are negative go against the Creator, that we sometimes call the devil's side. And we certainly would like to be on the positive side.

Our goal as Silva Mind Control graduates, then, is to reach peak perfection in everything and to solve as many problems as we are supposed to be solving.

In this we are on our way, and this is where we fit in today's belief system.

Each one of us is emitting positive mental energies which taken together constitute a formidable force for the better.

This is really what Silva Mind Control is all about.

12 One Program Helps Everyone Who Uses It *(1984)*

There have been thousands of books and courses created to help people achieve more success, and they prove useful for a very few people. In fact, only about one person in ten receives any significant benefit from most of these books and courses.

There is one notable exception. One program has helped virtually everyone who has learned it, and several million people worldwide have learned it.

The program, of course, is the Silva Method of Mind Development, which is now (in 1984) being presented in fourteen languages in more than sixty countries and territories worldwide.

Why has the Silva Method been successful with everybody?

To answer that, let's look first at what makes successful people successful. Not the people with average success, but the people with outstanding success.

And not just success in one field, but success in many fields.

These very successful people have goals, of course, and a strong commitment to reach their goals. They are persistent, and are hard workers.

They are reasonably intelligent, and relate well to other people.

But many people with average success share these same traits.

So What Is the Difference?

The difference is this: People who achieve outstanding success use more of their brains and minds than those who achieve average success.

Most people, approximately ninety percent, use only the left half of the brain for thinking, while the other ten percent use both sides of the brain to think with.

Does this make the ninety percent who are left brain thinkers just half as effective?

No, they are usually much less than half as effective. For example, try lifting a bulky object with just one arm instead of two.

Now back to the question of why the Silva Method of Mind Development has helped so many people.

While most books and courses motivate people and tell them how to set goals and be more persistent in striving for them, these programs do not teach people how to use the right side of the brain.

The Silva Method is the first program ever created that guides people to start using the right side of the brain to think with.

To develop all of your potential, it is essential that you use both brain hemispheres to think with, because each functions in its own way.

The left brain hemisphere stores information we collect with our physical senses.

The right brain hemisphere stores a different kind of information: it stores data that you collect with your subjective senses—your mind.

Just take a look at the people who achieve above average success. When they talk, they seem to have a better grasp of things. They understand more quickly. They are more sensitive to people, and seem to know exactly how to deal with them.

And they make correct decisions. They make more correct decisions than the average person.

While the left brain hemisphere is limited to only information that you have collected with the physical senses, the right brain hemisphere is not limited in this way. It has access to more information than the left brain hemisphere because it deals with information stored on other peoples brain neurons.

Intuition—Hunches—Are a Phenomenon of the Right-Brain Hemisphere

The right brain hemisphere perceives information that the logical left brain hemisphere misses. When you have access to information from both brain hemispheres, you have much more going for you than if you are limited to only one.

How Can You Learn to Use Your Right Brain Hemisphere?

First, learn to relax and slow your brain until you are at a level comparable to light sleep.

Then practice using visualization and imagination, and you are using your right brain hemisphere.

With practice, you can learn to reach this level without going through those steps. The fastest way to learn is by taking the Silva ESP training.

When you have practiced enough, and practiced the proper way, then you can evoke that special feeling associated with using the right brain hemisphere at any time, so you will have access to the right brain's abilities whenever you need them.

People who achieve outstanding success do this. But they might not realize that most people do not function the same way they do. Remember this when you read their books and take their courses.

If you apply their techniques with your right brain hemisphere, then you will achieve the way they do.

13 What's New With the Silva Method?
(1985)

We have been presenting the Silva Method Basic Lecture Series to the public for almost two decades. It has helped millions of people worldwide change their lives for the better by developing their clairvoyant abilities.

This is the main purpose of the Basic Lecture Series: to center yourself and learn to function in other dimensions.

We want to learn to communicate subjectively, because this is so valuable in *every* area of life.

The Basic Lecture Series has not been changed in all this time. It was designed to do a job, and it does it well.

What's New?

But this does not mean that there is nothing new in the Silva Method. There is a lot new.

What's new is the way our research and experience have led us to find new ways to *apply* the Silva Method.

Here in Laredo, we have recently developed special applications of the Silva Method for athletes and for people interested in physical fitness.

Tag Powell, with our assistance and guidance, has developed a two-day seminar with applications of the Silva Method in business and industry. Harry McKnight and Dr. George DeSau are developing a comprehensive program for management personnel utilizing the Silva techniques.

Burt Goldman has developed the Silva Supermind Seminar to help people apply the Silva Method to achieve more of their goals in life.

In its first year, the Silva Supermind Seminar has already attracted thousands of participants who have been motivated and inspired by Burt Goldman.

Solid Silva

In all such programs, the basic Silva Method procedures and techniques are used because they are the best available.

New applications of the Silva Method make these programs new.

Besides these programs, most Silva Lecturers present one-evening workshops to graduates and sometimes to the public as well. Silva International Graduate Association (SIGA) hopes to harness some of this talent and make this available on a broader scale.

The key to the success of all of these programs is the solid foundation of the Silva Method.

The Silva Method is the first program ever developed that *guarantees* that you will learn to reach the alpha level and then learn to use both sides of your brain.

The Silva Method includes both carefully-crafted beneficial statements and unique visualization-imagination exercises to help you learn to use both sides of your brain.

With practice, you learn to do this so well that you can do it with eyes open. This is possible because every minute, for the new graduate, the brain dips into alpha about thirty times. If you have practiced going to level enough, doing it consciously and practicing the techniques, then during those fractions of a second when the brain dips into alpha, you will be able to use that level to get the information you need and program what you desire to program.

The best way is to become a graduate and to practice, and the best way to get the results you want, is to practice working health cases as often as possible.

This is the best way to learn to function in the subjective dimension, and it is within the subjective dimension that most of the good things we desire can be created.

Which brings us right back to the Basic Lecture Series.

What Counts the Most

Without subjective communication—case working—all of the other techniques become very limited.

What really counts is subjective communication. This is basic.

Subjective communication is necessary if you are to do all the rest effectively.

This is why our system is still the best, most effective program available despite imitators attempts to alter it.

They miss the point when they take away the very uniqueness that has made it work.

When you learn and begin practicing these new applications, keep in mind your roots. Keep your foundation solid:
- Enter level daily.
- Practice case working as often as possible.

Do this and be more successful than you ever imagined.

Note: If you have not taken any of our Courses, you can learn to enter the alpha level and use many of our techniques with the free training in the appendix.

14 Life Is More Than a Seventy-Year Coffee Break *(1982)*

Some people act like they came to this planet for a lifelong vacation, or for a seventy-year coffee break.

I believe we came to this planet to solve problems, and through this process, to learn and to grow.

By solving problems, I mean making this world a better place to live. This can be done many ways, like coming up with cures for diseases, or marketing products that make life easier, or simply by doing your assigned task better and more effectively.

Knowledge Is the Key to Success

To help each of us do our job better, we need knowledge and skill. We need effective ways of obtaining information. That is why, in the Silva Method, we have Dream Control and other techniques to help us obtain information.

The information we receive should serve a purpose. The purpose that has the most value is to use that information to solve present and future problems.

We should select and weed out information, not have it just to satisfy our curiosity, but to satisfy our needs. The correct application of information is to solve problems. There is no other need for information, except to solve problems.

Take Action and Do Worthwhile Things

I have never been idle in my life. I don't like to waste time. I need to be reading a book or some lesson, or doing something constructive, no matter what time of day or night it is.

I get up at five o'clock in the morning to start work, and no matter where I go, if I've got a book in my hand, it is going to be a book that has something constructive in it. I've never read novels, and the only time I read comic books was when I was studying to learn to speak English. I've never read a novel in my life. It has to be the real thing or I won't touch it. To me, fiction is like fairy tales. Some people say they learn from that.

Well, I think it is false learning.

That's why I was attracted to the life of Christ. He developed a system for solving problems.

There have been a lot of "Saintly" people in the world, but what I was going for was someone who found a system to solve problems. Not just a person who said he was divine and saintly and a good and kind person, but someone who solved people's problems.

We hear about people who try to get "Saintly" by holing up in caves and meditating all day. But they never help anybody else. They are not serving any purpose as far as serving others.

Your Purpose In Life

Our purpose is here before us, and it is easy to see. If you want to know why you came to this planet, to this physical dimension, then just look around you for the work that needs to be done. That is your purpose.

We are told that God worked to create the physical world.

And the entire story of Christ's life was one of working to correct the problems we created here on this planet through our ignorance and erroneous thinking.

If you want to be Christ-like, if you want to be God-like and be close to the Creator, then imitate Christ. Imitate the Creator. Use all the tools and talents you have to obtain correct information, and then get to work to put that information to use solving problems on this planet.

15 You Are Greater Than You Think
(1983)

There is much more to a human being than meets the eye.

That is something people have always sensed, and something that Rabbi Jesus came to earth to give us: the method to become more human, more spiritual, more successful in life.

The Purpose of Religion

My personal concept of religions is that religions exist to help us enhance our spiritual factor.

The spiritual factor is what distinguishes the human from the common animal. A person can have a human body and a human brain, but if that person does not have an enhanced spiritual factor, then that person functions like a beast.

The spiritual factor is enhanced in the subjective dimension, which we now know has been identified by science as the alpha dimension. Some people say that we cannot do anything to enhance the spiritual factor, but that it is strengthened only by grace when we have enough faith.

My personal concept is that we were created in the image of God, and were given spiritual tools to use, so that we could take action to strengthen our spiritual factor. It does not make sense to me that we would be given tools and told not to use them.

Strengthen the Spiritual Factor

We enter the subjective dimension mentally, and there we can use our spiritual tools to strengthen the spiritual factor.

The correct dimension can be recognized because of what we are able to do there.

The spiritual tools include visualization and imagination, and we can use these tools to strengthen the spiritual factor and to correct problems once we find the correct subjective dimension.

Visualization and imagination are faculties of human intelligence that function in a subjective dimension, the world of the mind dimension. This dimension exists ahead of the world of physics, and this is what makes it possible to use these tools in this dimension to solve problems of the physical dimension.

To me, that correct subjective dimension is the kingdom of heaven that Rabbi Jesus spoke of, a subjective dimension that we can learn to use while here on earth, not a "kingdom of God" that we might enter into when we die.

(*This is excerpted from José Silva's book,* The Mystery of the Keys to the Kingdom.)

16 How to Become More Human
(1983)

When you function at the alpha level at least fifteen minutes a day, you become more human.

What do we mean by that?

Religions are supposed to help human beings become more human. What do they recommend you do?

Pray.

And what is prayer?

Quiet down, close your eyes, meditate. And usually, bow your head. We think what they are looking for is that human dimension, that alpha dimension, ten cycles per second brain frequency.

To become more human, you must enter a spiritual dimension.

To become more human, you must become more spiritual.

Religions enhance the spiritual factor. And when religions enhance the spiritual factor, you become more human, because of the spiritual factor.

Animals Don't Have a Spiritual Factor

The stronger and more enhanced your spiritual factor is, the more human you are—the more difference between you and a common animal.

The more the similarity between you and the Creator.

We think that a human being is not one who looks like one, but one who acts like one. Some may look like human beings and function like beasts.

That goes along with the concept that we have been created in the image of the Creator.

Image.

Likeness.

But not bodily, not biologically, for we know we don't all look alike. Every human being is different from every other.

Then what do we mean by image, likeness?

In the power of mind; our human intelligence.

We should be as intelligent as God is. And we should use this intelligence to correct the problems on this planet like God corrects problems in the entire universe. We should have enough intelligence to correct at least that much.

So we are sons of God. Creatures of the Creator.

We have been created in the image, likeness, of the Creator, in the sense of how we use our human intelligence.

To enhance the spiritual factor, you must enter a non-physical dimension. And once in the non-physical dimension, you must use spiritual tools, to enhance the spiritual factor.

Now what are spiritual tools?

Visualization and imagination are spiritual tools.

Use these to help correct problems on our planet.

We Are Here to Help the Creator

My concept is that we human beings are on this planet to correct problems, to help our Creator with the problems that creation encounters.

We have been created in the image of our Creator in the ability to use our minds to correct problems.

We are a speck, a fraction of Higher Intelligence, our God.

Our mind functions in the same capacity; it has the same power as God has, but in a limited fashion.

We should be able to do on this planet what God, our Creator, can do in the whole universe.

We come from God, and evidently our Creator needed us to help Him with creation on this planet or else we wouldn't have been created; it's as simple as that.

So we were created to help our Creator with creation, which means solving problems, not destruction.

The Creator is not a destructor, He's a Creator.

So we, I believe, have been sent to the planet to convert this planet into a paradise, by solving all problems by using the power God gave us, mentally—mind-wise, mind-power.

We are like gods on the planet, and if we are like god's on the planet, we should be able to solve all problems, because God solves all problems. If we do not solve problems, we are not God-like.

Those who solve problems are God-like, because we are working for the Creator's creation, and solving the problems that face God's creatures, the creatures on the planet.

Enter your alpha level and ask why you are here, ask what you can do to help correct problems on this planet. Ask, and you will get answers. You may be surprised at the answers you receive, but you will receive answers.

Then take action, for, as the Bible says, faith without works is dead. Knowledge and wisdom are only that which, when applied, solves problems.

Claim your spiritual heritage; function in a god-like manner by helping to make this world a better place to live.

17 Our Practical Approach Is Popular in India *(1995)*

The Silva Method is a big success in the land where meditation began.

We just returned from a three-week visit to India and Bangladesh where more than 1,000 people came to the advanced Silva Method training with me.

Yoga is the oldest meditation system known. It began in India at least 5,000 years ago.

Yogis typically meditate at theta levels. This is why some of them are able to perform amazing feats with their bodies: sleeping on a bed of nails, slowing their metabolism so that they can be buried alive for a month, withstanding great pain.

But they cannot become mentally active at the theta level.

They told us that yoga feels wonderful. It can bring a sense of oneness, a feeling of euphoria. They say that they often gain great insight.

Yet with all of this, India still has a great amount of poverty and suffering.

Yoga is too slow, they report. It takes too long to learn how to solve the problems that they have here and now, and even then they seem limited compared to the techniques of the Silva Method.

We took the Ultra Seminar to India, presenting the two-day program in Bombay and New Delhi, and also to Bangladesh. In all, more than 1,000 Silva Method graduates attended.

They learned new techniques to use to heal themselves and others:

We taught them the Silva Rapid Hand Vibration Healing Method. We asked for volunteers, as we always do. Several people came up front who were in pain, or who had limited mobility. Several others came up who wanted to be healers. We showed the healers what to do, and, as always happens, the subjects showed substantial improvement.

They learned the complete laying on of hands system that has proven so successful, even for people with so-called "terminal" illnesses. They watched us demonstrate it, and then they practiced it themselves.

They learned how to read the Silva Standard Conditioning Cycle (Silva Centering Exercise) to their loved ones, and then practiced reading it to each other. Now they are able to help their family members by teaching them how to find their level and use the Silva Method formula-type techniques.

We showed them several additional ways that they can get a person into a receptive programming state, through confusion, suspense, and so forth.

We covered the use of reinforcing mechanisms so that their programming will continue to work even when they are not present. It is sort of like a "timed release" medicine.

They saw demonstrations of biofeedback equipment and learned many ways that it can help them to improve their lives. We showed them how to use a small audio player as a healing instrument.

They found out how to program for various business situations, such as learning how to use a reinforcing mechanism to program a person to have a desire to pay a debt.

They learned even more, such as how to use their level to strengthen family ties and build better relationships, the ideal time to program, special techniques to improve visualization, psychometry, and more.

It was only a few years ago that we first introduced the Silva Method in India. Dr. Robert Stone, the co-author of several of our books, opened the door for us.

Dr. Stone reported that the first time he went to India to talk about the Silva Method and how effective the techniques are, one member of the audience spoke up and said, "Dr. Stone, it seems like you are storming the gates of heaven."

Dr. Stone said that he took a deep breath, looked him in the eye and answered, "Well, maybe it's time that we did."

The audience applauded enthusiastically.

Bimolendu Rakshit is our director in India, and Mahee Quazi in Bangladesh. They are adding new scientific findings to an old tradition of meditation and introspection.

The result is that more problems are being solved, people's lives are improving, and the world is becoming a little better place to live.

18 The Seeds of Super Success Are Within You *(1995)*

Napoleon Hill spent twenty years observing the most successful people in the world and studying what they did and how they did it.

He wrote about what he observed, and taught courses on it.

He spoke of how they all had a definite chief aim in life, how they had great desire and enthusiasm, a strong work ethic, and much more.

All of these are mental traits, not physical. They all arise from within the person.

Yet Hill was only able to study them from an objective—outer—left-brain point of view.

He studied—and taught—the effect, not the cause.

He was not able to teach how to make changes within, so he taught people to imitate the actions of successful people. This is very different from becoming like the successful people.

So instead of installing these characteristics from within, he tried to force them in from the outside, because that's all he knew how to do.

If you imitate the actions of successful people, eventually you might internalize some of it. If you do enough, for long enough, it is sure to help you.

Some people are even able to internalize it, to make it their own, so that their actions spring from within, instead of merely being on the outside.

A few people—the ten percent or so who are natural alpha—right-brain—thinkers, were able to internalize these ideals, and they went on to become huge successes in their lives.

Meanwhile, all the other people who tried to follow the teachings and failed to achieve much success, thought of themselves as failures, as somehow falling short because they were lazy or dumb or something.

But that's not true! They often worked just as hard, acted just as enthusiastic as the most successful person, and imitated all of the other characteristics that Hill wrote about.

So why didn't they succeed?

Because they were trying to shove it in from the outside. They were dealing with effects, not causes.

Any success book or success course will work for some people. It will work for some of the ten percent who are natural alpha—right-brain—thinkers. That is why you will always see some people who swear by a success book or success course. They are the lucky few who can get it to work for them. These books and courses are always authored by successful people who are successful because they are natural alpha—right-brain—thinkers.

Some people who are not natural alpha—right-brain—thinkers can follow the instructions in the success books and imitate the successful and become successful themselves. These are usually people who have great energy and drive. But even then, their success is limited.

Not because they are lazy or dumb, but because they have never learned how to enter the alpha level with conscious awareness, and remain at the alpha level when they become mentally active, so that they can use their right brain hemisphere to think with, so that they can get subjective information through the right brain hemisphere—that is, they can read minds.

It is much more difficult to achieve much success when you are not able to enter alpha and think with your right brain hemisphere and detect information mentally, information that is not available to your physical senses, and send information mentally, through subjective means.

It is much like a person who has never learned to read or write. They can still get by in the world, but it is more difficult, and their options are more limited. There are many fields that are not open to a person who cannot read or write.

Even a person who is a slow reader and a mediocre writer can usually go much farther than a person with high energy and great intelligence who is illiterate.

A person who is illiterate is not dumb, is not necessarily lazy. A person who does not know how to enter the alpha level with conscious awareness, and become mentally active while remaining at the alpha level, is not dumb, is not necessarily lazy.

These are skills that anybody can learn by using the Silva techniques.

Everybody should learn, if we are to solve the problems of the world.

Note: If you have not taken any of our Courses, you can learn to enter the alpha level with the free training in the appendix.

19 Persistent Practice Produces Progress *(1983)*

One of the most important keys to success is persistence.

You see this throughout the Silva Method of Self-Mind Control.

We use repetition in our mental training exercises to persistently impress statements that insure your success. And by so doing, you learn the one skill, the one method of functioning, that is common to all of the very successful people:

How to use your right-brain hemisphere creatively and clairvoyantly.

You can see the persistence that went into the creation of the Silva Method when you hear the story of the twenty-two years of research that we did to perfect it.

During the seventeen years we have been presenting the Silva Method to the public, we have persistently maintained the high quality of the program, resisting efforts to alter it because some people thought we could sell it more easily.

Your Continued Success

To insure your continued success, you need to practice what you have learned: persistently.

Different people need different amounts of practice, but it is safe to say that when you have practiced 300, 400 or 500 health detection and correction cases, you will have developed into a very good clairvoyant.

When you learn the Silva Method, you learn to use subjective communication; that is, you learn to function as a psychic. This is the one most valuable skill you can ever develop. However, if you want to learn to use this ability naturally, on a daily basis in all of your activities, then you need to practice.

At first, you must practice consciously. Persistently. Then it will become a natural habit, and you will not have to think of it so much.

A Naturally Developed Psychic

I have been practicing since I was six years old. At that age, I began to use my right-brain hemisphere creatively to discover new ideas for earning money to help support my family. I began to use my right-brain hemisphere clairvoyantly to make correct decisions more often so that my efforts would end in success.

At the same time, I also learned to use my left-brain hemisphere the way it was intended to be used: to keep business records, and to help me with the objective, rational tasks: I had to perform.

Through years of practice and many successes, I developed considerable skill in using both brain hemispheres. And I developed a lot of confidence in my ability to function as I needed to.

It is easier to practice and maintain a persistent attitude when you have someone to help you, to encourage you. Throughout my twenty-two years of research, I was on my own much of the time, especially in the early days, pioneering this new field. But I always felt that High Intelligence was with me all the way. I felt that Jesus was guiding me and encouraging me.

To help encourage Silva graduates to practice, we have always done several things: We give discounts to immediate family members; we encourage graduates to repeat at no charge; and we encourage graduate clubs and graduate activities, although we make no money from any of this.

We are now carrying this a step further with formation of the Silva International Graduate Association, called SIGA. In Spanish, the word SIGA means "Keep on going." This is just what the organization is for.

SIGA is a non-profit association made up exclusively of Silva graduates.

Some graduates have asked questions about SIGA, so here are some answers.

The dues for SIGA are used to run the organization. None of the money goes to Silva Mind Control International. In fact, Silva Mind Control International has donated a great deal to get the organization started.

Now it is up to graduates to keep it going.

There are many expenses involved in a world-wide organization. So far, Silva Mind Control has paid for all the necessary travel and most of the telephone calls involved. We have also donated much of the printing that has been done, and time of many of our top staff members.

Ultimately, it will be up to Silva graduates to make SIGA a success. It will take persistence, but the benefits will be worth it.

This will be your way to insure your continued success by getting the necessary practice and developing the confidence you need.

20 The Commercial Aspect of Silva
(1980)

If there is one question that is asked of me, and I am certain of others within Silva Mind Control, it is that of the commercial aspect of our enterprise.

Why, I am, asked, "Is Silva Mind Control a commercial venture," one where people have to pay for the right to partake of the knowledge we possess?

The answer is quite simple, and, I feel, very much justified.

For one, and this is the view expressed in an article in this newsletter by Fr. John Rossner, Silva Mind Control is a very particular type of venture—one which, in a very real sense, demands a change in the traditional belief system people have had for centuries.

It is a belief system that deals with the brain—that part of the human anatomy which has perplexed laymen and scientists for generations simply because it is the only organ of the body that has organic qualities that are associated with the mind's spiritual functions.

The type of research that Silva Mind Control pioneered touches upon the fringes of both academic and religious beliefs people have attached to the function of the mind. This is why the holistic approach to human development espoused by us has brought us criticism—especially at the beginning of our research—from both the academic and religious fields.

Our research—now proven beyond a doubt by many scientists in various fields—required a refinement in the rough edges of mental rigidity which tradition and custom had given people, and was one reason why we had to be extremely careful on how our research was going to be presented.

It is not natural for people to accept change and discard the attitudes that have been ingrained within their system for at least four hundred years.

We need to present Silva Mind Control in a way that will not create a religious hysteria, for ours is not a religious movement, nor, for that matter, a movement dealing with the "occult."

Silva Mind Control, above everything else, seeks to acquaint students with the potential of their whole person and how, by using more of their mind, they can change their limiting ways of thinking and their unproductive habits to become, as we are fond of saying, "Better and Better."

There is nothing secret about our organization, nothing dramatic, no rituals or initiations. It is purely and simply the most effective way yet devised to make one's self a more effective human being on the planet.

Marketing our course in a commercial setting takes away whatever "religious" interpretation people might give it, thus perhaps salvaging the movement altogether because it operates not in a religious environment but in a secular and pluralistic one, where it is accepted on its merits, not on the belief systems of people.

Yet, even though our movement is commercial, much of what is earned—at least 90 percent—is put back into the program, primarily to reach other nations and to continue our research.

After all, ours is a strictly self-supporting program. We have not received one nickels worth of charity nor a dimes worth of grant money to do our research.

We are self supporting; this is why we need to be commercial.

Since we started our movement, we have indeed come a long way, and I believe our success is due to our having never wavered from our commitment to use our system for the betterment of humanity. We have stuck to a philosophy that "to be human one must do humanitarian acts."

And this is the reason why we attempted to provide our method—free of charge—to institutions that render a service to people: schools, universities, hospitals, etc.

We believe our system belongs, in the final analysis, to the furthering of human knowledge and human experience.

And we believe that the commercial aspects of Silva Mind Control contribute greatly in the final achievement of such a goal.

21 Personal Security is the Key to Peace *(1981)*

The shooting of Pope John Paul II and the attempt made on the life of President Reagan a couple of months prior, has made the world turn to analyzing the consequences and the roots that spawn violence and terrorism.

In a very definite way, the acts of terrorism that plague the planet are counter to the philosophy that we adhere to, and that can be summarized in three simple words: Better and Better.

There will, no doubt, be reams upon reams of reports seeking to determine why young men would attempt to assassinate respected world leaders such as Pope John Paul II and President Reagan.

And undoubtedly there will be many answers: some will blame the home environment of the would-be assassins, others will blame the inequities in our society that breed discontent and division, and others will focus their search on the fanatical way that political assassins view the world.

However, those of us who have become accustomed to viewing ourselves and the world through the objectivity that the Silva Mind Control Method has taught us to do, find a very disturbing aspect to what is going on in the world today. Disturbing not because we do not want to accept reality as it really is, but because we see the many positive changes that can be instituted through the practice of the Silva Mind Control Method.

There are far too many individuals who have allowed themselves to become insecure, frightened, alienated, disgusted, fatalistic and even paranoid by the pressures that this society imposes as the cost for its many blessings.

Our society has provided us with the best standard of living, the best scientific methodology.

Yet despite our affluence and blessings, we find many people grappling with fears that bear heavily upon our behavior towards ourselves and others.

The problem, really, is not society's but merely one of coping.

Many in the world today have not been able to cope with the realities that they feel have attained control over them. Being unable to cope forces an individual to seek escape mechanisms and alternatives that are not grounded in the realities of life.

This is why their acts—which to them may seem effective and perhaps even justified—shock society in very much the same manner that we were shocked with the attempted assassinations of John Paul II and President Reagan.

In Silva Mind Control, we teach people how to control their own mind and thereby alter their own behavior. Nobody controls anybody in Silva Mind Control, we merely offer the techniques to allow individuals to become better people as manifested in their relations with themselves and with those around them.

As a better person, the Silva Mind Control graduate talks of peace, not war; of love, not hate; of helping, not deterrence; of positive, not negative; of action, not passivity; of loyalty, not convenience; of optimism, not pessimism.

Going to level and practicing the techniques through which a person can be better fulfilled are some of the greatest contributions that anyone can provide to their fellow human beings.

The insecurity in the world cannot be abolished simply by the waving of a magic wand. We need to develop and nourish programs that will nourish and sustain those who feel they have something to contribute to the general well-being of the country.

Those of us who are aware of the benefits of Silva Mind Control know that the key to many of today's problems can be placed directly and unequivocally upon individuals themselves.

With the Silva Method we have the tools that an individual can use to become better realized as a member of this society and of this planet.

These tools fall under the slogan that we use:

"My increasing mental faculties are for serving humanity better."

This slogan, when properly applied, can be a tremendous factor in solving many of our problems dealing with violence.

It goes to the very essence of our existence for without the optimism, the hope, the joy and the faith that we bring one another through the Silva training, the world really would be a darker and more somber place to live.

Silva Mind Control has become a soothing force in a world of change and violence.

Note: If you have not taken any of our Courses, you can learn to enter the alpha level with the free training in the appendix.

22 Programming for Better Health
(1986)

The weakening of the body's immune system is believed to be a major cause of such serious illnesses as cancer, AIDS, leukemia and other so-called incurable diseases.

Whenever the immune system is weakened, life is threatened.

What weakens the immune system?

One answer to that question has been confirmed many times over.

The answer is tension and stress.

The Worst Stressors

Let us examine three major causes of stress.

1. Guilt. When you know that you are doing something wrong, and you continue to do it, you are inviting a weakening of your immune system.
2. A deep loss. When you lose something or someone of great value and are not able to recover that loss, great stress is caused and, again, you are inviting a weakening of your immune system.
3. Working or living in an environment or under conditions that you hate. This is chronic stress. Chronic stress is known to cause a weakening of the immune system.

There are many other causes of stress, and several of these small stress can add up to a big problem.

Relieving Tension and Stress

Knowing this about stress, what can we do about it?

The obvious answers are:

- do not behave in a way that will cause you guilt;
- accept your loss philosophically;
- change to a more pleasant job or environment; and solve small problems before they become big ones.

This advice is easy to give, but not that easy to take or apply.

Life is not always that closely under our control.

But our mind is, or should be, under our control.

With the Silva techniques, you can give yourself mental programming to change unwanted behavior. And it changes.

Taking Control

You can program yourself to change your habits, your attitudes, your self-image and your lifestyle so that you are living a life that is beneficial to yourself and others.

You can give yourself programming to accept your loss and go into higher levels of possessions or relationships.

You can program for the kind of life you want to live, and program that everyone will benefit from changes you make in your lifestyle, that the best thing be done for everyone concerned.

And you can solve problems at the alpha level, big or small.

While awaiting the results of your programming, you can go to your alpha level three times a day for fifteen minutes and enjoy serenity, tranquility and a vacation from stress, while also strengthening your immune system.

23 Some Ways to Clean Up Your Environment *(1986)*

People sometimes ask how they can use the Silva techniques to help detect and correct such problems as polluted air, water or food.

A word of caution first: negative thinking magnifies negative effects.

You might do more harm to yourself worrying about the chemicals injected into chickens, than in actually eating that chicken.

You might do more harm to yourself feeling guilty about ingesting all the sugar in that ice cream sundae than the sugar itself can cause.

Worry and guilt mean stress.

This kind of stress can do quicker harm than many environmental factors.

This is not meant as permission to do things that are harmful to your body or your health. Just a reminder that it is preferable to use more of your mind to make sensible choices where options exist than to worry.

Learn to Trust Your Intuition

If you are at the supermarket and wondering whether to buy the chopped beef or the pork chops, stop, defocus your eyes and ask yourself, "Which is better for me at this time, chopped beef or pork chops?"

Clear your mind by thinking of something else for a moment, then return to the job at hand, which is selecting one of the packages, and you will find yourself automatically moving your hand toward, say, the leaner chopped beef.

If you have pre-programmed the Three Fingers Technique, keep your three fingers together while marketing.

You will do this by going to level before going to the market and programming yourself in the following manner:

First, state the problem that you are not always certain which item is best for you.

Second, state what you want—that you always want to get what is best for you.

Third, establish the program you will use; program yourself that whenever you use your Three Fingers Technique, you will make the correct choice.

Fourth, use the Three Fingers Technique to help you with your shopping.

Fifth, take it for granted you have made the correct choices.

The more you have practiced the Silva techniques, the more centered you have become. As you know, a centered person is more likely to· make correct decisions because the two hemispheres of the brain are more balanced in their degree of functioning.

The most valuable technique to develop your intuition is case working—working health detection and correction cases as you learn in the Silva ESP training.

Occasionally, the need for detecting poisons, irritants or pollutants becomes more critical.

Thus it is best to go to alpha and follow a problem-solving procedure.

If you have a skin rash, indigestion, or some reoccurring allergic reaction, the wisest permanent approach is not just to treat the symptom. That is, you might begin by using the Mirror of the Mind or 3-Scenes Technique to treat the symptoms, But prevention is the main goal.

The best step for a permanent solution would be to detect what is causing the allergic reaction and then to avoid that food or substance.

You can use your case working procedures for this. You can ask about each food or substance whether it is causing you a problem.

Which answer seems right to you: yes or no. If you sense it is causing a problem, then eliminate it from your diet and see what happens.

Always remember, when working on health problems, consult your doctor and work under medical supervision.

Of course, the best doctor for you to work with is one who is a Silva graduate.

One quick word about cigarettes.

We know they cause harm.

We sometimes hear graduates claim that they will simply program that the cigarettes will not harm them. If they could do this, they could also program not to need cigarettes.

As mentioned above, if you insist on using products that create stresses on your body, at least avoid feeling guilty about it and thereby increasing the potential harm.

Avoid dwelling on it.

Best of all, use the Silva Habit Control Techniques and start some good new habits instead of continuing the habit that does you no good.

Note: If you have not yet learned our techniques, you can learn them with the free training included in the appendix.

24 The Human Factor . . . No Other Way
(1980)

When the seeds of what was later to become Silva Mind Control were first nourished back in 1944, the world was on the verge of tremendous technological advances.

Those also were the war years, and there were many of us who were greatly concerned about how humanity was going to utilize the tremendous knowledge it had acquired.

Technology had given us much to rejoice for; but it also clouded that optimism with uncertainty.

What new world was technology taking mankind to? And, more importantly, what type of future would it allow us to have?

There is no doubt that technology has given more dimension to ourselves.

Through the telephone, we can extend our voices throughout all comers of the world. Through the use of radio signals, our voices are indeed carried into space, even to the brink of infinity.

Television projects us to far away places, and our decisions—whether personal or commercial—are instantly relayed through the wizardry of computer technology.

But as our own selves are provided more dimensional latitudes through technology, we tend to become less personal:

- People hear our voices, but not gestures.
- People see our persons, but not the feelings that only personal contact can project.
- Computer-made decisions lack the compassion needed to provide warmth to human relations.

In a world of high technology, one needs to become aware of his personal individuality.

And, perhaps more important, people might lack awareness that they are also members of the human race.

This is why we say that "To qualify as humans we must take part in humanitarian acts."

There are now, in 1980, more than two million Silva Mind Control graduates all over the world, people whose lives have been enriched because they have been able to integrate themselves into a whole person, with the mind: that infinite guardian of our personalities and wellbeing and the fountainhead of the whole.

But the whole can only function if it is directed towards the person's own growth and development. The whole must never betray its own nature, the source of its destiny, the essence of its being.

We are, above all, humans, rational beings. But Silva Mind Control teaches that humanity can never be taken for granted, that rationality can malfunction, that people can act against themselves.

To qualify as humans we must take part in humanitarian acts. We must pay our dues and maintain humanity alive.

We are, after all, links in that human chain that transcends history.

Humanitarian acts are the ones that temper the steel, making it strong and durable so that it will remain true and strong until infinity.

This attitude forms the mainstay of our method, for our knowledge and our techniques, while personal, must be integrated with the whole, and humanity is the commonality we all share.

Let's never lose sight of our purpose, and let's keep humanitarian acts the cornerstone of our movement.

25 Reflections of the Christmas Season *(1982)*

When I think of Christmas; I think of Christ, and when I think of Christ, I think of that time in 1944 when, during the induction physical for the army, I encountered two things:
- the science of psychology
- the short story of the "One Solitary Life" of Christ

Somehow those two things stuck in my mind, and I have always felt that Christ wanted me to pursue the study of psychology.

Even later, when I was ready to quit studying and had put my books away in the attic, a painting of Christ came to me in a very strange circumstance, again as if Christ were directing me to study psychology.

When I look back at the life of Christ, and at what He was reported to have done, it seems clear that the message is that we should do all we can to solve problems on this planet.

My background is Christian—I was raised in the Catholic Church, and still go every Sunday when I am not presenting lectures—so the message came to me through a religious belief system I was familiar with.

But my studies have revealed to me that all religions are working towards the same end results: the enhancement of the spiritual factor that distinguishes the human being from a beast, directing their followers to strive for the betterment of humanity.

Christ seemed to be saying to me that there is another dimension, besides the physical dimension, which can influence the
physical dimension.

As I studied psychology, hypnosis, yoga, the Rosicrucian teachings, and of course the Christian Bible, I saw again and again that
all assumed the existence of a "spiritual dimension" that has dominion over the physical.

As I observed faith healers, I noticed that they, too, assumed
that they could make corrections in the "spiritual dimension" and
these corrections would often manifest in the physical as well.

From observing hypnotist, charismatic healers, witch doctors
and others I observed that all of the healings and corrections that
took place involved either the healer or the subject, or sometimes
both healer and subject, going into an altered state of consciousness.

Through a study of electronics and electroencephalography, I
learned this meant that the subjects were producing a slower brain
frequency, as though consciousness had regressed to an earlier time
on the scale of brain evolution.

This, then, made sense with what Christ said about entering
the "inner kingdom" by becoming "as a little child." At that earlier
point in the development of the brain, as children, we functioned at
slower brain frequencies.

Could this, then, unlock the secret of using the subjective
dimension to correct physical problems? Do we simply need to slow
our brain frequencies to those child-like frequencies, when we were
young and new to the physical dimension and thus not so physically-
oriented?

This is why I developed a method to help people regress back to
lower brain frequencies, and then developed techniques to use this
"alpha dimension," through the science of psychorientology, and to
use this dimension creatively and clairvoyantly, just as Christ used it.

We know now that about ten percent of the population use this
"alpha dimension" naturally, without training, which means that
they use the right-brain hemisphere creatively and clairvoyantly,
while the other 90 percent use only the logical left-brain hemisphere.

When we learn to use the right-brain hemisphere clairvoyantly, we all function as geniuses. Through clairvoyance, we can communicate more directly and more accurately than we can with words. And through clairvoyance, we can solve more problems than we can without clairvoyance.

This is the message—the message of all religions. All of the great leaders have used the right-brain hemisphere creatively and clairvoyantly. I think that Christ developed a method to train everyone to develop clairvoyance to save humanity from suffering due to ignorance.

Now we have this method. Its effectiveness has been proven with millions of people of all religions and races and ages and backgrounds, throughout the world.

We must move forward with this method, with a commitment to do what all the great religious leaders have urged for thousands of years: to help relieve suffering, to bring peace and understanding to all people throughout the world.

It matters little who gets the credit; so long as we get results.

It is our obligation to our Creator to help relieve the suffering of the Creator's creatures on this planet.

PART 2
SOME BASIC TECHNIQUES FOR YOU TO USE

by José Silva Jr.

The biggest factor my father found was foretold by Napoleon Hill in his *Reading Course In The Laws of Success*, is functioning at the alpha level and using your natural God-given intuition to help you detect the information you need to help you solve problems.

You can use your mind to help live matter return to normal. If someone has a malfunction heart for instance, you can visualize the heart functioning normally, the way the Creator intended, and your mental image will help attract matter (the heart) to return to its original—healthy—state.

That doesn't work the same way for inanimate matter. Your mental image can help to guide you to do the things that are necessary to achieve success. For instance, if your computer is malfunctioning, you can project your mind to locate the problem, then take action in the physical world to replace the broken part.

In the objective dimension—the world of the body—we use force to make things happen. In the subjective dimension—the world of the mind—we use visualization and imagination to attract solutions.

Read on to see a good example of this.

26 Resolutions: Are They What You Really Want? *(1981)*

January is the month for self-evaluation and for promises to do better in the incoming year. This is normally done in the traditional "New Year's Resolutions," promises that all too often remain unfulfilled.

All of us, no doubt, can become much better persons, and those of us who are involved in Silva Mind Control have made becoming better a continuing process, just as our way of greeting dictates—"Better and Better."

Perhaps more important is the fact that along with our commitment to self-betterment, Silva Mind Control offers the tools by which this can be accomplished, and it can be done personally or with the help of any professional counselors or therapists.

There are many references in the Silva Mind Control Method that allow us to individually modify our behavior for the better, and all we would need to do is review the concepts and literature of our method.

We must, first of all, view our behavior critically and judge it solely on the basis of whether it is our best choice for us as individuals deeply concerned with humanity.

In making this judgment, the Mirror of the Mind or the 3-Scenes technique can be extremely useful, and Silva Mind Control graduates should find this a relatively easy task.

We must, however, be certain that we are not influenced in our behavior modification by the countless pressures placed upon us by the media to conform to some standard established by them.

Any change should be done with a deep insight into our own humanity and realizing that ultimately our behavior should be judged not only on how it is affecting us but also how it is affecting humanity—particularly those close to us.

Fortunately, Silva Mind Control offers standards that we as individuals can use in determining any behavioral modification.

Understand What Counts the Most

We should understand the difference between how we *feel about* our behavior and how we are *acting because of* our behavior.

This point is very important because people can be acting in a very satisfying manner yet may feel they are not acting in a way that is personally gratifying to them.

Feelings, as I explain in my courses, are neither right nor wrong, and there may be a tendency for people to change their behavior simply because they are not feeling right about it.

The problem here is to determine why we feel this way instead of changing behavior automatically.

Interestingly enough, most people evaluate their behavior during the coming of the new year, which is the time of year when emotions are most active and sensitive.

The excitement of the time, the family gatherings, the joyful music and the festive and religious atmosphere often make it difficult for people to differentiate between feelings and actual behavior.

The Correct Attitude

It is much easier to modify behavior if the person has an attitude of success.

People who are depressed, lonely or who feel they are failures will find it much more difficult to change their behavior to one that will lead to success.

This is why in Silva Mind Control we put so much emphasis on recalling a feeling of success, and that is why our Mirror of the Mind and 3-Scenes techniques are so popular among our graduates. Through them, we can project a success image, recall the feeling of success, and then adapt our behavior to meet that image.

A person who has a success identity will be able to make whatever changes are necessary to become "better and better." Conversely, a person who identifies with failure will not be able to shed this behavior. They will find it impossible to do so.

This type of defeatist attitude is expressed in, "Yea, I know I ought to change, but this is all I can do. I know this is not the best, but what can I really do about it?"

Get Involved

We will find our choice of behavior much more fruitful if we become involved with humanity. In addition to being able to help our fellow humans, becoming involved will also tend to give us a new perspective on life. We will realize that our problems are not unique and that others with similar circumstances have changed for the better, and so can we.

We qualify as humans through our humanitarian acts, and helping humanity will reinforce a sense of fellowship, of belonging, of worthwhileness.

Visualizing ourselves as integral parts of humanity without losing our individuality is the key to personal fulfillment.

At Silva Mind Control, this is the essence of our existence, and as individuals we should always be striving to do this by becoming better and better.

May this year bring all of you your most cherished wishes.

27 Use Your Mind to Stay Alive
(1991)

If you want to stay alive and healthy in the world today, you need to use your mind.

I'm not talking about just programming. That's important, of course. You need to do more:

You need to use common sense, and avoid trouble.

We just received a report from the Webb County Medical Society that contains some alarming information about AIDS.

The report quotes the *Journal of the American Medical Association* of Nov. 15, 1991, that "In New York City, AIDS has become the leading cause of death in women ages twenty to forty."

Do you think that it can't happen here?

Consider this comment from the report:

"A handsome twenty year old male is infecting each month an average of three new girls in Laredo. He knows he has the disease but none of his victims are aware of his disease."

Seeking Protection

We've been asked by Silva graduates to help combat this problem in many ways.

Some want us to add a statement into the programming that they will never contract AIDS.

But a statement in a conditioning cycle isn't going to stop them from getting the disease if they do not change their risky behavior. The AIDS virus won't stay away just because we tell it to.

We already have plenty of statements in the conditioning cycles about the kind of life we should live if we want to be healthy, happy, and successful.

You need to live the kind of life that we recommend if you want to be healthier, happier, luckier, and more successful.

How We Can Help

There are those who want us to lead a worldwide effort to find a cure for AIDS. Let's talk about that.

There are many highly qualified people right now who are searching full time for a cure for this disease. We will be glad to train them in our System so that they can use their creative and intuitive faculties to find the cure they are seeking and solve this problem.

We know what we are good at:

We are good at teaching people how to actually use the untapped power of their minds to solve problems and reach goals in order to get whatever they need.

We will be happy to teach our System to researchers who are qualified to search for a cure for AIDS.

Meanwhile, we will continue to do what we do best: Teach people how to use more of their minds, how to live healthier, safer, more successful lives.

We need to learn to love one another. Not just have sex with as many people as possible that's not loving one another.

The medical society report concludes that "Movies, television, music lyrics, commercials, *must decrease the selling of sex to decrease promiscuity.*" (The emphasis is theirs.)

"Sexual transmitted disease control programs need to be expanded."

Dr. Robert C. Noble, an infectious disease physician with the University of Kentucky, is quoted as saying that "Passing out condoms to teenagers is like issuing squirt guns for a four-alarm blaze. Condoms just don't hack it. We should stop kidding ourselves.

"Abstinence, or sexual intercourse with one with whom one is mutually faithful who is an uninfected partner, are the only totally effective prevention strategies."

We've been saying the same thing, in a slightly different way, for years.

Many animals exhibit higher moral standards than many humans. Many animals are more faithful to their mates than a lot of people we know.

Sex is necessary for the survival of the species on the planet. Because of that, the Creator made it very enjoyable.

If people were not using sex so often only for fun and recreation, and were using it to bring new life to the planet, with one partner, then we would not be having this discussion; AIDS would not be a problem.

Our Natural Feedback System

The Creator established a pretty good feedback system: If you get hungry, you eat, and therefore you survive. When you do wrong, the automatic feedback mechanisms let you know by causing you to suffer. If you don't eat, you get hungry.

When you use sex to help perpetuate the species, you enjoy it, and you grow to love your partner more each year.

Many people who use sex primarily for pleasure, end up suffering by contracting sexually transmitted diseases. Such as AIDS.

If you want to stay healthy—in fact, if you want to stay alive—then start using your mind in the most basic way:

Use your common sense.

Stop doing things that could kill you.

Be careful.

28 Do You Know the Purpose of Your Life? *(1983)*

Many people wonder about the purpose of life. They ask: Why am I here? Where did I come from, and where am I going? What am I supposed to be doing while I am here?

For those who have not yet begun to discover the answers to those questions, time is growing short. We have but a few years on this planet to do what we were sent here to do. We are here to help the Creator correct the problems of creation.

For some of us it is later than we think. We have only a certain amount of time on this planet.

One second of time puts you in another dimension.

What have you done to help make this world a better place to live?

What have you done before that one second to help the Creator correct problems of creation?

Or are we just enjoying life, and "living it up"? That's a good question, you know, because so many people function like they are on a long coffee break.

Wrong Values

We have a tremendous wrong sense of values. Can you imagine paying twenty million dollars to two boxers to destroy each other on television for forty-five minutes? Twenty million dollars!

Entertainment, they call it.

And look what they are trying to do: to destroy the most precious creation of the Creator, this human being that the Creator put together to function correcting problems on planet Earth, and they are trying to destroy each other, and they get paid for it.

Twenty million dollars for forty-five minutes.

And we think it is too much to pay twenty thousand dollars to biologists who are trying to save lives.

That's too much money, you say?

How wrong can we be?

When the athletic hero comes to town: big celebration, parades, bands, ticker-tape and the whole bit. Have we ever done that for the man who discovered the polio vaccine? Penicillin? The sulfa drugs that have prevented thousands of human beings from suffering and dying? Have we done this?

No.

We don't even know when they come to town!

But that football hero, baseball hero, soccer hero . . . big deal!.

Do you see how wrong we are?

We Suffer Because of Ignorance

And we say, "God, please help me!" The help God can give is to help save us from ignorance. We are suffering because of ignorance.

It is my responsibility, and it is your responsibility, to try to straighten out this whole mess, because we were sent with the same power of mind to do this on this planet.

We were all created in the image of our Creator, not physically, but in the power of our minds to create solutions to problems and to help make this world a better place to live.

Center yourself and ask, "Whoever sent me here, what am I supposed to do here? I don't remember asking to come to planet earth, so somebody must have sent me. Now, what am I supposed to do here? I want to understand, I want to know, I want to do the right thing."

You'll be surprised what information will start coming to you.

You will discover how to use your money, because money is a tool to do the job with. If you need more of it, you center yourself, you are sincere about it, and ask for more money, and it will come to you, to do the job. Not extra money to pay more boxers to destroy themselves, but to do the job to correct problems.

If you are sincere it will come to you.

When you are fulfilling your mission on this planet, then you will be prosperous in all areas of your life. You will have health, wealth, and happiness. You will have everything you need to continue to do your job here.

If you have any lack in your life, look at how much you are helping to make this a better world to live in. Not just how much you are trying to help, but how much you are accomplishing.

If you need to practice more and develop more skills, then practice and develop more skills.

But practice on real, existing, problems.

For it is when you work on real problems that you obtain the best results.

Take action today, and build your prosperity on a foundation of service.

Note: If you have not taken any of our Courses, you can learn to enter the alpha level, and learn many of our techniques, with the free training in the appendix.

29 Great People Want to Serve, Not to Be Served *(1993)*

We can learn a lot by studying the lives of the greats who have come to the planet to teach us and to help us.

There are some common themes that run through the stories of their lives, almost as if they were all sent from the same source, with the same purpose:

To find out why humans are causing problems and destroying each other, and to teach us how to be more constructive and creative and to convert our planet into a paradise.

They have all made contributions, and have served as great examples of how to live. This is true of Moses and Abraham, of Zoroaster, Krishna, Buddha, Mohammed, Jesus, and many others.

Since I was born into a Catholic family in a Catholic community, I was brought up with the story of Christ. It is much the same as the stories of the others. But, because of my birth, Christ has been my inspiration.

It was through the study of Christ's life and teaching that I was guided to discover how humans can learn to actually use a new dimension of mind for problem solving.

There are other things that I learned too, about the best way to live.

For instance, none of the greats who came here to Planet Earth came to be served.

They all came to serve.

They did not come to destroy.

They came to build.

From Moses who climbed the mountain to bring his people a code of conduct called The Ten Commandments, to Jesus who washed his disciples feet at their Last Supper, we see these greats doing all that they could to solve problems and to help people have a better life.

They did not seek a better life for themselves. They did not seek greatness.

They Came to Serve

Isn't it interesting that those that we honor as the greatest who have ever walked the earth, are those who came to serve.

It was this kind of thinking that prompted me to write the final statements in the Silva Method:

"You will continue to strive to take part in constructive and creative activities to make this a better world to live in, so that when we move on, we shall have left behind a better world for those who follow.

"You will consider the whole of humanity, depending on their ages, as fathers or mothers, brothers or sisters, sons or daughters.

"You are a superior human being; you have greater understanding, compassion, and patience with others."

The Value of Forgiving

Another characteristic of these greats is their ability to forgive. They set wonderful examples for us.

You can see this throughout the story of Christ's life, from His parable about the Prodigal Son, to his words on the cross.

It is good for us to forgive.

Forgiveness will help you remove a tremendous load that's on your back.

If I was hurt by anybody, it is because that person didn't know any better.

They didn't know how to live like the great masters who have come to the planet. They are still ignorant of their purpose here on earth.

I do know better. I know more than the person who hurt me.

And since I know more, I should help those who do not yet know.

Since I know more than the person who hurt me, I should forgive that person. They hurt me through ignorance, by not knowing that they should not hurt me, so what else can I do but forgive?

That is what Christ did on the cross. He didn't complain about "those rotten so-and-so's who nailed me up here." Remember what he said?

"Forgive them Father, for they know not what they do."

If someone has hurt you, forgive them.

And if you have hurt someone, enter your level and imagine that they are forgiving you.

Get rid of those burdens now.

Use your level to make future decisions.

And live by those words that I put in the conditioning cycles:

"Continue to strive to take part in constructive and creative activities. . . ."

30 Learn to Be Successful by Acting Successful *(1995)*

If you want to be successful, then learn to do what successful people do.

Successful people have certain traits, they do certain things, and they function in certain ways.

Learn those things and do them, and you will be successful too.

Successful people want to be successful. They have a burning desire to succeed. They are willing to do whatever it takes to achieve their goals. This powerful desire propels them towards their goals, through obstacles, etc.

Successful people learn to believe in themselves. They turn away from thoughts of failure and focus their attention on success.

Successful people accomplish things.

First, they manage their own lives, so that they can direct their energy into activities that will help make them more successful.

Second, successful people get into action. They have strategies to help them determine what to do, and then get into action and do it. They have goals, and they go after those goals.

Successful people relate well to other people. You do not achieve great success in a vacuum. The better you are at dealing with other people, at knowing what other people want and need, and how to satisfy those needs, the more successful you will be.

Successful people are able to get the information that they need to make correct decisions. This enables them to solve more problems. There is no such thing as a problem without a solution; only problems for which we do not yet have enough information to know what the solution is.

Now scientific research has finally learned how to teach all of these traits to anyone who is willing to put in the time and energy to learn them.

Learning How to Succeed Is Not Enough

It is more than simply a matter of learning something—you have to take action. You learn a new way to function, to process information the way that the super successful people do.

And then you use your new abilities and apply them in the same manner that highly successful people do, so that you will be more successful also.

Once you have learned our System, practice what you have learned:

Practice the Long Relaxation Exercise (Silva Centering Exercise) once a week.

Work health detection and correction cases regularly, and establish more points of reference so that you will be able to use your clairvoyant faculties more effectively.

Help to correct problems whenever possible.

Persuade friends and family to learn the course too so that you have your own support group. Do not depend on your Silva lecturer to take care of your problems. Help each other.

If we all keep working to correct problems, then we can bring peace to the planet, and convert the planet into a paradise.

31 When You Encounter a Sticking Point *(1985)*

Why don't our techniques work every time they are applied by a Silva graduate?

There could be many reasons.

Perhaps there are factors involved in the situation that the graduate is not aware of. In that case, one of the information-gathering techniques can be used to find out what needs to be done.

Perhaps the graduate is not at level when programming the technique. The best way to learn that special feeling of being at level where you will be successful in using the subjective dimension is to practice working health cases regularly.

You can also use aids such as the Alpha Sound or Theta Sound recordings to help you remain at your level.

Maybe the graduate's faith is not strong enough. Check on your desire, belief and expectancy. Desire is especially important.

When you have a very strong desire, you will usually succeed even if the other two factors are weak.

Belief comes from experience—from having successful experiences. So practice solving problems at every opportunity and accumulate as many feelings of success as possible.

Accepting Responsibility

A technique by itself is not going to accomplish anything.

A technique works only when it is applied by a human being.

A technique works when you have desire, belief and expectancy.

It is up to you to manage your life.

If you expect the Silva techniques to take care of everything, then you are not really accepting responsibility for your own life.

You are responsible for your own life.

The more you take charge, the more successful you will be.

Applying a technique with the attitude that "it" will work is not the answer. Yet some people do this.

You Make the Difference

A camera doesn't make pictures. A camera is a tool used by a person to make pictures.

When people lift weights to become stronger, it is not the weights that make you strong. It is the effort you use to lift them.

If you apply a Silva technique with a "disinterested" attitude, with the attitude that it is the responsibility of the technique to solve the problem, then the results may not be what you wanted.

But when you use a technique as a tool to help you accomplish what you desire, and you apply the technique properly, you will probably get results that will satisfy you.

You Can Succeed

You have many tools to work with to improve your life, and you should take advantage of those tools when appropriate.

When dealing with your health, follow your doctor's advice.

In religious matters, listen to your religious leaders.

In education, your teachers know how to help you.

In business, apply proper business principles, use good accountants and other professionals to guide you.

And regardless what you are doing, use your mental tools also.

Use your Silva techniques just as you would any other tools to help you achieve your goals.

Remember, it is up to you to use the tools available to you.

When you do this, you will succeed more often than not.

32 Be More Successful by Dwelling on Success *(1995)*

When you succeed at something, you get a unique feeling of success. It is a special feeling that you only get by succeeding at something.

Even if you have only one talent, you can still solve more than one problem. You can have many successes.

When you use your one talent to solve many problems, you accumulate many feelings of success.

When you accumulate enough feelings of success, these serve as a key to discover a second talent.

Then you can use both talents to accumulate enough experience, enough feelings of success, to unlock another talent.

A Better Way to Achieve Success

They used to tell us to learn from our mistakes, that our success would be built on a ladder of failures.

Now we know better:

Greater success is built on a ladder of lesser successes.

The feelings of success that you accumulate from using the first talent may be enough to reveal a second talent, but not enough for the third talent. However, by using the two talents, you will be able to accumulate enough feelings of success to uncover the third talent.

Then you can use the three talents to help you develop a fourth talent.

The accumulation of successes equals wisdom.

We have demonstrated, through scientific research, that you can imagine doing something and it is almost as if you had actually done it—provided that you use your imagination at the alpha brain wave level.

Athletes who went to their level and imagined shooting at a goal for five minutes improved 68 percent, compared to athletes who physically shot at the goal for five minutes and improved 70 percent.

And a third group of athletes who played the game mentally for two and a half minutes and physically for two and a half minutes improved 160 percent!

If you have one success, and you enter your level and review that success, and especially review and recall that special feeling of success, then it is almost like having another success.

If you have one success and then review that success and the feeling of success at your level ten times, it is almost like having ten more successes.

So cancel-cancel your failures. Erase them, and replace them with memories of successes. And from then on, dwell on your successes. If you happen to think of a failure, cancel-cancel it and recall your success.

Using information correctly. Remember that it is not enough just to put together bits of information just to have knowledge. Knowledge is to be used, and to be used correctly.

The Correct Use of Knowledge is for Problem Solving

Truth and reality solve problems. If something creates problems, it goes in the other direction.

If we can get enough information, we can solve all problems, eliminate all suffering. So, perfect your information gathering techniques.

Our senses detect information, both biological (objective), and subjective.

Most people have been using only animal type senses, the senses of the body.

Now people are learning how to sense information with human intelligence type sensing.

Which senses are "extra"?

We feel that the fundamental senses are the senses of human intelligence, of the mind. The biological senses are an extension of these.

Clairvoyance is not an "extra" sense. It is a fundamental, or prior, sense. We had it before we had a body, and will have it after we no longer use the body. It is the biological senses that are the extensions, the "extra" senses.

Visualization is the fundamental detecting sense of physical eyesight.

The physical senses (the extensions) are limited. They can be fooled. If you put up a wall, you cannot see beyond the wall with the physical sense of eyesight.

You can see beyond the wall with the subjective senses of human intelligence.

You can't fool the human intelligence senses; you cannot hide from them.

When you function from the center of the universe of human intelligence—at ten cycles per second alpha—there are no limitations to what you can do, because there are no limitations to what the mind can do.

We are made in the image of our Creator, not in what we can see with our eyes, but by what we can do with our minds.

Practice entering your level. Practice working health cases. Regain the use of your fundamental, subjective, senses.

Note: If you have not taken any of our Courses, you can learn to enter the alpha level with the free training in the appendix.

33 Negative Thinking Can Sneak Up On You *(1987)*

Positive thinking is not just going around telling everybody that you are the greatest. It is not talking about how wonderful everything is.

Positive thinking is thinking and talking about what you want in your life, rather than what you do not want.

It is just like we teach in Mental Housecleaning: If you want to have a good memory, then do not talk about how bad your memory is.

Talk instead about having a good memory.

Cancel-Cancel

We teach you to "cancel-cancel" any negative statement that you put into your bio-computer brain.

But cancel-cancel is not permission to go around being negative.

We sometimes hear people saying something like this:

"I 'cancel' forget 'cancel' to take my vitamins."

Regardless of the fact that they are putting the "cancel-cancel" in the sentence, they are still making a negative statement that creates a mental image on the brain of what they *don't* want.

Accentuate the Positive

We must learn to emphasize the words and statements that create positive mental images, not negative ones.

Some people make a big issue when they hear somebody make a negative statement.

It would probably be better if they would just remind the person to "cancel-cancel" the negative statement and make a positive statement.

Remember, a negative statement is anything that creates a mental picture of something you *do not* desire, anything that is *not* beneficial for you.

A positive statement is anything that you do desire, that is good for you.

A Case Study

Sometimes people do not completely understand the difference.

I remember one graduate who told me that he wanted to come to the International Convention in Laredo, but did not have the money and could not think of any way to get the money. He kept programming to get the money, he told me.

Then he realized that getting the money was the problem.

Being in Laredo and attending the Convention was the solution.

When he changed his programming to focus on the solution—attending the Convention—instead of the problem—getting the money—then he quickly found a way to get the money.

Why Have Insurance?

Someone asked recently if it was negative to wear seat belts. Doesn't that put the idea in the bio-computer that we could have an accident?

What mental movies do you make when you buckle your seat belt?

Do you have a fear of crashing, or do you remind yourself how safe you are? One is a negative thought, the other positive.

But the main reason for wearing seat belts is that not everybody is as positive as you are.

We can't control other people. And many of those other people have not yet learned the Silva techniques.

When everybody on the road—and in the world—knows these mental techniques and practices them regularly, then we will have a safe world to live in.

Until then, buckle your seat belt.

You might even program yourself that buckling your seat belt will be a reminder to tell somebody else about the Silva training, and tell them how it has helped you.

They will benefit, and so will you.

34 How to Handle Programming Conflicts *(1987)*

Q: Sometimes my partner and I program for different things. That is, we program for the same subject but for opposite results.

There are times when we go to level and ask for guidance, and the answers we get are opposite. I'll be guided to do one thing, my partner another.

Can you explain why this occurs, and how we should handle this.

When two people are programming for opposite things, what determines which one gets it?

When two people both want the same thing, but only one can have it (like a particular job), what factors determine which one gets it?

Remove All Doubt
A: (by José Silva) Any time you are not sure of what you should be programming for, the first thing you must do is to remove all doubt.

You can enter your level, analyze the problem, and analyze potential solutions.

After you are sure of what you should be programming for, then you can program with complete confidence.

Different Goals

If your partner programs and gets a different answer, that could be because the two of you have different goals, because of your background and experience, your philosophy, or other factors.

For instance, in business, one partner may feel that long term growth is more important than immediate cash flow, while the other feels just the opposite.

Both partners could be correct—for themselves.

But what is best for one may not always be what is best for the other.

You can include a phrase such as, "May the best thing be done for all concerned."

You can also program for the conflict to be resolved, but since we are all human beings and not God, we do not always resolve every difference of opinion.

Most Deserving

If two people are programming for the same thing but only one can get it, it will go to the one who is most deserving.

That is a good principle to remember in all of your programming. To receive good things, we must qualify for them.

How do we qualify?

By helping to correct problems.

The more problems you "correct" without creating new problems—the more you qualify to receive the things you desire.

When I program, I do not program to receive money. I program to provide service, and I keep in mind what my needs are—plus a little bit more.

Higher Intelligence

It is important when you are programming, especially when you are at the intuitive level, that you be in a sitting position with your head lowered (bowed) about 20 degrees, and your eyes turned upwards about 20 degrees. This position aligns you with higher intelligence.

It is important that you align yourself with higher intelligence when you are programming so that higher intelligence knows you qualify for help.

To seek help from higher intelligence, you must first attempt to correct the problem yourself. After you have made a strong effort, if you still cannot correct the problem, then you can seek help from higher intelligence with the MentalVideo Technique.

If you qualify for help because you have been correcting problems, and you have attempted to correct this problem yourself, then higher intelligence will help you.

Higher intelligence may not correct the problem for you, but will help you correct the problem yourself.

You can learn the MentalVideo Technique right now in the appendix and start using it tonight if you need to.

We do not have all the answers yet—nobody does. But by using our Silva techniques correctly, we will get the correct answers most of the time, and this will make our life much better than it would be if we did not use these techniques.

35 Who Answers Questions in the Newsletter? *(1987)*

Q: Who answers the questions in the Newsletter about using the Silva techniques?

A: Newsletter editor Ed Bernd Jr. is responsible for all of the content of the Newsletter. Questions come from many sources: from graduates who call or write, from lecturers who get the questions in class, and even from your editor himself. Here is how they are handled:

Many of the questions concern subjects that have come up before, during lecturer training or seminars, and José Silva has discussed and answered them, often in great detail. When this is the case, then your editor answers the questions. Sometimes he shows them to Mr. Silva to insure that they are accurate, and other times José Silva does not see the answers until after the Newsletter is published.

If one of those answers were to be wrong, then Ed would correct it in the next issue of the Newsletter.

Fortunately, during the six years Ed has been Editor, that has not happened.

Any time that Ed is not absolutely certain of how José Silva would answer the question, he goes to Mr. Silva and gets his answer. Many follow up questions are asked to insure that the answer will be comprehensive, clear, and easy to understand.

The discussion is usually recorded on a micro cassette recorder, then transcribed and edited, and given to Mr. Silva for approval. When this is done, Mr. Silva is generally identified as the source of the answer.

Sometimes it is felt that either José or Juan Silva can give some special insight on a situation. In that case, they are consulted, usually with the micro cassette recorder in hand. They are usually identified as the source of the answer, or else quoted directly within the article.

Of course, answers could come from other sources.

Sometimes when talking with lecturers, they are asked how they would answer, and they often give ideas to use.

In all instances, steps are taken to insure that the answers in the Silva Newsletter are based on, and are consistent with, José Silva's research, as well as the vast experience of both José Silva and his brother Juan.

This has been the case during the last six years, so that you can be sure that all information you read in the Silva Newsletter comes directly from the source, and you can depend on it.

Ed has asked so many questions that when Mr. Silva sees him coming with recorder in hand, he sighs and mutters, "Here we go again." But he always spends as much time as necessary to answer the questions completely, and he answers all follow-up questions, to insure that there will be no misunderstanding or doubt.

So, ask anything you like about using the Silva techniques. You will get answers that you can depend on.

(This question was asked by Teresa Chavez, Silva Lecturer in El Paso, Texas, and answered by Ed Bernd Jr.)

36 Are There People Who Can't Learn Our Method? *(1987)*

Q: I'm interested in learning the Silva Method. Is there a specific group of personality traits a person possesses that would make the course more beneficial for one type of person than another?

If a person is not very responsive to hypnosis, would they still be able to achieve the goals of the Silva Method?

In other words, is this something that would be beneficial for just about anybody, or are there certain limitations?

A: The only thing required for a person to be successful with the Silva Method is that you have a desire to solve problems, and be willing to use the techniques.

We like skeptics, because when they are convinced, then they are really good at using the techniques.

The only people who have difficulty gaining much benefit from the Silva Method are those people who have closed minds, who say, "You can't teach me anything." Of course, most of those people never even attend the training.

If they are coerced into attending (by a spouse or an employer for instance) then they often receive only minimal benefit.

This is not hypnosis—it is just the opposite of hypnosis. We encourage people to have more control mentally, not to give control over to someone else.

They say that ·the most difficult people to hypnotize are hypnotists, because they already know all about it. Yet hypnotists are just as successful with the Silva techniques as anyone else.

We've taught young and old, rich and poor, and they all succeed if they follow instructions and stick with it.

We currently offer the program in seventy-three countries and sixteen languages, to people of all races and religions, as well as those with no religious beliefs.

Everybody who wants to, learns to use the techniques successfully.

We guarantee it:

Anybody who is not completely satisfied, by the end of the training, can get a refund, no hesitation, no questions asked.

Fair enough?

It is very rare that anyone asks for a refund, which is good feedback to us that the program works for all who want it to.

If you are interested, we have reprints of research reports on the results of the Silva training with all kinds of people:

- teenage students,
- athletes,
- alcoholics,
- mothers on welfare,
- mental patients,
- average people from the general public.

You can get copies from your local Silva lecturer, or from the SilvaESP.com website.

37 Ancient Writings Aid Research
(1990)

Many of my ideas for research came from my study of ancient literature, especially the Bible.

But sometimes these writings can be quite confusing.

On the other hand, we have found that our scientific research sometimes helps us understand what the ancient teachers were attempting to teach us.

Some really interesting ideas can come from meditating on these matters.

For instance, consider the line from the Lord's Prayer, where we are told to implore God, "Lead us not into temptation."

People have questioned that particular line. Why, they ask, would a kind and loving God who always encourages us to stay on the path of righteousness, even consider leading us "into temptation"?

When you read those same words another way, and apply what we have learned about programming, you might draw a different conclusion.

Three Requests

When you study that section of the Lord's Prayer, it appears that we are told to make three requests. These requests deal with the present, the past, and the future.

First we deal with the present:

"Give us this day our daily bread." Survival is always the first order of business, for if we do not survive we cannot help other humans, we cannot grow spiritually, or any of the other things we might want to do.

Then we deal with the past:

"Forgive us our debts as we forgive our debtors." As soon as we are born we begin learning. And we continue to learn throughout our lives. Part of the learning process is making mistakes.

We all make mistakes, and we should learn from those mistakes, and not continue to make the same mistakes.

By the same token, we should be tolerant of others when they make mistakes.

Many sermons can be based on these ideas, and undoubtedly have been.

Finally, we turn to the future:

"Lead us . . ."

How to Program

Now let's pause here for just a moment, and consider what we have learned about programming.

When we want to program for something we desire to have, or desire to do, or desire to be, we use the Mirror of the Mind or the 3-Scenes Technique.

Our research indicated that we must first identify and visualize the problem, or the existing situation.

Then we must imagine the solution, or our goal.

Now, back to the Lord's Prayer: ". . . not into temptation, but deliver us from evil."

Could it be that the author wanted us to visualize the problem (our debts, that we have already asked forgiveness for), and our goal: to continue to learn and grow.

Could it be that the intent was to express movement and growth, from ignorance to knowledge?

The Cause of Evil

Ignorance does not exempt us from suffering. If we are ignorant of the law of gravity and step off the top of a building, we will probably suffer. You don't break laws. Laws don't break, people do.

Suffering is evil. Could it be that those who say we were born in sin, were trying to tell us that we were born in ignorance, and therefore, would suffer until we learned better? Did they mean that ignorance is bad, and knowledge is good?

Sometimes the ancient writings help us better understand how to function, and sometimes our scientific research helps us to better understand what the ancients were trying to teach us.

It certainly gives us some interesting topics to meditate on.

38 José Silva Answers a Question About Time *(1987)*

Q: Could you please help me out of my confusion. In José Silva's book, he says to move the blue framed mirror (of your mind) to the right and away. My lecturer said to move it to the left in your head, and the New York people say to just break it. Just what is the correct thing to do, or does it matter that much as long as it is gone?

A: (by José Silva) A couple of people have asked this same question recently, so let's clear up the confusion.

The technique in *The Silva Mind Control Method* book is not the Mirror of the Mind. It is a different technique, designed for people who have not attended the Silva training.

Let me explain.

The whole concept of the movement of time from a psychic (mental) point of view came about when I was conducting age regression experiments with children. Sometimes I would regress them back to a time before they were born, and they would tell me stories as if they were living another life.

With some of the children, I could take them back many years, even many centuries, through many lifetimes.

With children who were very good subjects, I could take them back very rapidly. I noticed that when I did that, they would lean to the side.

When I was taking them back in time, they would lean towards their right, and when I was bringing them forward in time, they would lean towards their left.

When I questioned them about this, they said that the images from the past were coming from their right, very rapidly, and it was a little bit like having a rug pulled out from under them.

That's why they were leaning.

The images of the future came from their left.

When I wrote the material in *The Silva Mind Control Method* book, I wanted to use this same kind of idea. That's why I suggest that, onto your mental screen, you "slide on an image" (a solution image) from the left.

However, the Mirror of the Mind is a completely different technique.

With the Mirror of the Mind Technique, you project an image of a full length mirror onto your mental screen. The mirror is directly in front of you (the present), and has a blue frame around it.

After projecting the problem image into the blue framed mirror and making a good study of it, you then erase the problem image.

Now there is no image.

So you take the empty mirror and move it towards the left, towards the left side of your mental screen where the images of the future are (from a psychic point of view).

Then you change the frame to white, which symbolizes that you are changing from the problem to the solution, and you create, with your imagination, and project onto the white-framed Mirror of the Mind, your solution image.

Please note that we are not going "against the grain" when we do this. We are just moving the mirror over to the side of the mental screen where it will be closer to the images of the future.

If you do not like the idea of moving the mirror, then you can leave it directly in front of you, on your mental screen. Just erase the problem image, change the mirror's frame to white and create and project onto it your solution image.

In the future, whenever you think of your project, visualize (recall) the solution image you created in your white-framed Mirror of the Mind.

Do this whether the mirror is directly in front of you, or towards your left.

Some people like to smash the blue-framed mirror, but personally I do not like this. I prefer not to break or destroy anything at my level. I prefer to use these levels for constructive and creative activities.

If you are working more than one project, then you can proceed this way:

After you are finished with the first project, you can slide the entire mirror, with its solution image, off of your mental screen towards your right (put the problem into the past).

Then bring a new mirror onto your mental screen from your left, and work your next project.

Or if you prefer, you can just snap your fingers and cause the first mirror to disappear, and a second mirror to appear in its place.

Note: If you are not familiar with the Mirror of the Mind Technique you can learn it in the appendix.

39 Practice Prepares You to Handle Emergencies *(1985)*

Among the many calls and requests we receive here at world head-quarters are ones like these:

"I just discovered I have cancer. What can I do?"

"I'm taking a test Monday to get a job with the Post Office. What techniques can I use?"

"I have a really big meeting with a client tomorrow morning. How can I be certain I will say the right thing?"

"My daughter has run away. How can I find out where she is?"

"I need to sell my house right away. Can I program to find a buyer?"

Answers Are Easy

Now, requests such as these are easy enough to answer. There are many techniques that can be applied simultaneously to each of those problems.

But what occasionally disappoints our headquarters staff is the answer we sometimes get to the very first question we ask:

"What have you already been doing? Which techniques have you developed proficiency in?"

The majority of the time, callers admit that they have not been practicing "because I didn't need it until now."

And we find that the caller has not taken the time to practice the various techniques and develop proficiency with them.

Solving Serious Problems

The best way to solve serious problems is to keep them from becoming serious problems in the first place.

How does one do that? By entering level every single day for at least five minutes (even though fifteen minutes is better), this will guarantee your centering yourself so that you will avoid many of the problems that the un-centered (eccentrics) encounter.

And when you practice the various techniques and develop proficiency with them, you will be able to correct problems as soon as they begin, before they become serious.

Keep Practicing

I like to remind our staff here that the people they hear from are usually the graduates who do not practice. Those who practice are usually able to correct the problems by themselves.

Of course, whenever you want any help, suggestions, guidance, or just some reassurance and motivation, please call on us. All of us here, as well as your local Silva lecturer, stand ready to help any way we can.

But nobody can do things for you.

The only solutions that are really permanent are those you attain yourself.

A doctor can treat you, but if you don't do something yourself, the same condition might reappear, or another condition.

If somebody gives you the answers to a test, that will help you temporarily, but not in the future. You must do for yourself, learn for yourself, if you wish to change your life.

The best time to practice is when you don't need to, because then, when you are relaxed and not under pressure, you can establish deep and very healthy points of reference.

Repeat the Silva training.

Learn new ways to apply the techniques in Silva workshops.

Participate in local graduate activities.

Read the authentic Silva newsletters and books that are available.

Practice, and help yourself.

Whenever you desire, call on us to assist you.

And keep getting better, better and better.

Note: If you have not taken any of our Courses, you can learn to enter the alpha level with any of the free training options in the appendix.

40 How to Generate More Problem Solving Ideas (1985)

People sometimes ask if the Silva techniques always work. I don't know of anything that works every time, but the Silva techniques work so much of the time that they are an extremely valuable tool to use on the challenges we face in life.

There could be many reasons why you might not get the results you program for. The time might not be right, or the project itself may need to be altered.

What could you do if your programming is not working the way you think it should work?

Here are some ideas that we recommend to graduates who ask such questions.

Getting It Working

The first step, of course, is to practice regularly.

That means *every single day.*

It is best to practice going to level for five, ten or fifteen minutes, two or three times a day.

When you enter level, make sure that you relax and remain at your level. You need to learn to establish deep, healthy levels of mind. There are aids available to help you do this, such as the Alpha and Theta Sound recordings.

You also want to make certain that you are applying the mental techniques correctly. Review your course manual and make sure you are doing them exactly as I wrote them. The wording is based on many years of research, and it is the very best we could come up with.

Some people want to modify techniques because they think they will work better for them. This could be true, but first practice with the techniques the way I wrote them. After you are successful, then you might try changing them to suit yourself.

Check your desire, belief and expectancy—your faith. Desire is a vital factor. The more desire you have, the more energy you have towards reaching your goal.

You can increase your desire by thinking of more reasons why it will be beneficial for you to achieve your goal. If you have five reasons for wanting to reach the goal, you have a certain amount of desire. You will have more desire if you think of ten reasons for wanting to succeed.

You can increase all three factors—desire, belief, and expectancy (hope)—by repeating mentally or verbally what it is that you want to accomplish. It will continue to get stronger and stronger, until you have enough mental energy to reach your goals.

Creative Solutions

Most people, when they first complete the Silva training, program for things. They program to get things, to do things, and perhaps to be a certain way.

This is one type of creative work, for you are creating for yourself just the kind of life and lifestyle that you want to have.

But there is another way to utilize your creative potential.

Let's say you have been programming for something, and it has not yet manifested in the physical world.

Your faith is strong, you are applying the techniques properly, it is a project that will benefit everybody, yet you still are not getting results.

In that case, you can use your techniques to determine what to do next. In other words, at your level, with the use of your Silva techniques, come up with some creative ideas to guide you in your future efforts.

A good technique for this is Dream Control Step 3. Another is the MentalVideo.

Mirror of the Mind and the 3-Scenes Techniques could be used for this also, as you mentally picture yourself in the solution image learning what you must do to reach your goal.

You can also use the case working model, like you do when working health detection and correction cases: Examine the existing situation and look for problem areas, sticking points. Then use your imagination to correct the problems.

It all becomes easier and more effective with practice.

I know graduates who have been practicing for ten years and more, who use the techniques very effectively, who tell me they continue learning new ways that the Silva techniques can help them live the kind of lives they desire.

If you work, so do the Silva techniques. You can review the techniques right now in the appendix of this book.

41 How to Break Through Limitations
(1990)

Your limits are set by the amount of knowledge you have, or from your ignorance.

The less knowledge you have, the less you can do to solve problems.

The more knowledge you have, the more problems you can solve.

We say there is no such thing as a problem without a solution, only problems for which we do not yet have enough information to know what the solution is.

That's why we have included so many techniques in the Silva Method to help you get information.

Information Tools

In the MC101 section of the Silva Basic Lecture Series you have Dream Control Step 3. Of course, you may need to practice Dream Control Steps 1 and 2 first. Many times graduates become impatient and want Step 3 to work right away.

First practice remembering a dream, until you can recall a dream every night. Then practice remembering dreams.

After you are good at remembering dreams every night, then you are ready to program to generate dreams that contain information you can use to make decisions and solve problems.

Dream Control is a wonderful technique. It is a very natural technique, and that is why we are able to present it so early in the training.

You can begin to use it with only a minimum amount of practice at your level. People have been using dreams to solve problems for thousands of years. We see it used repeatedly in the Bible.

In MC404, as well as the Silva UltraMind ESP Systems, you have case working, another tool to obtain information that you can use to correct problems.

You have already established points of reference for a healthy body, so now you can search for unhealthy ones.

We call this "mental projection."

We do not wait to "perceive" some kind of information that somehow mysteriously appears.

You can use mental projection to get information from the subjective dimension. Ask questions, clear your mind for a moment by thinking of a different subject, then come back to your question and expect an answer. Then start thinking again to figure out the answer.

Once you have an answer, then come out of level and get your body involved, try out your idea and observe the results.

We begin by detecting information about physical health problems. After you have practiced working a few dozen health cases and are satisfied with your results, then you can begin working cases on other types of problems.

You can practice detecting information about animals.

Then after you have become effective at that, begin working with plants.

After that, inanimate matter.

You can learn to work cases on business projects, on relationships, on anything.

Whenever you need more information so that you can solve more problems, you have the tools to use.

All of these tools help you to get information from or through the subjective dimension, to help you correct problems in the objective, or physical, dimension.

For best results, practice and develop all of them.

Help from Higher Intelligence

When you are stumped, we have a technique to ask for and receive guidance from higher intelligence: the MentalVideo.

This technique is only to be used after you have tried, but are not making any progress on the case. We teach the MentalVideo in the Silva UltraMind ESP System. You can learn it in appendix D.

If you still have limitations in your life, if you still feel limited, then pick your favorite technique and practice it. Once you are satisfied with your results, select another technique and start practicing it also.

When it comes to solving problems, the more techniques you have that you can use, the better off you are.

Note: You can learn the MentalVideo Technique and many other techniques in the appendix.

42 Use Your Mental Screen to Repair Things *(1984)*

The Mental Screen is a tool that is used for some very important purposes: first, it is a selected area for you to use to project and develop your ability to use visualization and imagination.

As you develop this ability, the Mental Screen serves a more important purpose: it permits you to mentally correct anything that needs correction.

The Mental Screen is a device that enables you to use visualization to transfer that which exists in physics from the physical dimension back into the mental dimension where it came from, so that you can then use imagination to make alterations.

Once the change is made at the fundamental dimension, then it can manifest in physics as well.

While something is in its physical form, we cannot change it with mental energy. We must project it back to the subjective dimension, and in that dimension we can use mental energy, in the form of imagination, to make the alterations. Once the alterations, or corrections, are made at this fundamental dimension (the subjective dimension), then the change can take place in physics.

We need a place to make such corrections in the subjective dimension, and the place to do it is the Mental Screen.

We have special places for certain tasks: a kitchen for cooking, a bedroom for sleeping, and so forth. Thus, we have a Mental Screen to use for transferring between the mental and physical dimensions.

Everything that exists was created first in the subjective, dimension. It is the fundamental dimension.

Everything had to be thought of first, before it became a physical reality. The Mental Screen is a special place to transfer from the physical to the mental, where alterations can be made.

When you desire to create something new, you do so in the subjective dimension. After that, it can manifest in the physical dimension. The Mental Screen is an aid in focusing your thoughts to make this process easier and more efficient.

The imagination is an energy-gathering concept, or means, to alter whatever needs altering, at the fundamental dimension, so the alteration (the correction) can take place in physics, too.

So we take whatever is malfunctioning, project it back and then make alterations to get it to function correctly.

Remember that all mental energy is an attractive energy; that is, it cannot push, but can only attract. This is why we can not cause harm, or create problems in physics with the use of our mental energy. We can only attract back to the perfect blueprint that is right for whatever we are working with.

Such things as "mentally" bending a spoon actually use physical energy, part of the body's aura, that is channeled through the use of your thought processes. It is a physical force that causes a distortion to occur.

That is something different from what we are talking about.

Imagination used in the subjective dimension cannot force the way physical energy can; mental energy can only attract. Thus, we can use mental energy, imagination, in the subjective dimension to correct problems, to fix what is broken, but it is impossible to use this energy of attraction to break anything.

Note: You can learn the Mental Screen technique and how to use it to correct problems and achieve success in the appendix.

43 Memory Pegs Are Good Training
(1984)

The main reason Memory Pegs are included in the Silva Method is to give you practice using visualization and imagination so you can function better in the subjective dimension. You recall (visualize) something familiar, then use imagination to create something you have not observed before.

This is good practice for the process of using visualization (memory) to transfer something back to the subjective dimension, and imagination (a creative process) to alter it and correct whatever needs correcting.

Of course, Memory Pegs are an excellent tool to help you improve your memory. Here's why:

Usually people can recall something they have seen more easily than a description they have heard. The brain and mind prefer to function with images, rather than with abstract representations that we call words.

Thus, it is valuable for us to practice thinking in visual terms.

When somebody is talking to you and says, "Do you see what I mean?" you should do just that: make mental movies of what the person is telling you. This way, you will recall it more easily.

When programming for something it is also important to use mental pictures so the brain and mind can function most efficiently.

The best tool we have found for beginners to use to develop their visualization and imagination is the memory peg system.

While we recommend that you practice the memory pegs to improve your visualization and imagination, and thus become a superior clairvoyant, this will also help you to improve your memory as well.

Definitions

Remember that visualizing is different from seeing; you see with your eyes, and visualize with your mind. Visualizing is not seeing; it is recalling something you have seen before, and remembering what it looks like.

Webster's dictionary says that to visualize is "To form a mental image of something."

It is a passive process of recalling the appearance of something that exists, something you have already seen.

Imagination is a creative process. Webster's says it is the "act or power of forming a mental image of something not present to the senses or not previously known or experienced."

"Act" is a verb, an action word. Thus imagination can be used to take action (mentally) and create something that you have never seen or visualized before.

After you have used your imagination to create something in the mental dimension, then it exists as a mental picture, and in the future when you recall the mental image you created, this is known as visualization. In fact, when you function at your level you can perceive mental images that others have created, and others functioning at their level can perceive your mental creations. Imagination is very real.

This sometimes explains why children have nightmares and "see" monsters: they reach a mental level where they begin to perceive fantasies that have been created by themselves and others.

Better Memory

Memory is the product of visualization, imagination, association, and exaggeration:

You visualize what you want to remember, then use your imagination to associate it with something familiar.

If you exaggerate the size or amount or color or action, it will be easier to remember, and will also be great practice to help develop your imagination.

Once you learn the memory pegs, they are familiar to you. Images of a glass of tea, or of Noah, or a calendar, are easier to recall than the numbers 1, 2, and 3. You can hang your mental pictures of the things you wish to recall on your memory pegs.

When you associate the objects to be remembered with the familiar pegs in a strange or unusual way, it will be much easier for you to recall them. Make your associations as outlandish as possible; exaggerate in size or quantity; use bright colors in your images; give them action.

As we say, geniuses are people who use more of their minds, and use them in a special manner. This is one of the ways.

44 Why Visualization and Imagination Work *(1984)*

Silva techniques will bring about changes for the better in every area of your life: health, relationships, business, learning, self-confidence—anything you desire to change.

Why do they work so well? What mechanisms are involved in making these changes?

The key is functioning in the subjective dimension.

When you enter your level, you are then functioning in the invisible world of the mind, and you are able to make changes in the visible world of the body.

The tools of the subjective dimension are visualization and imagination. They are two faculties of genius.

Let's take a close look at these tools so you will understand exactly what they are and how to use them in the subjective dimension to make the needed changes.

How to Get Good Results

Remember that it is important to use visualization and imagination in the subjective dimension, that is, at your level.

Many books tell you to visualize your goals, but if they do not teach you a method for doing so in the subjective dimension, then this will do you little good.

Visualization is memory. Visualization is remembering what something looks like.

Visualization is a receiving mechanism. In the subjective dimension, you receive a mental image of what something looks like. If your mental image is not as clear as you would like it, simply recall what the subject looks like. Recalling what some thing looks like is visualization.

Recall the details and the colors.

Imagination is a creative process.

With imagination, you create a mental image of something you have not seen previously.

With imagination, you create whatever you desire.

When you create something in the subjective dimension, with your imagination, then it actually exists—in the subjective dimension—and can be perceived by other people when they are functioning in the subjective dimension.

Everything must first be created in the subjective dimension; then it can manifest in the physical (objective) dimension also.

Imagination is a transmitting mechanism. With imagination, you can transmit your desired end result to the physical dimension.

There is no time or space in the subjective dimension. When you create something, it exists as of that moment.

But the physical dimension does have time and space, so it may take time before your desires manifest in physics.

Visualization is the receiving mechanism, imagination is the transmitting mechanism.

How do you put these to use?

Using Visualization and Imagination

Use the Mirror of the Mind or the 3-Scenes Technique.

In the first Scene—the blue framed mirror—use visualization to receive (recall) a mental image of the situation as it exists now, the problem. Then erase it, move your attention to your left (the future in the subjective dimension), change the frame to white and with your imagination create and transmit to the physical dimension the desired end result, your goal.

Use this same technique to create better health, better relationships, get a better job or increased business, make better grades, any traits or characteristics you desire for yourself—anything at all that you want to have, to do, or to be.

You can use the same technique to help other people. First, recall (receive information) about the existing situation (the problem), then use your imagination to create a solution (goal) and transmit it to the physical dimension. Just be certain you do your programming in the subjective dimension, while at your level.

In the future, when you think of your project, visualize (recall what it looks like) the goal you created with your imagination in the subjective dimension. Take it for granted that the solution already exists, and is being transmitted to the physical dimension so it can manifest in the physical world of the body dimension.

This is what is meant by the phrase "Pray believing you have already received." Our way of saying it is to "Program in the future in a past tense sense."

Take it for granted, and you will get your results.

Note: You can learn the 3-Scenes Technique and other techniques in the appendix.

45 Imagination Can Solve Many Problems *(1984)*

Imagination serves many purposes.

We have always used imagination for making things up, make believe, fiction, things that have never happened, will never happen.

Once we learn to enter the subjective dimension and use the Mental Screen to transfer present reality into the subjective dimension, then we can use imagination as a creative tool to alter that, change it, and create something else.

We can also use imagination to create that which has never existed before.

That is true creativity.

We can also use imagination as a communication tool.

We can send information and we can receive information by using our visualization/imagination faculty.

Working health cases is an example of a way to use imagination. We use our visualization/imagination faculty to obtain information about a person's health, then we use imagination to alter the existing conditions and change to perfection, and finally we use imagination to transmit this correction back to the person who needs it.

To know—to really know—that we are using imagination as an information tool, and as a creative tool, we must practice. There is a slightly different feeling for each use: making things up, communications, alteration, and creation.

When you first begin to practice working health cases, it does not make much difference whether you are "right" or "wrong." Every experience you have is beneficial to you. That is why the orientologist encourages you to "say everything that comes to mind. You may feel as though you are making it up. This is the correct feeling."

Some things, you may be making up. Other things will be real information. Until you become accustomed to functioning in this dimension in this manner, you will probably find it difficult to tell the difference. But with practice you will learn.

After you have given a complete report on the case, and while still at your level, the orientologist will give you feedback on the case. You will learn which times you were receiving accurate information, and which times you were making it up. It is all done with the process we have labeled "imagination."

And just like a child learning to walk, we must continue to practice, learning how far we can lean before we lose our balance. The more we learn, the more we stretch to the limit, the more effective we will be in our functioning.

How many cases does it take before you really begin to get the feel of it? You will be quite accurate and quite confident when you have worked the Magic 50 health cases as you are instructed in the human anatomy conditioning cycle.

Some people ask: Are you accurate because you are confident, or are you confident because you are accurate?

The answer is, Yes.

But more importantly, you are both accurate and confident because you have practiced and because of the practice, you have developed your sensitivity and your ability to discern the difference between fantasy and fact in the subjective dimension.

46 The Worst Enemies of Your Immune System *(1985)*

There are certain steps we can take to protect our health so that we not only will live a long life, but will live a healthy life for as long as we live. To understand these steps better, let's take a look at the main reasons the immune system breaks down and allows us to become ill.

Three Main Stressors

There are three main stressors that attack the human immune system, as well as many smaller ones.

The worst one of all is doing something wrong, and you know it is wrong, and you continue to do it; the guilt complex.

Number two is having lost something of great value and feeling hopeless, that you are not able to recover it.

Number three is working and living under conditions you hate, and you have to continue whether you like it or not.

Minor Stressors

There are many minor stressors, also. When you have several minor stressors working against you, they can add up to the same effect as one of the major ones.

Minor ones include the fear that you will not have what you need, too little money to make car payments and so forth.

Many small negative stressors can accumulate and equal a major one.

These hurt the immune system by creating a stress enzyme in the blood stream. Lactic acids can accumulate and create problems for us when we are suffering from these kinds of stresses.

Imagination

Humans are blessed with a great imagination. This imagination has helped us create the beautiful world we live in. But it can also create problems for us.

The more vivid the imagination, the more potential to create beneficial things, and the more potential to cause serious problems.

You can use your imagination to create the kind of world you want to live in. But you must take control if you desire to do this. A mind out of control is always destructive, because of the strong biological programming we have to be constantly on the watch for potential danger in order to preserve physical life.

To take advantage of your human potential and put it to use for constructive purposes, you must learn to focus your attention on positive goals.

Enter Level Daily

The best, most positive thing you can do to strengthen your immune system and protect yourself from negative stressors, while at the same time putting your human potential to work for you in all areas of life, is to enter level every day and use your imagination for constructive, creative purposes, to help make this world a better place to live.

When you are doing constructive, creative things, you will eliminate guilt feelings.

Since you are constantly using your creative talents to make your life better and better, you will not mourn the loss of what you enjoyed previously, but will realize that life is a cycle and that the cycle continues on and on.

And since you will be developing your ability to use your imagination to convert your portion of the world into a paradise, you will never have to remain in conditions you do not enjoy.

When you are happy, truly happy deep within, because you are leading a constructive, creative life, then you will also be healthy.

To accomplish, you must be certain you are entering deep levels every day, and this comes with practice.

So make a commitment to yourself right now to practice every day. Starting right now.

Note: If you don't already know how, you can learn to enter the alpha level right now in the appendix.

47 Balancing Humanity Is Our Goal
(1981)

While traveling throughout the world in conjunction with my duties with Silva Mind Control International, Inc., I often hear about the imbalances present in our planet.

Mostly, these imbalances are generalized such as the poor and the rich, the healthy and the sick, the productive and the unproductive, etc.

It is interesting to hear comments like this because in Silva Mind Control, imbalances (and balances) are very much a part of how we function.

To become a self-actualized human being, we need to become a totally integrated person, a holistic man or woman.

Being able to achieve this state of being is fundamental to our method, and much of our course deals with helping people help themselves to become a more integrated human.

In these general statements that are voiced to me—and I am certain many of you have been told about the same imbalances in the world today—one thing is perfectly evident: the source of these imbalances is the people themselves.

Imbalances are not created by themselves, nor are they the product of nature.

Nature, as any Silva graduate knows, is in perfect balance. Humans, through their individual actions, make imbalances.

However, in today's society—where value systems and value judgment are in many ways commercialized—it is very difficult for individuals to achieve balance in their systems.

Finding this line of balance and adapting our behavior to it and making our decisions based upon this balance are some of the critical aspects of humanity today.

To do so requires great effort on the part of the individual, as well as tremendous strength of character and discipline plus a wide knowledge of various academic, religious and medical disciplines.

Oftentimes, a person may confuse a state of balance because of the acts they undertake.

A sense of balance, for example, is not achieved only through good deeds, for those good deeds may have been performed out of fear, out of selfishness, out of pity or out of prejudice.

If those good deeds are performed out of a genuine sense of service to humanity and because you want to give each person the value and respect they deserve, balance can then be achieved.

In achieving balance in ourselves, we must first of all attempt to make sound value judgments regarding our own personal behavior.

There are many individuals who may examine their behavior critically and objectively and find that certain changes need to be made, but who may not really know how to plan for a more integrated and successful life. These individuals often reach out for professionals to help them and to guide them, only to find out that there is still something lacking in their self-fulfillment.

Our method is based on the belief that every person can develop realistic plans for becoming a more integrated human being and that no one—neither parents nor teachers, husbands nor wives, employers nor ministers—knows better than the person themself what is best.

All individuals have at their disposal all the knowledge that is required to make them more self-fulfilling and self-actualized.

The key is to allow the individual to allow Higher Intelligence to guide them, for within each individual lies all the knowledge that that individual will ever need for self-betterment.

However, one must be careful not to attempt too much because setting unrealistic goals will usually fail and failing will only help to reinforce the feeling of failure. A person who lacks integration also lacks success and a failing person needs to have success.

People who have admitted that they possess many bad habits that are preventing this balance, will probably want to set up goals of eliminating one habit at a time, and not all of them at once.

Once one bad habit is eliminated, others will eventually follow until total integration is achieved and a more perfect balance is obtained.

Once the bad habits are eliminated, good "habits" in the form of attitudes take their place:

- Instead of failure, we have success
- Instead of sickness we have health
- Instead of envy, we have charity
- Instead of slothfulness we have industry
- Instead of loneliness we have companionship
- Instead of rejection we have acceptance.

Becoming fully integrated is not an easy task, and it may take us all of our life to reach that stage. Yet, we can make humanity much better if we attempt to do so starting today and every other day for the rest of our lives.

In this manner, we can indeed become "better and better" for the service of humanity.

48 Uri Geller Impressed Us
(1992)

I'm glad that Uri Geller has joined us.

We met Uri at the Silva 1992 World Convention in Greece and were so impressed with him that we invited him to our annual International Convention in Laredo in August.

Uri is probably best known for his ability to hold a spoon in his hand and hold a thought of bending the spoon in his mind—and the spoon bends.

This seems to have little value, except to demonstrate that he can use his mind to direct some form of energy to alter matter. It is probably part of the aura—the body's electromagnetic radiation—that causes the molecules to expand and thus bend the spoon.

If Uri can do this, then anyone should be able to learn to do the same thing.

This sort of demonstration serves to show people that they have more abilities than they may have realized.

But what other practical value does it have?

That's the question I've always asked.

It turns out that Uri Geller has been asking the same question.

In Greece, and again in Laredo last August, Uri stood on stage and held a spoon that someone in the audience gave to him. As he stood there, surrounded by children, the spoon bent right before our eyes.

There are a couple of waiters at the Holiday Inn in Laredo who are still wide-eyed after Uri bent a spoon for them in the hotel dining room.

But what does this accomplish, Uri wonders.

Even more impressive than the spoon bending is when Uri holds a handful of seeds and—still surrounded by children and a few adults—wills the seeds to sprout, and sure enough, one of them does sprout.

"There must be some way to apply this to help heal the human body," Uri told us.

We told him that there is. And he immediately said that he wants to take the Silva training.

Uri's great natural ability, combined with the reliable structure of the Silva training, creates something very special.

We put the two together—Uri Geller and one of our best Silva lecturers, Burt Goldman—to present a series of weekend seminars to give people an idea of how much more they can accomplish.

Uri can sprout seeds in his hands. If you want to learn how to use your hands to help heal people, then learn the Silva Holistic Faith Healing techniques.

These things are real—whether it is Uri Geller sprouting seeds or bending spoons that he holds in his hands, or Silva graduates using the "Laying on of hands" techniques from our Holistic Faith Healing Home Study Course to heal someone with cancer.

I learned, as Uri has learned, that what he and I are able to do is not nearly as important as the fact that you can learn to do the same thing, and even more.

Note: As a reader of this book you are entitled to a discount on the Holistic Faith Healing home study course. You can order it at SilvaESP.com and when you check out enter coupon code MM15 for your discount.

49 Holistic Faith Healing Workshops Are Popular *(1984)*

Our Holistic Faith Healing Workshop and our two-day Ultra Seminar have been so popular that we are training more people to go forth and present them to the public.

Everywhere we go, scores of people attend and learn to heal by laying on of hands.

This is valuable. This restores health so people can be better problem solving agents on our planet.

This is what Christ instructed His followers to do.

Christ said of His followers that "these signs shall follow them that believe, they shall lay hands on the sick, and they shall recover."

What I believe He meant by this was that those who seek and enter the kingdom of heaven, which we know as the alpha dimension, and seek God's righteousness, which means to function rightly, will be able to do all things.

This does not mean you have to belong to any particular religion, or have any special belief system. But you must know how to enter the alpha—subjective—dimension, and you must desire to create, not destroy. Then you can "lay hands on the sick, and they shall recover."

Many Techniques

We have been guided to discover many holistic faith healing techniques. In the one-night workshop, we present a simple technique that involves the healer vibrating their hands at ten vibrations a second to help bring about the proper state for healing. This technique seems to be effective for everyone, whether they know how to enter the alpha ten-cycle brain frequency or not.

In the Ultra Seminar, there are many more faith healing techniques that participants learn. Most of these require that the healer know how to enter the ten-cycle alpha dimension—what we believe was the Kingdom of Heaven that Christ spoke of.

When people enter that dimension and apply the healing techniques, then they get results.

This shows that we are, in fact, following Christ, doing what He said to do.

Our plans for the future call for these techniques to be presented four times a year in areas throughout the country.

Every three months, a lecturer will come to an area and present either the one-night workshop, or the Ultra Seminar, or both.

We will use many different lecturers for this. This is important for several reasons. It will let people know that these techniques are not limited to just a few special people.

There are quite a few healers in the world who go and show how much they are able to do. We are different: We want people to learn to do these things for themselves.

Also, people sometimes find they have better rapport with one person than with another. This does not necessarily have anything to do with how well you like a person. It appears to be on a more subjective level.

For instance, one healer may be very successful at using the faith healing techniques, but may get very little in the way of results with a particular patient.

Another healer, perhaps much less experienced, might get far better results with that patient.

Our goal is to train many of our most experienced lecturers to present these techniques, and, through them, to train as many people as possible to apply the healing techniques.

Through this, we can help relieve suffering and restore health to our planet so that we can get on with other work that needs to be done to convert this planet into a paradise.

Note: Times change. A few years after Mr. Silva wrote this, video technology had improved and it became easier to distribute videos online, so he asked us to make videos of the two holistic faith healing techniques in order to reach more people as quickly as possible. Now you can obtain the videos from our SilvaESP.com website, including instructions from José Silva himself about how to proceed. To activate your special discount, enter the coupon code MM15 when you check out.

50 Go Within and Get the Whole Story *(1997)*

Vibrations are related to, and depend on, the light of the sun.

Anything that produces light is a transmitter. It produces light energy. Light is energy.

The complete spectrum of energy covers all the vibrations that the body responds to, or has within it.

The visual spectrum is a complete spectrum which, when complete, produces white light. It goes from the red up to the violet.

This is what we can perceive with our senses.

Each of the vibrations of our senses responds and combines with specific frequencies. It detects and vibrates with these frequencies. It repels some of these frequencies, and it absorbs some of these frequencies.

When your sensing faculty detects a frequency, some of it is absorbed and some is repelled. The frequency that is absorbed is converted to a different frequency, which is then transmitted to the brain.

All senses receive energy from the electromagnetic spectrum, convert it to nerve energy, and transmit it to the brain.

The sense of sight receives light energy, converts it to nerve energy, and transmits it to the brain.

The same can be said of the sense of smell, sense of taste, touch, and hearing.

Our biological senses detect physical vibrations, convert them, and transmit them to the left brain hemisphere.

The brain receives nerve energy from the physical senses, converts it to subjective energy, and transmits it to the right brain hemisphere.

The right brain hemisphere also has a set of senses. They are subjective, at a different dimension, not within the physical electromagnetic spectrum that includes sound vibrations, visible light, etc.

We have two different things happening that we need to interpret:

When we talk about matter, matter is a composition of atomic structure. The vibration of the atomic structure of a particular type of matter depends on the distance of electrons that are circling around the nucleus, or heart, of the atom.

The number of atoms, and their distance from the nucleus, and the rate of circling around the nucleus, produces the rate of vibration.

The sum total of all atoms of a specific type of matter is the fundamental frequency of that type of matter.

All inanimate matter—the mineral world—has these vibrations.

When your sense of sight detect vibration from matter, your senses detect what is reflected by the object.

Your biological senses detect what is reflected from the object.

Your subjective senses detect what is absorbed by the object.

Every object has a different rate of vibration because of the different composition of matter—atomic structure—and the vibration is different.

The object's vibration collides with the vibration of the electromagnetic energy—light for instance. Now we have two fundamentals: the fundamental frequency of the object, and the fundamental of light, for instance.

When they come together, they add to one another, so we have the sum of both; and when they collide with each other, one neutralizes some of the other, and we have the difference between the two.

So we have four fundamentals:
- The object
- Light
- The sum of both
- The difference between them

It is like a frequency multiplier, or divider, that can reduce the frequency from a very high rate, to a rate that the senses can perceive.

Take the eye for instance:
- The eye has its own radiating vibration
- The reflected object has its own.

Now when light strikes the object, the difference between the fundamental frequency of the object and the fundamental frequency of the light will reflect and be detected by the eye.

When the difference between the object and the light, collides with the eye, it interacts with the fundamental of the eye, and the difference is detected by the eye, converted to nerve energy, and transmitted to the brain.

Each sense does the same thing.

Everything has to do with vibrations: Sense of touch, sense of smell, all of them.

Now the right brain hemisphere is connected to the subjective senses. The subjective senses detect subjective information, the vibrations that are absorbed by the object.

The left brain hemisphere detects information that is reflected by the object.

The right brain hemisphere detects what is absorbed by the object.

Now which of the two would you say would be the most accurate information about the object: What is reflected from it, or what is absorbed?

- What's absorbed is not distorted by anything.
- What's reflected can be distorted by other reflections.

There are many other reflections that can contaminate the reflection from the object—the reflection that is detected by the physical senses.

But there is nothing to distort or contaminate the inner vibrations that are detected by the subjective senses and transmitted to the right brain hemisphere.

So the right brain hemisphere, the subjective senses, detect things more accurately.

Your thought—your mind—is what locks in on something and detects it.

- At alpha, you can detect the object from within.
- At beta, you can only detect what is reflected from it.

Being within, since there is no "law of physics" involved, it is as though everything is together.

Your thoughts are the tuning mechanism to change from one frequency to another.

When you are thinking about a typewriter, for instance, you adjust yourself to the vibrating rate of the atomic structure that is absorbed by the typewriter. When you picture it in your mind and think about it, you are there already.

With the physical senses, you have to get it objectively. If you are not there, you have to go where it is in order to detect information about it.

But when you visualize it in your mind, at the alpha level, you are already there.

You can describe it from within, like you can describe it from the outside.

This is beyond physics: Metaphysics. That's the fourth dimension.

In physics you have the height, width, length. The fourth dimension is the depth—the inner dimension that you can detect only with your mind. Penetrating matter and detecting information from the inside.

- We say that spiritual medicine operates from within the inner layers of matter, to the outer layers of matter.
- Physical medicine operates, or helps, from the outer layers to the inner layers of matter.

Now we can help from both ends: From within, or from without, to solve the problem much faster.

Neither one covers everything. We need both of them. It is like saying, I need the sense of sight, and the sense of hearing also. Not just one. It depends on what is required—whether you need to see, or need to hear.

We cannot hear at the frequency of sight, and cannot see at the frequency of hearing.

We need different channels in order to do both.

The same thing with left and right brain hemispheres: We have to attune to them, and use the appropriate one, depending on what is required to correct a problem.

They operate on two different bands—they are two different ways of communicating, like AM radio and FM radio. You cannot hear AM stations on the FM band, and you cannot hear FM stations on the AM band. You have to tune to the correct one.

To learn everything about matter, you need to use both bands: One external, the other internal. One objective, the other subjective. One left brain, the other right brain.

We need to train our mind to do this.

Healing Subjectively

When it comes to correcting problems subjectively, inanimate matter is one thing, animate matter is another.

With inanimate matter, the law of physics takes over. There are a lot of things that cannot be done to inanimate matter except through the laws of physics—through physical means:

If you want to move something, you move it physically.

Right brain thinking—subjective thinking—imagination—has an energy to cause life to move. Not inanimate matter, though.

But animate matter will follow a blueprint that you create with your mind.

If a plant is not producing what it should, you imagine it producing it. You are going to help it do what it is supposed to do. You cannot get the plant to do something it is not supposed to do.

You cannot get an apple tree to produce oranges. That is impossible, because that does not conform to the original blueprint.

But you can help it produce more apples.

Objectively, you can hurt an apple tree and cause it to produce fewer apples, or more apples.

Subjectively, you can help it produce more apples, but you cannot change the normal to the abnormal, to produce fewer apples.

You can only influence, subjectively—within—what the plant is supposed to do, not what it is unable to do.

If the plant is supposed to produce, it is going to produce. You cannot get it to not produce through subjective means.

With the left brain hemisphere, you can help or you can hurt. You can help it to produce more, or keep it from producing.

You can hurt it or you can help it through objective means.

Subjectively you can never hurt anything. You can only help it to do what it is supposed to do.

The subjective, right brain energy, controls the creative process.

In order to create something, you need to first have a blueprint. You create the blueprint with imagination, then matter will conform to the image that you have in your mind. But you must have animate matter; you cannot do it with inanimate matter, because it has no intelligence.

Inanimate matter cannot move, because there are no cells there, no life. Animate matter can move towards perfection, towards the original blueprint.

Imagination has the power to correct problems with animate matter. But it has to be done with the right brain, with subjective energy.

It could be that the person developed a bad habit that damaged part of their body, the heart for instance. Or it could be that somebody along the way made a mistake—papa or mama for instance, in conceiving, or because they had a health problem while conceiving and it was transferred to the child. Now we have to correct it.

Psychometry

Everything vibrates, and we sense information through the internal vibrations of an object.

Your body's vibrations penetrate objects within your presence and affect the internal vibrations of the objects. Your body radiation charges up the object with your own frequencies. When you touch a ring, for instance, it becomes an extension of you; it is saturated with your own vibrations.

Later, someone else can hold the object and project into it subjectively and sense the vibrations of the previous owner.

In order to do this, you need to go to alpha, use right brain thinking, and desire to want to know about the person who owned the object.

What are you looking for? Color of hair? Color of eyes? What information do you want to know? It does not just come to you automatically. You have to know what you want to know.

This can make case working more effective.

If you are seeking information about a missing person, it would be good if you had something that the person had worn, to hold in your hand. It would make it easier for you to tune in to the person.

If you are programming to help someone who is ill, it would help to have something of theirs to hold in your hand.

Relationships

Husband and wife need to have the same vibrations in order to get along.

The vibrations change in the bodies of individuals.

How do you start loving somebody? Or anything?

By changing whatever it is to your vibrations, or to similar vibrations, to be alike.

The way it starts is like this:

A boy is walking on one side of the street, and a girl is walking down the other side of the street.

They see each other and they like what they see.

Energy radiates about eight meters from the body. So if they are within 16 meters of each other—about 50 feet—then their auras are contacting each other.

What are they trying to do?

He is trying to change her aura to be more like his, and she's trying to change his aura to hers.

Their body radiations are different, but when they spend enough time together, they finally match.

There are several stages to contact:

First is sight.

Then the sense of touch.

Voice, and so on.

The closer they get, the stronger the changes. It is a battle between two auras, trying to change each other.

Finally, kissing, hugging, and the sex act—Bingo!—the chemistry is completely changed now.

If either one finds somebody else that they like, and their aura starts changing to be similar to the other person, they start having problems because they don't match anymore. They don't synchronize. There is something about each other that they don't like, and they start having problems.

That's why you should not let yourself become attracted to someone else. If you start seeing another person, then you weaken what you have with your mate. If it weakens too much, they will go find somebody else.

A husband and wife should not be too far apart. It is best for them to sleep in the same bed. When they are together a lot, this will keep the vibrations strong, they will not change. If the vibrations start to change, get closer to your partner and strengthen them again, bring them back into harmony, synchronized, matched.

The same thing happens with objects, too. You love your coat, your shoes. You don't want to throw them away because they are part of your body, they are saturated with your own energy.

Even though they may be worn out and look bad, you don't want to throw them away. You keep them in a corner, in a closet.

The same thing happens to a plant, to a pet, and even more to other human beings. It hurts when you break a connection. When you lose a friend, it hurts, because you break the radiations.

51 How to Get Help from High Intelligence *(1994)*

When a left brain person guesses, they might as well flip a coin.

When a person who also has the right brain going guesses—as I do—that person has help from a larger mind—a higher intelligence.

When we are Godly inspired, our guess is right. When we are not Godly inspired, our guess is governed by chance. It can be wrong.

When a guess is right we are Godly inspired. When we guess wrong we are not Godly inspired.

So wrong is not desired by God, only right is desired by God.

Knowing What's Right

God being the Creator, it is easy to understand right from wrong:

Right is to create and, wrong is to destroy.

Alleviating suffering is constructive; it is right.

Causing suffering is destructive; it is wrong.

What all humans should be doing on planet earth is being constructive and doing what is right.

Connection With God

For humanity to survive on planet earth, humanity must establish a connection with God.

To be able to establish a connection with God, you have to learn to use your intuitive right brain hemisphere, so that you will be correct by guessing right, because you are Godly inspired.

This is the main reason why we need to learn how to develop in our children the use of the right brain hemisphere, so that they will all be prophets, wise men, geniuses, clairvoyants.

They will be Godly inspired to correct all past, present and future problems that plague humanity on our planet.

Reinforce Life

One key to right or wrong is: Does it interfere with life, or reinforce life?

If a decision reinforces life, it must be right.

When you activate the right hemisphere, you improve the ability of your mind to affect your body:

You can relieve stress which when prolonged can be fatal.

You can stimulate your immune system to reverse a disease.

You can change abnormality into normality.

All of this—and more—can quickly add up to more years of your life and more life in your years.

Note: If you have not taken any of our Courses, you can learn to enter the alpha level with any of the free training options in the appendix.

52 Brain Wave Study Shows the Power of Alpha *(1996)*

When I was studying psychology, I came across the term "hypnosis" and I went into that field to study it.

Then I came across "parapsychology" and I went into that field to study it.

Along came the term "electroencephalography" and I went into electroencephalography to study it. I started experimenting, checking people's brains.

I started thinking about what I could do with the electroencephalograph. It measures brain frequencies, so I decided to check the brain frequencies of people doing various things.

Which Level Do People Use?

First I decided to investigate to find out which is the strongest of all these frequencies. I thought that this should tell me which level we should operate on more than anywhere else.

I put a digital counter on the EEG to see the brain frequency in numbers, not wiggles on a chart. I found that on average, 90 percent of the people I tested were thinking on beta, at 20 cycles per second (cps).

I would look at the digital counter when I would start talking to an individual. I would ask him a question, and he would answer the question while his brain was functioning at 20 cycles per second.

I would ask him how he would solve a problem. When he answered, his brain was still functioning at 20 cycles beta.

But 10 percent of the subjects I tested, when I would ask them a question, they would go to 10 cycles alpha, and then come back to 20 cycles beta and give me the answer. It was as though they went to alpha to get the answer, and would give it to me on 20 cycles.

I said, What's going on here?

I realized that 90 percent of people were using 20 cycles to think on, and 10 percent were using 10.

I wanted to know, Which is the better of the two?

Which Level Is Strongest?

First I went for synchronization. Which is the more stable of the two? Is 10 more stable than 20? Or 20 more stable than 10? Which is more synchronized? I found that 10 is more synchronized than 20.

Interesting, I said. Now what else could I do?

I decided to check and see which is the stronger of the two. Again, 10 was stronger than 20.

I thought, Can you imagine, if 10 cycles is the best place to think on, and 90 percent of the people are doing their thinking on 20?

Researching With Children

Now you can hook up a child: 20 cps. Then ask them, How would you solve this problem? What would you do about this problem?

Take a child, maybe 10 or 12 years old, and ask, "How would you clean a car? How would you brighten it up?"

"Well," the child might answer, "I would wash the car."

"What else would you do? Just the car?"

"No, the wheels too."

"Okay, the car, the wheels . . ."

"Well, the radiator, also. And then I could polish it up . . ." The child would continue until they ran out of ideas. All of this would come at 20 cycles per second.

Then, get the child to 10 cycles per second, and the child gives you more ideas.

You can ask other things like: "How could you use a pencil? How many uses can you think of for a pencil?"

They might answer, "Well, to erase, to write, to stick in my ear." They give you all kinds of uses for the pencil.

But at 20 they run out of answers, or ideas, and when you get them to 10, they come up with more, even though they thought they had run out of them.

More Information at Alpha

There is more information at alpha. That is the benefit.

The benefit is, you have information to solve more problems.

All problems require information to get the solution, to correct them. And information is spiritual. Information is mental.

This is one of the major benefits of alpha.

Whenever you need information to help you correct a problem, whenever you need ideas, then enter your alpha level and do your thinking at the alpha level. Then come back to beta and implement your ideas.

Notice which ideas produce the best results—which ideas are the best for correcting problems—and let this guide you in your future efforts, so that you will continue to get better and better.

53 Problems Can Serve a Purpose in Life *(1985)*

Have you been looking for a method of eliminating all of the problems in your life? Would you like to get rid of every disagreeable, negative situation you might encounter?

Before you answer "yes," let me remind you that we are not here on earth for a vacation. We are not here on a long coffee break.

We are here to correct problems. If problems are negative, then goals are positive, and the combination gives us energy.

When dealing with energy, you have both positive and negative.

The battery in your automobile has a positive side and a negative side.

In the early days, many people thought that current (energy) flowed from positive to negative, that negative was lower in something.

But just the opposite is true: the negative terminal has an excess of electrons, the negative particles, while the positive terminal has a deficiency of electrons and is out of balance because it has an excess of protons.

It is the attempt to bring about a balance that causes the current of electrons to flow from negative to positive through the circuit.

Likewise in our lives, we have both positive and negative.

A lack of health or a lack of money could be considered a negative situation.

It is such negative situations that give us the motivation, the incentive, to strive to correct problems.

The negative in our lives pushes us towards balance, towards solutions and the creation of new things that benefit us in many ways takes place.

Your goal is like the positive terminal on the battery, while the problem, or the situation you wish to alter, is like the negative terminal. The goal attracts, while the problem pushes you onward.

We are here on planet earth working with human energy, moving from the negative to the positive. While we do not desire to have the negative things in our lives, we should not despise them. We should be grateful for them because they motivate us towards our good.

We must have both to propel us to seek something better.

Challenges are there for a reason, perhaps to help us learn and develop our skills and grow so that we can accept greater responsibility later on and take better care of our planet.

Here's How You Can Overcome Obstacles

People sometimes want to know how to keep working towards a goal when faced with many obstacles. That's something I've had a lot of experience with.

It takes persistence. You can achieve any kind of goal you set for yourself if you make it the most important thing in your life and sacrifice everything else for it.

There are people who do that, but I would not necessarily call that success. You have to learn when to continue fighting for your goal with everything you've got, and when to stand back, take a deep breath, and see if there is another path that will get you to your desired end results.

How can you learn to determine when you should stand and fight, and when you should seek another path?

There were times when I decided to stop my research because of obstacles I was facing.

But I was guided to continue.

Once I dreamed of numbers, and purchased a lottery ticket with those numbers. The ticket paid $10,000. Adjusted for inflation it would be about $130,000 in 2023.

Another time, as I sat reflecting on my decision to stop my research, my son brought me a picture he had found in the street—a picture of Christ.

As you know, I continued my research.

Enter your level, seek guidance from High Intelligence, and you will be guided as to what to do to reach your life goals.

Note: You can learn how to enter the alpha level and how to use the Mental Video to communicate with higher intelligence in the appendix.

54 Your Strength Is Within You
(1984)

Always remember that your strength is within you. You reach your source by going within, not by anything from without.

We find people sometimes who keep going from one program to another, from course to course, from teacher to teacher, book to book, always looking for "The Answer."

They keep looking, which means they never find the answer. For the answers are within.

I do not mean you should not seek help when you need it. But do avoid overdoing it. Techniques are a means to an end, not the end itself.

In the Silva Method, you learn ways to go within and find the answers you need.

You have methods for seeking guidance from High Intelligence.

When you first learn, use the techniques exactly the way they were designed to be used. While doing this, establish internal points of reference so you can function as you need to in the future.

People function differently.

Some are visually oriented. Some audibly. Others are sensitive. We make allowances for all modes in the Silva Method. That's why the directions that orientologists read during case working say, "Sense it. Feel it. Visualize it. Know it is there." You may detect information in any number of ways. You may imagine asking for the answer, and imagine an answer being spoken to you.

By whatever means you perceive information, use it.

But remember to do this: if you "feel" the information, if you imagine that you hear it, or if you just have a general sense of knowing, once you have the information, imagine what it would look like.

Develop your visual senses along with the others.

To begin with, you will use a specific ritual to enter your level and work cases. With practice, you can shorten the ritual, until finally you can do without it. You will have your own internal points of reference—you will recognize that special mental or emotional feeling associated with being at your Clairvoyant Level—and you will be able to work cases without having to go through the ritual first.

Develop confidence in yourself, for it is *you* who is doing the work, it is *you* who is getting the information, it is *you* who is responsible for *your* success.

How do you develop confidence? By experiencing success. Collect as many successes as possible, big or small. Review them at level, and this will help you to develop more confidence.

Techniques are a tool to help you get there, to help you learn.

You will learn that "special feeling" you have when you make correct decisions, and you will not have to use any techniques for those decisions. Only when you do not have that feeling of being right will you need to apply one of the techniques you have learned to help you out.

Developing such self-confidence is difficult for some people. But it is the goal you are seeking. Learn to rely on yourself.

Use your mind and your mental abilities to go directly to your source, for you have all that you need to insure your success.

55 We All Have a Responsibility
(1984)

God solves all problems. The more problems you can solve, the more God-like you are.

This thought is always brought home to me when I witness the birth of a newcomer to this planet.

Although I have witnessed birth many times and have ten children and twenty-three grandchildren (with the twenty-fourth expected in June), I am still fascinated and awed when a new child is born.

A birth always reminds me of the responsibility I have, as every human being on this planet has, to continue to work to help make this world a better place to live for those who will follow us.

The ability to have children is a power God has given us to create.

With Power Comes Responsibility

It is the most divine power we have, to create another human being. But with this power and privilege comes responsibility. We have a responsibility to care for these newcomers, to educate them, to protect them, to help them survive.

Those who came before helped us. It could be something like this idea that I have developed through many years of meditating and seeking guidance.

My idea might not be exactly right, but it is certainly a strong possibility, the best possibility in sight, so why not go for it rather than take a chance on getting zero.

It is our obligation to help.

When we have passed on from this plane, we will be asked what we did to help.

Our answer will determine whether we get a promotion. We might get a promotion to a little more obligation and responsibility to serve, at a higher level.

We might be assigned to more highly evolved planets, or galaxies, or dimensions.

If we did little to help, we could be required to continue at the same level. Or we might even get a demotion, and be sent to a place that is even less evolved, more primitive.

For some of us it is later than we think. Tomorrow we might not be around any more. Maybe we will be sent somewhere else. By serving here and now, we will guarantee that we will be sent somewhere better where we can serve even more.

It is our obligation, our way of helping God, to create newcomers on this planet, and to help those newcomers as much as we can. We should be thinking every single day how we can help make this planet a better place for these newcomers.

When we get up in the morning, we should think of how we can help God with creation today, how we can help relieve suffering, how we can help guide the newcomers.

At night, we should review how we did on this day to help God with creation, to help relieve suffering, help guide the newcomers to do better and better.

I have heard people suggest that we will be asked, when we pass on, how much we have loved and how much we have learned.

Service Is Love In Action

To me, the only question is how much we have served. The more we learn, the more we can serve.

And service is love in action.

There are many people who learn, and who think they have learned something valuable. But the only way to determine whether it is valuable or not is to take action, put it to the test and see how many problems it solves.

That is what Christ meant when he told us that "By their fruits ye shall know them." Does your knowledge produce good fruits? If so, it is good.

And love for one's fellow human beings cannot be an abstract thing. Anybody can sit and think about others. Love is action, action that solves problems.

That is what St. Paul explained in I Corinthians 13, when he first spoke of the importance of love and then gave a list of actions that express love.

So the final question still remains:

What have you done today to help make this a better world to live in?

Take action, in the subjective dimension as well as in the objective dimension. Go to level and find out what you are supposed to be doing with your life, how you can serve, and then get to work.

Note: If you don't already know how, you can learn many of our techniques in the appendix of this book.

PART 3
SOME PERSONAL REFLECTIONS

by José Silva Jr.

My father practiced what he preached. When he was young, he learned to fight in order to defend himself, and he became a very good boxer. When we became interested in fighting, he taught us how to win.

He also kept things in perspective, and advised us to go into martial arts rather than boxing, because of the danger of brain injuries from repeated punches to the head.

It paid off for me, and for my children too. Both of my children, Ruthie and David, are 5th Degree Black Belts, and David was so successful that he was inducted into the National Hispanic Sports Hall of Fame.

My father paid attention to feedback in other ways too: When he tried to give his research away, nobody took it, so when a group of artists wanted to develop their clairvoyant ability, he taught them.

What did he like about the experience? Instead of spending an afternoon in the hot sun installing a television antenna and earning $50, he sat in an air conditioned meeting room, talked for 4 days, and earned $5,000. Let the feedback guide you.

He used the same idea to help us earn higher test scores and make better grades in school. He taught us to learn by doing what children do naturally: Use visualization, imagination, along with our natural creativity and enthusiasm.

Now let's turn the floor over to him for his explanation.

56 Teach Children Visualization & Imagination *(1983)*

Children from seven to fourteen years of age are at a very important point in life. It is at this time that a child can learn naturally to use both the left and the right hemispheres of the brain.

By the time a child is fourteen years old, it is too late to learn by natural means to use the right brain hemisphere.

Up to seven years old, a child uses mostly the delta and theta portions of the brain—that is, the parts of the brain that emit the slower brain frequencies.

By the age of fourteen, a child is using mostly the part of the brain that vibrates at the beta frequencies, from fourteen to twenty-one cycles per second.

It is between the ages of seven and fourteen, when a child is functioning primarily at the alpha brain wave level, that the choice is made regarding the use of one or both halves of the cortex of the brain.

Ninety percent of humanity takes the path of least resistance when that crucial time comes; most choose to use the objective half of the brain, the part of the brain associated with objective, physical senses such as sight, taste, smell, touch and hearing.

Very few—only about ten percent of humanity—choose to think with the right brain hemisphere.

Perhaps many of those were forced to think creatively and intuitively in order to survive. Perhaps, then, what appeared to be a hardship actually turned out to be a blessing.

A Hardship Leads to an Advantage

Take my own life, for instance. By the time I was seven years old, I had made a decision to earn money to help support my family. Perhaps it was through necessity that I thought creatively, that I used my imagination, that I called on my intuitive faculties and functioned clairvoyantly. By doing these things, I was better able to find ways to help support my grandmother, my uncle, and my brothers and sisters.

Therefore, I grew up using both brain hemispheres, which has given me a definite advantage in life.

When I began to research the potential of the human mind, I began to realize that there was something different about the ten percent of humanity who achieve outstanding success; these ten percenters function differently than the rest of humanity.

Is there a way, I wondered, to help the ninety percent who use only the logical left brain hemisphere to learn to do their thinking with the creative and intuitive right hemisphere?

The way seemed to be to regress back in time, to recreate the situation that existed at the age of seven. That is, to function at the alpha brain wave frequency—at what we call the Basic Plane Level, or seven cycles per second—and at that level, practice using visualization and imagination.

At the same time, we use very carefully worded statements to program into the bio-computer (the brain) the belief and expectancy to be able to function clairvoyantly.

Thus, in the first half of our Silva Mind Control Basic Lecture Series, participants learn how to use the right brain hemisphere and to think more creatively; and in the second half, they learn how to function with control and full awareness in the subjective dimension.

If all parents will take our training and learn how to help their children develop the use of the right hemisphere prior to the age of fourteen, then all children will grow up to be geniuses; these children will not need our training.

Note: There are techniques you and your children can start learning now in the appendix in this book. There are even more techniques on our SilvaESP.com website including a Speed Learning workshop. As an owner of this book you can claim a discount for our online courses. Details are in the appendix.

57 Silva's Work Ahead of Times
(1980)

There was a recent article published in the mass media that made me somewhat reflective about what we have accomplished at Silva Mind Control over the years we have been in operation.

This article, more than anything, reinforced my great conviction on the value of our method and more especially on the tremendously humanitarian benefit that can be gleaned from it.

My only regret, and this I say whimsically because our work speaks for itself, is that I feel our strenuous work and painstaking research has not been given the recognition it should by those who are following in our footsteps.

Let me illustrate.

In the article, released by United Press International, the folk medicine practices of certain Peruvian tribes were examined by a team representing medical doctors, anthropologists and health organizations.

The article quoted an anthropology professor from the University of Southern California—who had been studying these Peruvian practices for twelve years—as saying:

"For developing nations to reach the World Health Organization's goal of total health by the year 2000 they are going to have to build on what they have—natural medicine.

"These folk medicine doctors deal chiefly with peoples psychological and psychosomatic problems that are caused by disruptions in the social organism.

"If someone believes they have been hexed, they usually have had an argument with someone and becomes sick because the social organism is upset. They'll convince themself that they are sick and go to the shaman (folk doctor) to cure it."

If the anthropology and medicine fields are just beginning to go into this type of research, then they ought to become familiar with our method, for this is what we have been doing for the last 20 years.

Our research works on the premise that we can control our mind so that it can function more effectively, in effect preventing the disruption of the social organism.

For example, what really happens many times today in the so called Western civilized countries is that a person becomes sick mostly through problems and tension disrupting their social organism. Instead of a folk doctor, they go to a psychiatrist or psychologist, and in some cases they are given nothing more than a placebo.

Through our method, the mind can program itself to avoid the tensions and problems that originally cause the disruption of the social organism. This we have known for three decades; yet, the anthropologists in the article say that learning the ways of folk medicine "is the first step in adopting it for modern medical use."

Surely these scientists could save themselves a lot of time and money by becoming familiar with our method, as have more than 2 million people throughout the world.

We know, for example, that the basic element of healing is that both the healer and the patient operate at a brain frequency of 10 cycles. At this frequency, both are mentally in attunement, and healing can take place.

In effect, what the medicine man is doing—what an anthropologist may call the ritual or the "magic"—is nothing more than getting themself and the patient operating at 10 cycles.

I agree with the anthropologist about the tremendous value of folk medicine, but this is something that we at Silva Mind Control have been researching and studying for three decades.

To see that much of the recent research is a reconfirmation of what we have for decades developed on our own is a tremendous source of inspiration.

Studies like the one cited in the UPI article illustrates that we are a pacesetter in the field of the use of mental energy.

And all this time we have used our knowledge for the betterment of humanity.

Isn't this something to be proud of?

58 Lone Pioneer Attracted Scientists to His Work *(1995)*

In the beginning, José Silva was all alone in his research.

Even his wife Paula was skeptical and cautious until she eventually saw the benefits in the work he was doing with their children.

A few friends in Laredo became interested and listened to his ideas and helped him when he asked them to, but many more were suspicious and even hostile.

Eventually Silva's work attracted the attention of one scientist, who became a close friend and associate, and who brought the research findings to the attention of many other scientists.

This pioneering research, overcoming many obstacles and challenges, has provided José Silva with many wonderful memories of the people and events that helped us to take the first step into the second phase of human evolution on the planet by succeeding with metaphysics.

This is the story about how scientists became aware of the new science that José Silva has named "psychorientology."

A Scientist Takes a Peek

The first scientist who came to Laredo, Texas, to investigate the research that Silva was doing was Dr. J.W. Hahn, director of the Mind Science Foundation in San Antonio, Texas. Through Dr. Hahn, many more scientists became interested in the pioneering research into the mind and human potential.

Mind Science Foundation was founded by millionaire oil man Tom Slick Sr. It was Mr. Slick who asked Dr. Hahn to checkout Silva's work. He took back a very favorable report.

In fact, Dr. Hahn took the first step that led to the Silva Method being taught to the public for the very first time. Here's how it happened.

Better Results Than University Researchers Got

After Dr. Hahn's visit to Laredo, he called Dr. N.E. West, the head of the Department of Psychology at Wayland Baptist University in Plainview, Texas, and arranged for him to visit Laredo and inspect Silva's findings.

Dr. West was impressed. Even though he had visited the laboratories of Dr. J.B. Rhine at Duke University on two occasions, he said that he had never seen so much valid scientific work done on ESP.

A Very Successful Visit

That led to an invitation by Dr. West for Silva to come to Plainview and present a lecture to the psychology students at the college.

The visit was so successful that Dr. West told his friend Dord Fitz, an art professor in nearby Amarillo, that he should invite Silva to come speak to his art students. When several of the art students expressed an interest in learning Silva's techniques, Fitz suggested that Silva come teach a class in Amarillo.

Almost eighty students attended that first Silva Mind Control course. Even before they had finished their training, they were telling Silva that their relatives and friends were also interested, so Silva scheduled another class.

Silva Mind Control continued to grow by word of mouth until today it is being offered in more than 100 countries worldwide, in twenty-nine different languages, and millions of people have benefited.

First Presentation to a Scientific Panel

Meanwhile, while Silva was impressing students and artists with his findings, Dr. Hahn was arranging for a visit to the leading parapsychology laboratory in the world: The Mind Science Foundation Laboratory in Los Angeles, California.

It was here that Silva observed a scientific project with a plant that convinced him that the human mind could alter matter just by thinking.

Verified Results

Silva continued teaching, and Dr. Hahn continued encouraging him. But not everyone believed that such trailblazing research and results were coming out of Laredo, Texas.

Dr. Hahn needed to demonstrate to the Mind Science Foundation board of directors that Silva's program was valid, so he undertook a major survey.

Detailed, comprehensive survey forms were mailed to 10,000 Silva Method graduates. More than 1,100 of them took the time to fill out the forms and return them, an unusually high percentage. The graduates seemed eager to express their opinions.

The results were spectacular. Not only were people receiving all of the benefits they had sought when they first came to the course, they were benefiting in ways they had not expected. They were using the Silva techniques to correct problems that they had not even considered correcting before they attended the training.

There was also a question about the graduates overall opinion of Silva Mind Control. Only half a dozen had any complaint, while the rest—99.6% of the graduates—were satisfied.

To validate the survey, Dr. Hahn conducted another survey. In this one, he got responses from every person who attended a Silva Method Basic Lecture Series in Albuquerque, New Mexico.

The results in Albuquerque were the same as the results from the other survey, and every person was satisfied with the course.

Voluntary Control of Brain Waves

Armed with proof that the Silva Method works and that graduates were reporting outstanding benefits, Dr. Hahn now approached other scientists and encouraged them to investigate Silva's work.

He helped arrange with clinical psychologist Dr. Puryear to hold a Silva class at the Trinity University campus in San Antonio.

Then Dr. Hahn approached the University of Texas Medical School in San Antonio. He arranged for Dr. Robert Barns, head of the Psychiatry Department, and Dr. Richard McKenzie, head of the Psychology Department, to invite Silva to present a lecture and demonstration of how to control brain waves consciously.

Students and professors were impressed, because at that time, scientists believed that brain waves were under autonomic control, and could not be altered by individuals.

Later Dr. Hahn arranged with Dr. Fred Bremner, head of the Department of Psychology at Trinity University, to test Silva and some of the people that Silva had trained.

For the first time, scientists verified in a scientific laboratory that people could learn to control their brain waves.

They also conducted a scientific experiment that involved Silva teaching his method to twenty of the students at the university. As usual, the results were successful. They were reported in the British scientific journal *Neuropsychologia*, Vol.10, pages 307–312, and pages 467–469.

New Projects Suggested

While visiting the Mind Science Foundation in Los Angeles, Dr. Hahn suggested three projects to Silva:

Investigate a Brazilian psychic surgeon by the name of Arrigo.

To bring Uri Geller to the US to study the energy that he used to bend spoons.

To teach the Silva Method to forty-nine Ph.D. geologists and petroleum engineers of the McCullough Oil Corp.

Before the project with Arrigo could be started, he died in an automobile accident.

Silva decided not to go to the expense of bringing Geller to the US for research because he could not find any useful application for the spoon bending ability. "If he could straighten them out, it would be different," Silva explained. "Our goal is to correct problems, not to cause them."

The forty-nine Ph.D.s with the oil company were given special training to see if they could use their minds to locate undiscovered deposits of oil, using ESP. The oil company never released the results of their efforts.

At this time Dr. Hahn decided to leave the Mind Science Foundation and join Silva in Laredo.

More scientists joined him. Dr. George DeSau conducted numerous studies of the changes that take place in people after completing the Silva training.

Dr. DeSau conducted research on varied groups of people, from junior high and high school students, to alcoholics, welfare mothers, business executives, and others who learned the Silva Method.

One of Dr. DeSau's first projects involved more than 2,000 adolescent girls at an inner city school in Philadelphia, Pennsylvania: Hallahan High School.

Dr. DeSau later conducted similar research on schools in Guam, as well as in Venezuela for the Venezuelan government.

Silva met Dr. Richard McKenzie at the University of Texas Medical School and invited him to join the staff in Laredo.

Presentation to Leading Scientists

The three scientists who were on the Silva International staff, Dr. Hahn, Dr. DeSau, and Dr. McKenzie, were instrumental in arranging for forty scientists from all over the United States to come and meet Silva in Houston, Texas, so that he could explain to them what he had done and what his future plans were.

The meeting took place on Friday night and all day Saturday. On Sunday the group was given a tour of NASA facilities in Houston.

Those in attendance were: Rev. Marzel Allard, S.J., from Montreal, Quebec;

V.A. Benignus, Ph.D., University of North Carolina;

Mrs. Gayla Benignus, M.S., University of North Carolina;

Mrs. Lendell W. Braud, M.A., Texas Southern University;

William G. Braud, Ph.D., University of Houston;

Frederick J. Bremner, Ph.D., and his wife, from Trinity University;

Barbara B. Brown. Ph.D., Veterans Administration Hospital, Sepulveda, California;

Melvin Bucholtz, emissary for Dr. David Shapiro, Harvard Medical School;

Thomas H. Budzynski, Ph.D., the University of Colorado Medical Center;

Jeffery P. Chang, Ph.D., University of Texas Medical Branch;

Leslie M. Cooper, Ph.D., Brigham Young University;

Arthur J. Deikman, M.D., Mills Valley, California;

George T. DeSau, Ed.D., Silva International;

Paul Dunn, M.D., Oak Park, Illinois;

Doug Eddy, Ph.D., Carnegie-Mellon, Pittsburgh;

Stan L. Falor, M.D., McMurray, Pennsylvania;

Lester G. Fehmi, Ph.D., New York State University;

Rev. John Frizelle, Ph.D., Incarnate Word College, San Antonio;

Irving Geller, Ph.D., Texas Tech University School of Medicine;

J.W. Hahn, Ph.D., Silva International;

Dr. Paul Henchaw, Tucson Arizona;

W. Lindsay Jacob, M.D., Pittsburgh, Pennsylvania;

Kendall Johnson, emissary for Thelma Moss, Ph.D., UCLA Medical Center, Los Angeles;

Bonnie Kaplan, emissary for Thomas B. Mulholland, Ph.d., Veterans Administration Hospital, Bedford, Massachusetts;

Perry London, Ph.D., University of Southern California, Los Angeles;

Alejandro Martinez Marquez, Ph.D., National Polytechnic Institute, Mexico, D.F.;

Clancy McKenzie, M.D., and wife, Bala Cynwyd, Pennsylvania;

Richard E. McKenzie, Ph.D., Silva International;

Prof. John Mihalasky, Ed.D., Newark College of Engineering;

William "Bill" Opel, documentary film maker;

Dr. Robert E. Ornstein, Langley Porter Institute, University of California Medical Center, San Francisco;

Bari Payne, Ph.D., Wayland, Massachusetts;

Erik Peper, Berkley, California;

William G. Roll, Psychical Research Foundation, Dulce Station, Durham, North Carolina;

Arq. Jose Zarul.Braiz, emissary for Ing. Benjamin Rubio, National Polytechnic Institute, Mexico, D.F.;

Milan Ryzl, Ph.D., San Jose, California;

Gertrude Schmeidler, Ph.D., City College of the City University of New York;

Max Toth, Queens, New York;

N.E. West, Ph.D., and wife, Veterans Administration Hospital, Fort Meade, South Dakota;

Ian Wickramasekera, Ph.D., University of Illinois, Peoria.

The following doctors, Ph.D.s and Silva International staff members took part in introducing Silva's work to the visiting scientists:

Dr. J.W. Hahn, Dr. George DeSau, Dr. Richard McKenzie, Dr. N.W. West, Dr. Fred Bremner, Dr. William Braud, Dr. Jeffery Chang, Dr. Gayla Benignus, Dr. Paul Dunn, Dr. Stan Falor, Rev. John Frizelle, Dr. Irving Geller, Dr. Alejandro Martinez Marquez, Dr. Clancy McKenzie, Bill Opel, James Needham, and Harry McKnight.

59 Why the World Needs Silva Mind Control *(1980)*

The world needs the Silva mind training systems now more than ever!

Do you find this statement too boastful?

Perhaps it is, but it also is a reality.

Our society is fraught with loneliness and failure, and the medical field is much too concerned with the relief of pain and suffering, often by the prescription of pain-relieving drugs and tranquilizers.

The established professions, such as psychiatry, psychology, social work and counseling, are now augmenting their forces through a variety of semi-professional agencies such as halfway houses, retreat houses and settlement houses.

Alcohol continues in wide use, all to the detriment of many families and individuals. Narcotics—whether hard or even prescribed—all to often are taken to combat a depression or a loneliness that is never fully understood at all by the patient.

And it is in the understanding of that loneliness and that failure, and even of that pain, that the true answer to these illnesses may lie.

Yet, this is a very difficult task for some, at least for those individuals who are not trained to listen to their bodies and their minds, such as Silva Mind Control graduates are trained.

For some reason or another, our society is not accustomed to listening inward. In our success-oriented society, failure—whether real or imagined—is accompanied by tremendous pain, and it becomes very hard to change.

Consider, for example, the often-repeated situation of loss of job.

When someone goes through this situation, they become extremely negative and depressed, a sense of failure overwhelms them.

There is a strong belief that with the loss of that job, there has also been a loss of self-esteem, that the individual has lost value in the eyes of friends, neighbors and even their family.

Unless the individual finds an equally good job, the depression and attitude of failure continues.

And this in itself increases; and for the most part people may begin to shun their "successful" friends, or even their relatives, whom they feel they have let down.

As people lose value in their own eyes, they tend to separate from others, and the painful agony of fear, anxiety and depression begins to set in even more deeply.

Eventually, the depression itself allows the individual to rationalize their condition, and the excuse may be given that "It is no use. How can things go right for me. I am a loser."

Silva Mind Control teaches us to identify with success, not with failure. This, I believe, is among the most rewarding gratifications I get by being associated with the founding of the method.

For in teaching individuals how to identify with success, the need for hospitals, clinics, halfway houses, and sanitariums diminishes, as does the need for the chemical elimination of pain, suffering and other psychosomatic illnesses.

By allowing people to see themselves through the eyes of Silva Mind Control, graduates begin to understand all the positive aspects of themselves.

They begin to understand that failure is a state of mind, an aberration of the spirit and a condition that is not natural to the individual.

But the benefits of Silva Mind Control are not only personal. They also are transferable; for as people begin to see themselves in a positive manner, it then becomes possible for them to transfer that positive energy—or feeling—to others.

This, then, is our base, our own method of creating a society—or a community of societies—to provide people the opportunity to fail, and also provides people with the means to turn that failure into a positive force.

Through Silva Mind Control techniques, we can, indeed, begin this experiment in earnest.

By going to level every day and focusing on the positive, the successful, we will start visualizing a new attitude, one that will undoubtedly catch on.

One person may feel that their efforts will not count that much, but remember that there are more than 2 million Silva Mind Control graduates throughout the world.

That person is not alone by any means. There are many others with them.

Isn't it really exciting to belong to this type of involvement?

Yes, the world does need Silva Mind Control more than ever.

And Silva Mind Control is really each and every individual who tries, each in their own way, to achieve more positive things in the world.

60 A Turning Point in the History of the Planet *(1980)*

As the time approaches once again for our annual Silva Mind Control International Convention, the theme of the convention seems more and more relevant.

The theme is, "Innergizing the 1980s."

But what does the slogan mean? And, perhaps more important, why was it chosen?

First of all, the theme is relevant because the 1980s are much more than just the beginning of a new decade. This decade, more than any other one in history, can truly be said to be a crucial turning point in the history of the planet.

The 1980s is destined to be the decade in which the world sheds much of its old self—including attitudes and ways of doing things—and adopts attitudes and feelings shaped by the multitude of dynamic forces born during the previous decade.

In this regard, Silvans ought to be justly proud, for our movement is pretty much a creation of the 1960s and one that is destined to shape the way we live in the 1980s and beyond.

The Silva Mind Control Method is destined to play a big role throughout the planet as to how the world reshapes itself and adapts itself for the survival of its people.

This is why we selected the theme of, "Innergizing the 1980s."

To begin with, during the last two decades we have focused outward, influenced by the forces outside of ourselves.

And because these forces were often not understood, humanity was plagued by anger and frustration. Unfortunately, not knowing many times who or what was the direct result of our ills, people directed their anger at third parties, often innocent ones.

We witness this phenomenon by merely looking at the world wars and conflicts that engulf mankind.

But as Silvans, we know that the real answer to the true development and evolution of the human potential is not outward but inward.

We Are the Answer to Our Problems

We need to look to ourselves, for if we learn to solve the frustrations that cause anger without antagonizing other people that we need and love, the frustrations soon pass, and—painful as these may have been—they have provided us with an experience that we can use later to develop more as human beings.

If, however, we do not learn either how to relieve our frustrations or to understand their source, the underlying anger and frustrations remain—in effect making us the eternal victims of our own inability to "look inward effectively."

And this is what we must do, look inward, "Innergize" ourselves through the methods learned in the Silva Mind Control Method. By doing so, we will be providing ourselves with successful identities.

What will this mean?

Steps to Success

First, as successful people, we will learn to control immediate and angry emotions so that we can be assertive and aggressive in an effective manner.

This can be done without the need to enter into any irrationality and simply by going to level and understanding ourselves as we are.

Success is contagious. If we become successful individuals, our attitudes are going to expand to others we deal with, particularly our families and close friends.

The more success-oriented we become, the more we are going to teach behavior that leads to success.

Unless we "Innergize," we will continue to be plagued by attitudes and feelings that lead us to failure in our attempts to develop our human potential.

Failures cannot understand the nature of their being, and therefore find it difficult to get rid of their anger or frustrations.

More often than not, they remain depressed because their frustrations do not allow them to get involved with humanity, and they throw a barrier that prevents humanity from getting involved with them.

But "Innergizing the 1980s" does not mean that we all should look inward and continue to live there without interacting with others. Far from it.

Serving Humanity Better

"Innergizing" means only looking inward to gather the strength and fortitude necessary to share with others.

Only in sharing ourselves with others, in committing ourselves to helping humanity, can we become really "Innergized."

As Silvans, we must look with optimism to the future, and we must begin to "Innergize" ourselves into success-oriented personalities.

The answer lies within each of us, and we must, in turn, share each other in a bond of humanity.

Our planet has seen humanity emerge from very primitive societies concerned only with the ability to survive to one in which the essence of life is the development of human potential. How we handle this transition will determine the type of planet we will have.

"Innergizing the 1980s" is a good pathway to follow towards the achievement of this goal of actualizing human potential and "serving humanity better" as we say in the very first Beneficial Statement in the course.

61 | Motto Symbolizes Our Commitment to Humanity *(1988)*

"Better and Better."

This is the Silva motto, the goal of our very existence, and I feel there can be no better one.

My commitment to this motto was enhanced recently when my wife Paula and I attended Sunday church services at our local parish church. We have belonged to this church for years, ever since our children were mere tots, and I like to worship there every time my demanding schedule allows me to.

I thoroughly enjoy attending this particular church, not because it is particularly beautiful in an architectural point of view nor because it is elaborately decorated, but because of the people who worship there almost every Sunday.

You see, these people have been my neighbors and friends for years, people I grew up with and with whom I have shared experiences as a community.

Many of them I find with faces that are markedly more wrinkled than when I saw them last; and some of them I find sitting down with members of their own family—young men and women who seem to have reached adulthood unnoticed before our eyes.

Each one of them pursues a different career, some known to me, others unknown.

And although I do not interact with them very often, we are gathered for church services.

There, in that church, like in countless other churches throughout the world, are gathered ordinary human beings giving of themselves, at least for an instant, so that they can be more at peace with themselves and their maker.

"Better and Better."

Isn't that what we are all about?

Aren't we as human beings always seeking that impossible dream, the achievement of happiness, of love, of peace with ourselves, our neighbors and our God?

"Better and Better."

Not perfect by any means, for we know that perfection itself is merely the never-ending process of self-improvement that each of us performs at our own pace and direction.

Not hypocritical either, for the very essence of our method is a sincere desire to help humanity, and to set an example—not by words alone but by putting what we teach into practice.

"Better and Better."

Not conformity that settles by the mistaken belief that we have achieved a plateau of performance, but an ardent desire not to be satisfied, to strive for creativity, increase our humanity and involving ourselves more and more in motivating others to do likewise.

"Better and Better."

In a world burdened with insecurity, threatened by chaos, challenged by forces that most of us cannot fully understand, "Better and Better" becomes a beacon all of us can turn to, one which, if pursued ardently, can transform all our doubts and fears into mere illusions of the past.

The people in that church are a testimonial of people's inner desire to better themselves. It is not an easy task, especially with the constant bombardment of false priorities and warped motivations that are loose in the world.

Yet, amidst these turmoils, "Better and Better" continues to catch our spirit, channel our efforts and solidify our commitment to ourselves and to our neighbors, whoever they might be.

"Better and Better."

It is not just a slogan, but a way of life, the anchoring weight of our beliefs in a sea swollen with indecision and insecurity.

"Better and Better."

Can there really be any other three words that captivate our movement so adequately?

62 Guidelines for Moral Behavior
(1988)

We say that a human being is not one who looks like one, but one who acts like one.

What do we mean when we talk about acting like a human being?

Are we talking about morality and the ethical standards established by government and religion, by politicians and preachers?

Through the ages, the rules keep changing. The Old Testament tells us that the law demands an eye for an eye, a tooth for a tooth.

The New Testament says that no longer applies, but that we should answer evil with kindness.

In modern times, legislative bodies keep passing laws that change the meaning of right and wrong.

And if that were not enough, the judicial system keeps changing the interpretation of those laws. In a single instant in the United States, abortion changed from wrong to right.

How Can We Tell Right From Wrong?

Should we depend on people who proclaim themselves as our moral leaders? We have seen many of our self-professed leaders fall from grace in recent years. Who can you trust?

The judges at the Nuremberg trials ruled that we must each ultimately determine for ourselves the difference between right and wrong.

That was reaffirmed in Judge Sirica's courtroom during the Watergate scandal.

Even if your commander in chief orders you to do something that is illegal and is morally and ethically wrong, you still have a higher duty, to humanity and to yourself.

Is there a yardstick we can use to help us determine what is right, what we should do in any circumstance?

We have found only one reliable test to guide us in making these decisions:

Ask This Question:

Does it help correct problems, without creating any new problems?

Ask yourself that question when faced with a choice.

Avoid making the mistake President Nixon made when he chose a course of action that solved an immediate personal problem but created a much larger problem when people felt they could no longer trust the man they had elected to be their leader.

Attempting to solve a problem by using deceit can magnify your problems. The television evangelist who confessed his mistake has not been punished as severely as the one who used church funds to try to cover up his mistake.

Any one of us could make a mistake. We could say something that hurts someone, and wish we had never said it. We might fail to do something that should be done, and this could hurt someone.

But this should never stop us from doing what we can to correct problems on our planet.

We should continue to strive to make our world a better place to live.

Use Your Silva Tools

As Silva graduates, we have tools to help us make the correct choices more often.

When faced with a decision, and you are not certain which course of action will do the most to correct problems and make our world a better place to live, then take time to enter your level and use those deep alpha levels to help you.

Analyze the situation at alpha.

By doing this, you can minimize the emotion of the moment, you can view the situation from a higher perspective, you can free yourself of your fears and frustrations and anger.

There are many techniques in the Silva Method that you can use to help you make decisions,

In the UltraMind ESP System you learn a technique called the MentalVideo for calling on Higher Intelligence for guidance.

This technique is used only after you have attempted to solve the problem yourself, but have been unable to do so. You can learn this technique in the appendix of this book.

Just remember: society's moral standards change with the times.

Even the courts have ruled that ultimately you must make your own decision and refuse to do that which is wrong.

Keep in mind that the best be done for everyone involved. Then make your decisions at level with the confidence that you are doing your best to convert our planet into a paradise.

Note: If you haven't already learned to use the Silva Techniques you can learn many of them in the appendix.

63 First Identify Problems, Then Correct Them *(1990)*

Sometimes people ask why we mention all of those diseases in the Preventive Statements in the Basic Lecture Series (BLS). Let me explain:

One of the basic principles of our system is that we correct specific problems.

Those diseases are definitely problems.

We have heard about those diseases for years.

- Do this or don't do that and you could get cancer.
- Live a certain way and you will suffer hypertension and heart disease.
- Smoke, or just breathe big-city air, and you will have respiratory problems.

And so on and on and on.

So we want to identify the problems and develop tools that we can use later to combat those illnesses.

It is easy to understand when we use the analogy that Dr. J. Wilfred Hahn developed. Dr. Hahn identifies the logical part of himself as Wilfred, the left-brained scientist. The creative and intuitive part he calls Willie.

It is Willie that takes care of the body. But Willie is dominated by Wilfred.

So logical Wilfred has been bombarding Willie for years with warnings about all of those diseases we are likely to get because of the lifestyles we live.

Now we need to give Willie another message.

So in the Preventive Statements, we advise Willie that he never needs to learn to develop those diseases.

Those statements are programmed in very deeply. We do not put them in your student manual, because you cannot program them as deeply on your own as your lecturer can during the BLS.

Once Willie gets the new message, then all you need to do is to use the techniques you have been taught.

The Ideal Answer

Whenever anyone asks you how you are, answer "Better and Better."

That phrase has been programmed at a very deep level of mind and is associated with not being able to develop those diseases, and with maintaining a perfectly healthy body and mind.

In fact, the simple act of going to level once every day activates all of the helpful phrases in our mind training programs.

When you couple this with the natural benefits of spending time at alpha every day, you then have powerful protection from illness.

Relaxing while your brain pulses at the alpha level—which you learn to do in all of the Silva courses—automatically strengthens your immune mechanism. And since that level is associated with all of those helpful phrases, you get even more benefit.

This is something that is not available from our imitators.

Take Advantage of Our Many Years of Research

People who do not understand, people who have not conducted all of the years of research that I have, think that they can leave something out without hurting the course.

They do not understand that they are hurting their customers by not providing them with the tools they need to correct problems and maintain good health.

Many of the other techniques we have work on the same principle:

- First, identify the problem.
- Develop tools to use to correct it.
- Then correct the problem.

Mirror of the Mind and the 3-Scenes Technique—what is the first thing you do?

You visualize the problem.

How about the Headache Control Technique—what is the first thing you say? "I have a headache, I feel a headache."

You state the problem.

How do you work a case? What do you do after you have an image of the subject's body? You scan the body to locate any problems.

How about Awake Control; for remaining awake longer. What's the first thing you say?

"I am drowsy and sleepy . . ."

In every instance, we start by recognizing the problem.

The Preventive Statements are the same.

We are stating the problem, so that the mind—Willie—knows what direction to take.

We have to know two things in order to chart a course: Where we are, and where we're going.

Some systems try to deny that the problem exists. That's one major difference between them and the Silva Method.

You have some very powerful tools to use. To activate them, just practice what you have been taught.

Spend time at level every day and you should stay healthy.

And if you do have one of those illnesses, then work a case on your own body and correct it.

You have the tools. All you need to do now is use them

Note: If you haven't already learned the Silva Techniques you can learn them now in the appendix of this book.

64 I Had a Different Kind of Education *(1993)*

When I began my research back in 1944 my main goal was to find ways to help my children improve their grades in school.

During twenty-two years of research, I learned a great deal about the human brain and mind, and how people learn.

Based on this research, it appears that our present educational system does not do a very good job of recognizing the learning potential of a human being. It is much too slow.

In emerging countries, where children are required to pitch in and help parents even as toddlers, they show remarkable ability to carry out simple tasks in a day or two of observation. Reeds are gathered, piled, and bundled by a three year old.

Goats are milked by a four year old. A two year old collects eggs in a henhouse.

In many European countries, pre-school children help in the markets, bagging merchandise and making change.

Others offer trinkets to tourists or work in the fields.

My Education

I was four years old when my father died in a terrorist act during the Mexican revolution. My mother remarried and moved to another city in Texas and I lived with my grandmother and my Uncle Manuel.

Uncle Manuel made me a shoe shine box and I began to make extra money for our household by shining shoes.

It was fun. I enjoyed the people. I decided I could do more and I began selling newspapers. If I didn't shine somebody's shoes I sold them a newspaper.

Uncle Manuel helped me prepare separate lists. On one were the names, addresses, and office numbers of those who wanted shoe shines and when. On the other, those who wanted daily newspapers. On a third, those who wanted both.

These lists helped me be in the right place at the right time, giving my customers better service from me. Looking back, I consider this experience a lot better than knowledge I could have acquired in first grade.

A Complete Education

Looking back, I also see that I was using my left brain to keep records and supplies, and my right brain to come up with imaginative ideas to better serve my customers, I'm not saying I was a genius, but what I was doing was giving me a better real life education than a classroom.

Soon I was earning a dollar a day, then two dollars a day. This was now more than Uncle Manuel was making in the laundry where he worked. Because the family was in such a financial struggle, it was decided that I would continue working rather than start school.

What was I missing out on at school?

- One and one make two, while I was counting my profits for the day.
- C-A-T spells cat, while I was calling out the newspaper headline of the day.
- Coloring with crayons, while I was solving problems by polishing furniture and shining shoes.

I'm sure my six and seven year old education in the outside world can be topped by many other children forced by economic circumstances to educate themselves. The point is: Your child should not be spared any opportunity that arises for exposure to expanded experiences, for investigating unknown places, for trying out new skills, and for imaginative new games, toys, and entertainment.

My non-instructional education snowballed. As a teenager I was driving 150 miles to San Antonio to buy merchandise at wholesale not available in Laredo and peddle it door-to-door.

Soon I hired a crew of youngsters to work for part of the profits.

I asked them what they were learning in school. It did not click with me because I saw no purpose in it. Was it plane geometry? English? History? Whatever.

At any rate, the unschooled boy was the boss, and the school boys were his workers. Symbolic.

Let Children Learn

I don't intend to demean the educational system.

However, going to school and entering the classroom each day should involve, like life, a new adventure.

Children have a natural curiosity about nature, people, the out-of-doors, business, manufacture, farming, and other life activities.

Instead of exploiting this, the current system of learning often suppresses it.

Children are expected to learn about real life in an artificial environment.

- No tree, but a picture of a tree.
- No fish, just a picture of a fish.
- No survival problem, just a blackboard problem.

What motivation can there possibly be each day being in the same classroom with the same people, the same scene out the window, the same smells.

Traditional classroom teaching runs 180 degrees counter to the way the brain learns new things.

The brain learns new things not by knowing about these new things but directly experiencing new things. Students need to experience the things they are studying.

Add Another Dimension

Your child should not leave school, but you can add another dimension of education to the classroom education they are now receiving. That dimension can be summed up as:

Real life experiences.

Your budding genius deserves more than the incredible boredom and drudgery of one room.

School field trips provide occasional opportunities for "hands on" education, but they are far too infrequent.

How about adding some home "field trips."

Where?

Well, perhaps out to where some new home is being built, or to where dad or mom work, or to the airport.

Give it to your child as a case or problem to solve: "What kind of a field trip would you benefit most from?"

Natural Is Best

There is research being done now on neuro-chemically boosting intelligence.

One basic vitamin and mineral supplement was found to boost IQ over five points.

Hydergine is claimed to be a cognitive enhancer, improving memory and clarity of thinking.

Psychedelic plants are being touted in some areas as an aid to the learning process.

I vote *no, no, no!*

These are material world—left brain—approaches that are a far cry from the natural genius of the other side and its blessings of intuition, creativity, and inspiration that we wish to create.

You might as well use some electronic machine that promises instant theta or mind-altering moodscapes or "brain tune-ups."

It's all so simple once you remember that we all were born to be geniuses and we would continue to be geniuses if we did not mature.

Implant Images of Success In Your Children

Our parents interfere with dismal evaluations of us.

"Wet your bed once more and I'll rub your face in it."

"No television for one week."

"You're grounded!"

"I'm stopping your allowance."

"You're a clumsy brat!"

"Don't tell me that baloney."

"Go to bed."

This is all demeaning to a child. It gives the child feelings of guilt for not having done better or differently.

It puts down the child.

A genius needs to be put up.

Remember that "Mind guides brain and brain guides body" and after correcting a child, leave them with a positive thought in their mind.

A genius thrives on recognition of accomplishment, of appreciation of ability and efforts, and reinforcement of special skills and expertise.

Parents should never put the child down with destructive criticism. Boost the child's self-esteem rather than cloud it. That self-esteem is saying to the brain neurons, "You're tops." So the brain neurons behave "tops."

It would be disastrous to a genius-in-the-making to provide input that decreases expectations of wondrous accomplishments.

That high expectation is the backbone of a genius-to-be. You don't have to lie.

Just don't comment on shortcomings, or use words that are less judgmental.

There is always a way of avoiding the negative and emphasizing the positive.

We all function to the limits of our own self-image, but not beyond. Don't worry about ego, conceit, or bragging. That will very likely be a phase, but only a phase. Children will simmer down as they mature.

Meanwhile, the realization of superior work, talented creativity, and above average intellectual ability is the power that drives the genius-to-be to ever new heights of growth and maturity.

(This information is excerpted from the book from José Silva and Dr. Robert Stone, Create a Genius. *It is available from online booksellers worldwide.)*

65 Here's How José Silva Uses His Mind
(1983)

Here is a rare opportunity for a glimpse into the mind of a naturally developed clairvoyant, José Silva, who created a method so everyone could function in this manner. This gives us a very valuable clue as to how we, as Silva graduates, can function better in our day-to-day lives.

The following is an exact, unedited transcript of a conversation with José Silva, conducted in 1983 in Mr. Silva's office in Laredo. Your editor had been waiting for an opportunity when Mr. Silva was obviously functioning creatively and clairvoyantly, and was "tuning in" to get answers and information.

The physical signs included a sort of "far away" look, eyes turned upward and towards the left, and eyelids fluttering from time to time. The tone of voice was soft and thoughtful, the words flowing out smoothly and making a lot of sense. When all of these signs were noticed, the interviewer asked:

Q: Stop and think for just a moment, if you would: exactly what kind of mental process were you going through when you were giving me that answer?

Silva: Whenever I need to find the answer, I am accustomed to getting a feeling, to remember a feeling I get to enhance my ability to get information. I am familiar with this feeling because of practice and experience.

For instance, when I was working with Harry McKnight to develop a glossary of terms in the Graduate Seminar manual, I would get into a state of concentration and an idea would come, in many and different ways, many descriptions for one word, many kinds of meanings for the same situations.

When I would come out, it would not always make the same kind of sense that it made within. So I always try to go with it as I sense it, and if it continues to make sense at the outer levels, then I'd go with it.

(**Note:** Throughout this interview, he continued to show the same physiological signs of "tuning in" as the signs that prompted the question.)

Q: You said a "feeling." Is it like a physical feeling?

Silva: It is like an emotional feeling more than anything else. Kind of a mental thing. You cannot explain it. It is not physical.

It is a feeling you get through experience, of having come up with information successfully before, and you have detected that feeling when that took place.

I notice on this book that I'm writing now, that I get stuck sometimes and don't know where to go from that place. Then I concentrate and immediately the doors are opened and I start off writing again, with more information.

Q: What do you mean "concentrate"? Exactly what mental process?
Silva: Just quiet down your mind and go back to thinking the way you have thought before when you were successful.

Q: Do you review a success?
Silva: No, not necessarily.

You could do that too. Go back to the level where you learned to go. But the thing is, eventually you don't have to review a success, you just provoke that feeling, or desire that feeling, and you are back to the level where you should come up with the information. Just by knowing that you want the information, automatically you will become attuned, because of your desire, to the same level.

Q: How does the information come? Do you hear it?
Silva: No, it just occurs to you.

Q: Just like your own thoughts?
Silva: Like as though it is a natural thing, you knew it all the time, and you have to say it.

Q: Can you tell me how you, personally, invoke that feeling?
Silva: It is automatic once you get used to doing it, because you have been doing it for so long you know. You need to concentrate because you need the information, and you need some way to get the information. You just develop a way of getting the information you need, in a way that starts the information flowing in to you again.

It's as though you are asking for the information and it is flowing to you.

I always believe that when Rabbi Jesus said, "Ask and you shall receive, knock and it shall be opened." It is something like that; it is as though when I desire to have information, I am asking and it comes.

It comes from the inner dimension, not the outer dimension. It is a special type of concentration.

You are looking for that feeling that you have developed, have eventually developed, through practice.

Q: That "Special feeling that comes with success" that you have talked about before?
Silva: That would be it. That's it, because actually you recognize that feeling and you like that feeling, because when you have succeeded, you stay on it a little longer because it is a good feeling to be successful. So the more times you get to feel that feeling of success, the easier it comes to you. Like, practice makes perfect.

Q: In the Basic Lecture Series, you mention that after practicing enough successful health cases, you no longer need the 3 to 1 and 10 to 1 ritual, but can simply "daydream" and the daydreaming becomes "creative and the true reality." Is that what you're doing?
Silva: Yes. That's what we're talking about. That's the best way I can explain it. You're not really seeing anything, you let your eyes go wherever they want to go, but usually it's to the left, you see? To the left and slightly upwards.

And then you start daydreaming. You stare, defocus your vision, and information starts coming to you, when you desire it, and when there's a need for it. You don't just play with it, but when you need to have information, then you use your method for provoking the feeling, to open the door to the information.

Q: Then it is not necessarily an image? You are not necessarily daydreaming in pictures?

Silva: No. Well, it would be similar to daydreaming, because when you start getting information you start making images of it, for it, or with it. But you don't make the images before the information comes. You make the images after the information comes.

Q: And it is not clairaudience, like hearing a voice or something?
Silva: No. It is just like your own thoughts coming to you. But it is the information you desire from the inner dimension.

(**Note:** After this interview, conducted in 1983, your editor practiced working a lot of health detection and correction cases, reviewed successes, and did the other things we are taught to do in the Silva ESP training. The result: We now function the same way, and have written several books doing exactly what José Silva described. The keys to success: Practice and purpose. Practice the techniques so that you can do a better job of improving living conditions on the planet.)

66 Help Your Children Get Better Grades in School *(1982)*

The traditional way that parents try to help their children get better grades in schoolwork is to encourage, praise, threaten, and condemn.

As you know, "mind guides brain and brain guides body." That is why encouragement and praise generally have good effects on youngsters, but the condemnation and threats often lead children to develop a negative self-image and doubts about their ability.

Now you have another alternative: Help your children learn and use the Silva techniques. You can help your children develop specific applications of the standard techniques for their situation.

First, of course, help your children learn to manage bodily energies by learning the stress management techniques to reduce tension and stress, including the ability to relax physically and mentally on demand, and the ability to get to sleep and wake up when desired.

You can also help children develop special applications of techniques such as the Three Fingers Trigger Mechanism to help maintain a state of relaxation.

For instance, before the first day of school, have your children enter their level, put their three fingers together and program that if they feel nervous or tense, then they will relax simply by bringing together the tips of the first two fingers and thumb of either hand, taking a deep breath, and relaxing.

Of course, also reinforce the programming for using the Three Fingers Technique for study and test taking.

Make a game of memory pegs. While driving, see who can recall the most objects along the way. Needless to say, this will help you improve your own abilities, too, including the ability to visualize and use your imagination creatively.

You can help your children with goal setting, and imagine those goals successfully accomplished in the Mirror of the Mind or the 3-Scenes Technique. After creating the solution image, you and your child can enter level together and visualize the goals from time to time.

The benefits of using the Silva techniques in school situations are well documented in research projects conducted at various high schools. And now, more and more schools, such as the Ninos Cantores del Zulia in Venezuela, are making the Silva training a standard part of their program.

Developing That "Something Extra"

Of course, one of the biggest benefits of practicing all of the various techniques is that this helps develop the intuition. The more people exercise their mind, the better able they are to obtain information stored on brain cells; their own brain neurons, and the brain neurons of others.

Intuition is not a substitute study. To be as effective as possible with intuition and creativity, you need to first gather as much data as you can in your area of interest. This helps your mind to seek the right channel where additional information is available.

There are many ways to impress information. Besides having children use the Three Fingers Technique on their own, you can also help by reading a lesson to the children while they are at level.

In our early research, we found that the strongest way to impress information was to read it to the person three times, at three different levels of mind. After you read it to them, you can either have them do something else while at level, or bring them out of level and then later have them enter level and read it to them again.

As you can see, there are many ways you can help your children do better in school. Enter level yourself, and decide how you want to begin. It is a project that will bring benefits to both you and your children.

Note: If you haven't yet learned these techniques, you can start right now with the free lessons in the appendix of this book.

67 We Must Live Up to Our Image
(1993)

Planet earth is a creative problem-solving laboratory.

Humankind itself is an experiment. The Creator has many such laboratories and many such experiments.

What is the Creator seeking?

All this space and all these forms of life—what is in the making?

We cannot know, but we can make an intelligent guess. We can start by eliminating some of the goals that are quite likely not worthy of the Creator's infinite intelligence.

I'd like to eliminate such products of planet earth's civilization as: highest paid football quarterback, fastest racehorse, and largest ocean liner. Somehow, those kinds of sensational attainments don't seem to fit into the cosmic scheme of things. Nor do packaged cereals, automobiles, or cigarettes.

Be a Co-Creator

The Creator has to expect more from humanity than this. We are created, says the good book, in His image.

If you think all you have to do is look in the mirror and you will see the Creator, don't waste your time.

The image of God, the Creator, must be you, the creation. This is simple left brain logic.

It means you and I are supposed to be co-creators with the Creator, continuing to perfect this microcosm called earth, as the Creator continues to perfect the macrocosm called the universe.

You and I did not come easily to the Creator. Many a try failed. Species of life came and went. Even when we did arrive we were a mess. We were as bad as the animals that preceded us.

Anthropologists still find it hard to place us very far above some of them.

We continue to ravage the planet's mineral riches, harm the flora, and destroy the fauna. Instead of creating a better planet on which to live, we create more and more ways to kill each other.

It Is Time to Act

I personally believe that the Creator may be on the verge of letting humanity move towards its own extinction and start over with another creative idea.

All of my life's work has been devoted to doing better so the Creator will give us another chance.

I do not want to force you to hear my personal beliefs. But maybe they will inspire you to consider these matters yourself and maybe by such personal thought you will be convinced that it is your duty to create a genius.

Live Up to Your Image

There must be a hierarchy of intelligence in the universe. Some scientists see a global brain that devises unique ways to help correct our abuses to the planet.

Our solar system may have a somewhat higher level of intelligence, the galaxy even higher, all of the galaxies perhaps highest intelligence which we call God.

The higher we go, the better things are. It is down here on earth, that the level of intelligence permeating life must be elevated, if we are to survive.

We need to create more geniuses.

We need to raise the level of what Jung called the collective unconscious and what English botanist Rupert Sheldrake now calls the morphogenetic field of intelligence.

We have been created in the image of God. We need to live up to our image.

Be a Spiritual Being

Continued left brain dominated thinking will only carry us further along the way toward being rubber stamped by the Creator as "obsolete."

By activating our right brain hemisphere and becoming centered in our thinking, we put ourselves on the Creator's team.

We live up to our image.

As we solve problems, the right hemisphere acts as our connection to the rest of intelligence to higher intelligence and to highest intelligence.

Our solutions and decisions vault to a more lofty-in-wisdom level.

We become co-creators. The more problems you solve, the more creator-like or God-like you are. The more you become on the Creator's side and, of course, the more the Creator is on your side.

So, using the simple methodologies of the Silva Method to correct problems is helping the Creator.

Going to the alpha brain frequency, identifying the problem, mentally picturing a solution replacing the problem, returning to beta brain frequency and seeing it happen in the material world just as you pictured it mentally, is a spiritual act.

Enter your level once, twice, three times a day. Help correct problems.

68 You Can Call On Us for Help
(1982)

Our business is to help solve problems on this planet, to help do the Creator's work, to help relieve suffering, to help bring knowledge where there is ignorance, to help people not merely survive, but thrive.

This statement is true not only for Silva Mind Control International, but for each individual on this planet as well.

We are not limited to only one dimension or one technique for solving problems. When there is a problem, we should do everything within our power to help bring about the solution to the problem as soon as possible.

We should use the physical dimension, of course. And we should use the subjective dimension, also.

We should ask for help when we need it, from other people and from higher intelligence. We are not asking for someone else to do our work for us, but to help us do our work.

When we are doing work and serving, then all our needs will be met. We need only to know that we are providing service and expect that service to be returned, and we will receive in proportion to what we give.

Call On Us for Help
We often receive calls here in Laredo from people asking help, sometimes for themselves, usually for a loved one.

We have several ways to help.

As soon as we get a call, staff members here at headquarters "work cases" on the project, and send energy subjectively.

We have an active Silva Mind Control Graduate Club in Laredo, with many members of the healing hotline who get busy to send help.

And we have a technique that is available to anyone, that has proven itself very valuable and effective: the Alpha Uni-Mold.

Combining Our Energies

The concept of the Alpha Uni-Mold (AUM) is similar to a prayer group where members combine efforts to help solve problems. Here is the procedure:

Enter your level. Lower (bow) your head slightly and imagine the center to the galaxy behind you, so you can project what you visualize to it. Then on your mental screen, imagine an outline of a perfect human body of pure white light tinged with a little blue.

Visualize (recall) or imagine the appearance of the body of the person whose case you are working as being placed in that pure mold of light, being perfectly balanced as energy expression.

Send or think that perfect pattern of energy as a thought to your case, and imagine the person expressing that pattern of life, light and love as perfect balance.

Do this whenever you think of the project. Do it with the knowledge and conviction that the person is healed and in perfect health.

Once we create the image of perfection in the subjective (imaginative) dimension, then simply visualize (recall the image you have created) in the future, and the physical correction will take place.

An ideal time to use this technique is just before going to sleep at night. Or you can program to awaken automatically when the subject is most receptive, and program at that time.

With graduates all around the world programming, as well as psychics here in Laredo, we can get very rapid corrections to problems.

69 We Must All Learn Tolerance and Respect *(1997)*

This column will not be popular with some people. I've been advised not to talk about politics and religion. Well, I'll meet them halfway: I won't talk about politics.

Why talk about religion? Because we hope that this will get you to examine your beliefs, to analyze why you believe what you believe.

Throughout history we have seen that virtually every religion insists that their followers accept their doctrines. Some religions become very violent if you do not accept their doctrines—sometimes they become violent if you only question them. Unfortunately, we have experienced that personally.

But we are not the first to face this kind of arrogance and fear. Yes, fear. History has shown us that some religious leaders are so afraid of being proven wrong that they will even kill those who dare to challenge their dogma.

A Torturous Experience

Take Galileo for instance. More than 300 years ago, he confirmed what Copernicus had figured out: That the sun and stars and planets do not revolve around the earth; it is just the opposite: the earth and planets revolve around the sun.

That was unacceptable to the Catholic church. They insisted that since man was made in the image of God, it had to follow that everything revolved around man—that man was at the center of the universe.

This was not their first mistake, of course. For centuries everybody agreed that the earth was flat. Wrong.

In Galileo's case, his discovery proved to be very painful. He verified Copernicus' explanation of why some planets—like Mercury—seem to stop and back up from time to time. But they only *appear* to back up—which would be a physical impossibility of course—if you think that they revolve around the earth. Once you realize that they revolve around the sun—as does the earth—then you realize that they all keep going the same direction all the time.

But the church didn't like their teachings being challenged. After all, according to them they got their messages directly from God. So church officials took him into custody and tortured him until he recanted, and agreed to agree with them that everything revolved around man.

A few years ago, the Catholic church officially apologized to Galileo—three centuries too late to make any difference to him, and a feeble gesture that could never erase the horrible pain that they inflicted upon him.

Truth Evolves Slowly

We could give many more examples to illustrate the mistakes that people made in times past. Even religion has evolved through the years. We have moved from human and animal sacrifices, and from worshiping animals and idols, into the multitude of religions that we have in the world today.

Yet for all of that religious evolution, there is still no universal agreement.

All religions believe that they have *the* answer, and that others are wrong.

And unfortunately, most of those religious seem to be willing to fight to death for their beliefs!

They are very quick to destroy the highest creation of the Creator in the name of the very Creator that created that creation—and we're talking about human beings, of course.

Catholics and Christians are killing each other in Northern Ireland.

Arab and Jewish children are taught to hate and kill each other.

Hindus and Moslems and Sikhs and other religions are not exempt from this tendency to hate their rivals.

Just as Christians say that the only way to heaven is through Jesus Christ, most other religions can point to their scriptures—the divine messages that they believe that they get from God—to prove that *their* way is the only way!

Could they all be right?

Could be.

Might they all be wrong?

Could be.

Is it possible that there is some truth in every religion, but that no religion has the complete answer?

Could be.

By now you have probably figured out that when I say *could be*, it is because I know that we don't know all of the answers yet.

Who Has the Answers?

Doesn't it seem terribly arrogant for anyone—preacher or priest or philosopher or scientist or anybody else—to insist that they have all the answers, and refuse to listen to anybody else?

Scientists like Copernicus and Galileo, as well as explorers like Columbus, have expanded our knowledge far beyond what religious leaders and scientists of the day accepted as proven knowledge.

And they are still doing it.

We have put together a scientifically researched and proven program to help people actually use parts of their brain and mind that they have never consciously used before, to help correct problems and make the world a better place to live.

During our research in the 1950s and 1960s we were criticized—and yes, even condemned and threatened with excommunication—for daring to ask questions!

What were they afraid of?

What did we do that threatened them so badly that they were willing to go to all the trouble to call me in to consider kicking me out of the church?

Are they afraid of the truth?

Or are they afraid of losing some of their power over people if they are shown to be wrong about something?

Is it God who governs people, or is those who claim to represent God—the human beings who choose to take on the role of representing God?

Would an all-powerful God worry about a man—who was created by that God—assuming so much power that it would threaten the position of God?

On the other hand, what about humans—"mere mortals" as they say—who fear losing their tremendous power over people, a power they hold because they tell us from birth that they represent

God and that we will suffer forever in a fiery hell if we fail to do everything they tell us to do?

Is God running scared—or the people who claim to represent God?

The Struggle Continues

I had thought that this was all in the past. The Bible says, "By their fruits ye shall know them." If a tree bears good fruit, the Bible says, then it is a good tree.

For more than half a century we have been producing good fruit from the research that we began in 1944. But that doesn't stop religious leaders from panicking when I question one of their claims.

They point to the Bible and say that I have no right to question it.

I point to the fact that the Bible was written by human beings, often long after the events took place.

And then the Bible was translated into other languages—by humans.

And then various versions were written, to satisfy the needs and wishes of various people—like King James, who wanted permission to get a divorce. A version, in case you don't know, is defined by the dictionary as a variation of the original. That means that it is *different from* the original.

And I also point out that the people who wrote the original, and people who wrote the translations, and the people who wrote the variations, and the people who translated the variations—all of these humans lived in times when we didn't know very much about what was going on:

They thought the earth was flat.

They thought that the sun and stars and planets all revolved around the earth.

They thought that natural disasters represented the wrath of God.

They thought—and apparently many religious leaders still believe—that the Creator will approve of our destruction of other human beings because they do not believe the same things that we believe!

When Will We Ever Learn?

And I ask this question: If those men were wrong about so many other things, is it possible that they might also be wrong about some of the things that they wrote—or translated—in the Bible?

The Bible—and the other sacred books, such as the Bhagavad Gita, the Koran, the Book of Mormon, the Talmud, and others—were *not* written by God; they were written by *human beings*.

Were the writers inspired by God?

Could be.

Even if they were inspired by God, we know, from our scientific research, that even the best clairvoyants only average 80 percent accuracy.

Even though we know much more today than we ever knew before, we still know that at least 20 percent of what we think we know is wrong!

Is it worth fighting for every last word in the translation of the variation of the translation of the Bible that happens to be popular today?

Are we so sure that there are no errors, no mistakes, no misrepresentation, no misunderstandings, and no outright propaganda and lies inserted by someone for their own selfish purposes? Can we be sure of that?

Or should we be tolerant with one another.

Should we be patient with each other, and explore together to find out what will help us to solve more problems, and to make the world a better place to live?

Isn't it interesting that those who believe in devils, find devils everywhere they look for them?

We explain, at the beginning of the Silva Method Basic Lecture Series, how that happens—go back and review Mental Housecleaning.

People who believe in God—and do not believe that there is any such thing as the devil—find God everywhere.

In the Bible, we read many stories about Jesus practicing tolerance. "Let he who is without sin cast the first stone." "Forgive them, Father, for they know not what they do."

We also read stories about the religious leaders of the day accusing Jesus of being in league with the devil. They rationalized that the only way a person could be so good at casting out devils, was if he was in league with the devil.

It seems to me that times never change, for religious leaders have accused me in the same manner!

Well, at least we're in good company; while we in no way believe that we are as highly evolved as Jesus, we don't mind being compared with Him. It makes us believe that we might be on the right track, that we must be moving in the correct direction.

We don't want to go too far in that direction, though. Remember— they crucified Jesus!

Why Do You Believe What You Believe?

Well, we've gotten that off our chest. These ideas will surely be unpopular with some people. They will surely rationalize and find ways to condemn me for expressing my feelings.

But ask yourself: Throughout history, what kind of people have refused to tolerate people thinking for themselves? Dictators. Despots. Bigots. Totalitarians.

What kind of people welcome questions and new ideas? The constructive and creative people who lift humanity to new heights, who lead us to a better future, who do not cause suffering but who relieve suffering, who do not kill other human beings but who save the lives of human beings.

So ask yourself why you believe what you believe.

Does it make sense? Someone once said that there is nothing less common than common sense. What does common sense tell you?

Is it worth sacrificing all of the good work that a person has done because that person questions whether Jesus claimed to be God? After all, Jesus taught us to pray, "*Our* father . . ." He seems to be saying that He was one of us.

But even if this is wrong, why would religious leaders fear the question so much? Do they think that God cannot handle it?

Or do they fear that people might begin to question some of the demands that are placed on them by these people who claim to represent God? Do they fear the loss of their power over people?

Which is more valuable:

That religious leaders maintain their power over people, so that they can—hopefully—keep people in line.

That we continue to ask questions, to search for the real truth, even if that means that we have to stop believing that we humans are at the center of the universe and the sun and stars and planets all revolve around us.

We staked out our territory a long time ago: We'll keep searching for truth, and we will continue to do anything that helps to correct problems and make the world a better place to live.

And if they crucify us for doing that—if we must drink the cup—then so be it.

70 Love and Energy Fields
(1985)

(Recently, José Silva found a hand-written manuscript containing thoughts he had jotted down several years ago, and passed it on to your editor. It contains valuable information for everyone who is in love, or who wants to be. Here it is, just the way he wrote it.)

It is interesting to note that when researchers are researching in a specific field, some stumble onto bits of interesting information related to other fields. This is a report about such an observation.

When investigating a lead, a researcher often uncovers information that borders on other important fields.

The particular area of interest in this case has to do with love and energy fields.

Thirty years of research in the area of the mind, through which the Silva Mind Control programs were conceived, have taken us to many places; we have interviewed and investigated many people of both sexes, varying ages, many cultures, races and creeds.

On one occasion I would find myself face to face with people who performed with what I considered to be prophetic wisdom.

Some of these people, when relating their information, did not seem to make too much sense as perceived from a certain point of view. But from a different perspective the same information appears prophetic and carries great wisdom.

It appears that many years of research and experience are needed to develop the required factors that help the researcher reach his ideal baseline from which he can perceive prophetic wisdom with greater sensitivity.

To report these findings to you, the reader, the information has been arranged in an order that I thought would make the most sense. Since all this information has been compiled from the wise and prophetic sayings of so many individuals when at their wisest point in time, the title given this report is:

Wisdom Speaks

From here on, every time reference is made to any of the individuals interviewed or investigated, I will refer to their wisdom, saying, "Wisdom said . . ." or "Wisdom thought . . ." and so forth.

But keep in mind, this is not from only one person; it is the combined and agreed-upon wisdom of many wise people who shared their experience and insight.

"Wisdom Speaks" is the compilation of information of many individuals who, because of their experience, arrived at some conclusions or assumptions concerning a particular subject. Some of these subjects have not been researched by conventional scientific methods, and some may not be researched by conventional scientific methods for a long time.

It is interesting to note that all of these individuals who contributed information arrived at their conclusions or assumptions on their own, without knowing that others in the past had arrived at the same conclusions; or better still that others would in the future arrive at the same conclusions.

Before we enter our subject, "Love and energy fields," let us review basic principles offered by Wisdom.

Concepts of Wisdom

Wisdom refers to God or Creator as High Intelligence, and states that creation of the universe has not been completed, that it is still in an evolving process towards peak perfection.

Wisdom agrees that human beings, with human intelligence, are representatives of High Intelligence at the planetary plane of existence level.

Wisdom explains that the mission of the human being on this planet is to become aware of and remove all opposing forces that hinder the flow of the evolving process of creation as it moves towards peak perfection.

This is known as problem solving.

Wisdom also acknowledges the programming power of High Intelligence to program energy at all planes of existence, such as the spiritual, sub-atomic, atomic, molecular, cellular, organ, and organ system.

Energy and its field of radiation together have governing power in molding things according to environmental needs.

Wisdom has said that all human beings who have landed on this planet and are on their own personal journey while functioning as husbands, wives, fathers, mothers, sons or daughters, have landed here to help High Intelligence make this planet a better world to live in through problem solving.

Every human being arrives on the planet alone, is here for a short stay, and leaves alone, resuming the universal journey.

Wisdom says that all inhabitants of this planet, regardless of their race, creed, religion, or intelligence, leave this planet in a period of approximately one hundred years, to be replaced by newcomers arriving on the planet.

Wisdom's concept of High Intelligence is that the highest intelligence of all is in charge of the whole universe; that a lesser intelligence is in charge of a group of galaxies, and a still lesser intelligence is in charge of our galaxy.

Wisdom is convinced that the High Intelligence in charge of our solar system, our planet, and us does not watch over us or our planet every second of the day in order to help us or our planet.

Wisdom believes that High Intelligence automatically tunes into our planet in cycles of so many years. The same holds true for individual human beings, Wisdom feels.

There is only one other way for this attunement with High Intelligence to take place, Wisdom says. That is for the majority of the inhabitants of this planet to jointly enter a special dimension of the mind and jointly ask for help. Otherwise Wisdom believes that channels have been created to which the human being can become attuned to seek and get help when help is needed for taking care of creation.

Wisdom also believes that the urge to mate and conceive is due to fundamental programming by High Intelligence. This programming establishes marriage and conception of children as the system selected by High Intelligence to continue placing more inhabitants on this planet.

Wisdom says that the primary purpose why humans are on this planet is for making this planet a better world to live in; everything else is secondary.

So married or not, or married but with no children, the obligation of the human being remains the same: primarily to help make this planet a better place to live.

Wisdom says the so-called population explosion would not exist if every human being was on the job making this planet a better world to live in. Wisdom believes there is a balancing mechanism that automatically adjusts the planet's population in relation to the amount of work done by each human being. This adjustment would match the expected annual progress to the flow of the evolving process of creation that is taking place throughout our galaxy.

So, Wisdom says, as more work is done per human being to catch up with the expected progress of this planet, then fewer humans will be placed on this planet due to the automatic system created by High Intelligence.

The information discussed so far is valuable in helping us center our minds so as to function from a superior perspective and perceive information with greater understanding.

Wisdom Speaks About Love and Energy Fields

Wisdom believes that a specific compounded state of chemistry existing under a special set of environmental conditions is what allows a field of life-giving energy to be transferred from the spiritual dimension into the biological dimension. This is what we know as conception.

In the case of conception of a human being, the life-giving energy field serves as a mold that influences biological growth and development to conform to a human body. Once the body is formed, other energy fields come into being. These include energy fields caused by activity at the sub-atomic, atomic, molecular, cellular, organ, and organ system functioning levels.

The life-giving energy field that found its way through the chemistry from the spiritual dimension into the biological dimension is the basic fundamental life-giving energy field.

All of the other energy fields are artifact due to biological functioning.

Finally, a very complex aura of interlaced, interlocked energy fields is established, and surrounds the human body. Wisdom says that this aura that surrounds the human body is vibrating in a manner and at a rate influenced by the sum total of all influencing factors.

The influence from the genetic dimension is such a factor according to Wisdom.

Wisdom believes that all experiences of all of our ancestors have also been transferred from parent to child at the genetic level.

Then there is the influence of the heavenly bodies that influence matter, influencing the human being from conception on. There is also our own environmental, psychological, and physiological experiencing type of influence, along with the influence caused on us by the projected thoughts of others.

All of these contributed influences cause the human aura to vibrate at the rate that it does.

Keep in mind that the human aura is composed of several energy fields, each vibrating at its own rate.

When boy meets girl or better still, when boy sees girl and girl sees boy—if their auras are somewhat compatible, they will experience a body chemistry change because they like what they see.

Wisdom says that a body chemistry change is accompanied by an aura vibration rate change.

Wisdom knows that the aura of every human being, male or female, is different from every other human aura.

Wisdom also knows that when male and female see each other and like what they see, the aura of each starts changing in a direction to be more compatible with the other.

The next thing that will happen to the male and female in question is to get close to each other to talk. At this point, the sense of hearing comes into play, causing a greater chemical change, which in turn causes a greater degree of change in the rate of aura vibration.

This change of vibration is now assured of being in the direction of increased compatibility because when bodies are close to one another their auras are touching and interlaced with one another.

Next comes the sense of touch. Each desires to touch the other, bringing about a still greater change in the auras towards a greater compatibility.

At this point, Wisdom directs our attention to notice what is happening to two individuals who each possessed a very personal, and unique aura, different from any other aura possessed by anybody else on this planet. What is happening, of course, is that the auras of these individuals are changing towards the establishment of new and different rates of aura vibration brought about by the combined effects of two auras.

These new rates of vibration will still be different from the vibration rates of any other auras.

Maximum change of aura towards compatibility will take place when an exchange of body chemistry between the male and female is effected.

To maintain aura compatibility, Wisdom says that we need to reinforce the factors known to maintain compatibility. These factors are:

- Closeness of the physical bodies;
- Speaking frequently;
- Touching each other;
- Participation in the exchange of body chemistry through kissing and the sex act.

Wisdom has said that to maintain reinforced aura compatibility is to maintain reinforced love between husband and wife.

Aura compatibility and love between husband and wife are weakened when their bodies are kept distant from one another, and when there is no body chemistry exchange taking place between the two.

Wisdom recommends the following for the maintenance of strong love ties between husband and wife:

- Maintain frequent close range verbal contact.
- Practice frequent body contact.
- Practice kissing at every opportunity.
- Practice the sex act as frequently as possible.
- Do not sleep in separate rooms or in separate beds; sleep in the same bed.

Wisdom guarantees that when husband and wife comply with the five indicated steps, a strong love bond will be maintained that nothing except the power of God can separate.

This strong love bond is established through aura compatibility reinforcement.

Words From Wisdom

Remember husband, you were created to do everything within your power to make your wife happy first, and yourself second.

Remember wife, you were created to do everything within your power to make your husband happy first, and yourself second.

When the words of Wisdom are practiced, happiness is guaranteed for husband and wife.

Have a happy married life, Wisdom.

71 For a Better World, We Need Better Humans *(1995)*

Many people like to take time out at the beginning of the new year to pray for peace on earth.

There are new age groups that meditate on peace on earth. A lot of Silva Method graduates pray for it.

We certainly need it.

Look wherever you like, and you will see problems:

People trying to destroy whole races in the name of the Creator.

Governments treating their citizens like property to be used at their pleasure and then disposed of.

Politicians who fight any idea from the opposing party no matter how good the idea might be for the citizens.

Businesses taking advantage of every possible loophole—and even resorting to dishonesty and sabotage of their competitors—in order to improve the "bottom line."

Individuals hoping to "get rich quick" through any means possible, from lawsuits against corporations with "deep pockets" to gambling to fraud and theft whenever they think they can get away with it.

It is not all bad, of course. There are still people out there—and businesses and governments—that care about other people, who care about the effect that their actions have on other people, and who try to do what they honestly believe is best for all concerned.

A New Way

These problems are taking their toll. This has been recognized by individuals, by businesses, and by governments.

And this has spawned a whole new industry—an industry involved with "reinvention."

There are business gurus who want to help us "reinvent" business. And others who want to help us "reinvent" government.

They boast whenever they manage to get someone to do the right thing, the thing that is best for all concerned.

A politician goes on national television and boasts about how they got a government agency to stop paying 100 times more for some product than it is worth!

An officer of a corporation writes a best selling book about how their company has started to actually provide satisfactory service to its customers!

It is headline news nationwide when somebody returns a valuable item that they found to its owner!

Different Values

Thirty years ago in the United States a guru was a spiritual person who dedicated his or her life to helping people and uplifting the human spirit.

Now when you mention "guru" people want to know the title of his latest book, and what method he uses to help businesses be more competitive in the '90s.

And the new style of gurus oblige. They come up with new models for operating a business. You flatten out the organizational chart, or "empower" employees, or actually listen to your customers!

A Better Plan

As we begin this new year, I'd like to suggest another way to go about correcting our problems and bringing peace to the planet.

It is not the institutions that are at fault.

Not government.

Not business.

Not politicians.

Not lawyers.

Institutions are run by people. Decisions are made by people. Actions are taken by people.

If we make a better person, then the institutions will automatically be better.

They will function more efficiently. They will serve people better. We will all be happier and better off.

If we can somehow convince people to work for the common good, to do what is best for all concerned, then we will all be better off.

I am not saying that you should not stand up for what you believe in. You *should* fight for what you believe is right.

At the same time, you should realize that different people have different goals. They may have needs that are different from yours.

Respect for Everyone

Some people may want to worship in a different way than you do.

Let them!

Have you ever noticed that the people who start wars are the people with little minds who cannot conceive of anyone else being right except for themselves?

The people who say, "I believe I have found the correct answer, but I respect your right to differ with me," do not start wars.

It is the people who say, "My way is the *only* way." They are the ones who start wars.

It amazes me that the people who claim to be the most religious, those who profess their strong belief in their religion, are usually the ones who show the most disrespect for the Creator's greatest creation: other human beings.

Rather than supporting people and respecting their ideas and helping them to live productive, happy lives, they condemn them because their ideas about the Creator are different.

Most wars are started by people who are so narrow-minded, who have such little minds, that they cannot accept the fact that might not know everything there is to know.

These little-minded people act like they are some kind of god, with the right to tell everybody else how to live and how to believe and how to pray.

In order to have peace on this planet, we must learn to respect everyone. We must respect each other's right to do as we choose, so long as we are not harming anyone else.

How To Program

We are not going to bring peace to the planet just by wishing for it.

We are not going to correct the problems that face us by "reinventing" business and government.

All of the cute slogans that the gurus write about in their books and say so eloquently on their recordings may feel good for a moment, but they are not going to change the basic problems facing humanity today.

Those problems deal with humans . . . with people.

To make a better world, we need to make a better person.

Fortunately, there is a way to do that.

The people who correct the most problems, who bring the greatest benefits to humanity, are the people who do their thinking at the alpha brain wave level, where they can use their intuitive and creative right brain hemisphere to think with.

With your right brain hemisphere, you can get more information than you can from the left hemisphere alone. You can become aware of information that you detect intuitively, information that is not available to your physical senses. This will help you make better decisions.

The alpha brain wave level is the ideal level to think at, the ideal level for decision making.

When all people on the planet learn how to use the alpha level to think with, to get information and make decisions, then our institutions will work properly, nations will live in peace with each other, and we will actually have a paradise on earth.

At the alpha level, it is easier to determine what our purpose is in life. It is easier to understand and respect other people.

Those people who speak hateful words, who condemn others simply for being different, are not alpha thinkers. They are losers. They deserve our pity. We should try to help them, by showing them how to use both brain hemispheres to think with.

Teaching all of the 5 billion people on the planet to learn how to center themselves at alpha is too big a job for one person. It will take all of us, working together, to get the job done.

If you have children between the ages of seven and fourteen, then teach them to use visualization and imagination. Teach them to use their intuition. Just ask them to do it, and praise them every time they are correct.

If you do that, they will grow up with the ability to function at alpha whenever they desire. If you have questions about it, contact your local Silva instructor. We have written a book, and are putting together a home study course, to help parents help their children.

People older than fourteen need to take the Silva ESP training to regain the ability to function at alpha.

It can be done. It should be done. I believe that it must be done if we are to have peace on our planet.

And I believe that when we do this, when everyone can—and does—function at alpha, then we will have a paradise on earth.

Note: The book, titled Create a Genius, is available at bookstores worldwide, and the Speed Learning workshop is available at our SilvaESP.com website.

72 Live In Faith and Make Your Own Choices *(1986)*

Beware of those who try to keep you from learning all that you can, for knowledge is important to us. Ignorance does not exempt us from suffering; but knowledge exempts us from suffering.

Ignorance of the law of gravity will not exempt you from suffering if you jump off a tall building. Knowledge keeps us safe.

From time to time we encounter people who insist that we believe in whatever they tell us to believe, and to avoid what they tell us to avoid.

What do these people fear?

If they have confidence that what they have to say is right and is best, then why should they fear having people seek more knowledge?

The Silva Method encourages people to seek knowledge, to seek truth.

And the thing that threatens those who are insecure about their own faith is that the Silva training gives people tools to use to learn the truth . . . about anything and everything.

What do those who speak out against seeking knowledge have to hide?

Sometimes it is interesting to watch those people at work. Since they do not have substance, they resort to emotionalism and demagoguery to attract and keep followers. And since there is no substance to their appeal, they do not want people to learn how to find the truth.

Hitler operated that way. He aroused people to a high emotional state, to a state where their critical consciousness was suspended.

All the time, he was projecting very strongly his image of what he wanted. This image was able then to penetrate directly to the listeners' subconscious.

When people are fearful or confused, they suspend their ability to analyze, to make critical judgments. And the programming is done at a deep subjective level.

Since it is a subjective level, no impression is made on brain cells, and the person does not have any way to review the "program" that was impressed on the subconscious.

Please note that this is a type of objective programming that is, it is done through physical means, such as words, and the person's aura.

Silva graduates have programmed themselves to be protected from such tactics. And through the ability to enter level and to convert the subconscious into an inner conscious level they can learn the truth.

Religious revivals get a lot of converts through using such emotional approaches and powerful programming.

And be assured, the people who achieve prominence and power are the people who project strong subjective messages.

But revival conversions are usually not permanent.

This is because it takes continuous pressure to maintain such things.

The emotional level must be kept high, and the programming must be reinforced, or eventually people see through it.

On the other hand, Silva techniques are permanent because they are true. They are beneficial, they solve problems, they help people and help solve problems.

They are not based on imaginary stories and theories that can not be proven, but are based on principles that produce results.

All that is necessary with the Silva training is that you apply the techniques and get results.

When you get results and your life improves because of this, then you will keep seeking more and better results.

We think this is a much better way than constantly being fearful of things you cannot see, and that can not be proven. If there is a hell, then perhaps it is a condition created here on earth by people who spread fear, and hatred of their fellow humans, and who create problems instead of solving them.

Seek the truth, and the truth shall make you free—free to make your own choices. But some people want to insist that you choose *their* choice, choose only what *they* believe is right.

I don't call that freedom. It is not my way.

73 Become More Human With Silva Techniques *(1986)*

A human being is not someone who just looks like one; it is someone who acts like one.

Human beings have biological bodies, just like animals.

While the body is alive, it has biological needs, and it is programmed to strive for survival and to fear death.

But human beings alone are made in the image of their Creator.

What is meant by being made in the image of the Creator?

That does not mean in the way we look, because there are great differences in the way humans look.

It means the way we act. It means what we are capable of doing, and what we do with that capability.

What can humans do that animals cannot do?

First, humans have imagination, which is a creative faculty.

Animals can visualize. Animals can dream while sleeping, and recall things seen previously. But there is no good evidence that animals, on their own, use imagination to create something new the way humans do. Birds build the same kind of nest year after year after year.

What else do humans do that animals do not do?

Humans take care of other humans.

Animals take care of themselves and their blood kin, but not of other animals.

Humans take care of themselves and their families, and also of other humans. We often help people we've never even met.

But too few humans are doing this.

In fact, about 90 percent of humanity are causing more problems than they are correcting, and the other ten percent are trying to correct the problems that the 90 percent are creating.

Why does this situation exist?

Because only ten percent of humanity are centered. Only ten percent know how to center their brain frequency at the alpha brain wave level so that they can use both brain hemispheres to think with.

Ninety percent are using only their left brain hemisphere, the hemisphere associated with biological senses, the animal-like senses. Only ten percent are also using the right brain hemisphere, the hemisphere associated with spiritual senses, the human, God-like senses.

Ninety percent do not care if other people are suffering. This is not being human.

When people become centered and start using both brain hemispheres to think with to analyze problems with and to get information, several things happen.

First, the person becomes interested in helping others, and helping God with creation.

When this happens, the person receives many bonuses.

The person becomes more spiritual, more human, healthier, safer, more successful, and happier.

Besides all of this, we also qualify for more help from the Creator. If we are going in the wrong direction, creating problems and hurting other humans, then it does no good to ask for God's help. God will not help us to go in the wrong direction.

But when we are centered and using both brain hemispheres to think with and analyze problems and get information and make decisions, then we are going in the right direction. Then God will help us. God is always willing to help us when we are going in the right direction.

How do you become centered and receive all of the bonuses and qualify for God's help?

By practicing.

Enter your level three times a day, every day. Practice all of your Silva techniques.

Especially practice working health cases, every day.

When you do that, you are functioning like a human being.

Note: If you do not already know how to enter your level and use more of your mind to solve more problems, you can start learning right now with the lessons in the appendix of this book.

74 We Know That We Can't Ignore Problems *(1992)*

They say that it rains on both good people and bad. And the sun shines on saints and sinners and everybody in between.

Sometimes we meet people who hope to put an end to all their problems, and to live a life free of problems.

Life doesn't work that way.

It appears to me that we were put here to correct problems. Our task is not to avoid problems, but to correct them.

We can sometimes avoid them for a short period of time. But eventually they will catch up with us.

It is our job to correct them.

I have been very fortunate during my life, in many ways. I've been blessed with a lot of energy, and with a desire to solve problems and help people.

I've had good fortune in business.

I have a wonderful wife and family.

Many extras have been added unto me:

Athletic ability, the ability to sing, creative talents that have enabled me to invent electronic devices and to write books . . . and of course, to develop the Silva Method, a program that has helped millions of people worldwide to change their lives for the better.

In addition to all of that, I've had excellent health for the last 78 years. But recently I developed a health problem. I finally took my own advice and went to see a doctor—the first time I've ever seen a doctor for any kind of health problem.

It turned out to be serious. They put me in the hospital for a couple of weeks as they began to correct the abnormal situation that had developed in my urinary system.

There was a terrible strain on my body. As the doctors worked to correct the urinary problem, my body chemistry was thrown out of balance.

Things were critical for several days. During this time, I had my Alpha Sound recording, and I programmed as I used it.

But the efforts of the doctors, my programming, and the Alpha Sound tape might not have been enough if it had not been for thousands of Silva lecturers and graduates around the world who used the Silva techniques to help me.

Things are under control now.

There are some problems that we still need to correct, involving the prostate and the heart.

I want to thank everyone who helped, who programmed and who called our offices in Laredo to get feedback on my condition so that they could adjust their programming accordingly and keep working on me.

I especially want to thank my family. My wife Paula, my brother Juan, and all of my children who came to the hospital in Austin to be with me and to program and pray for me. Paula stood by my side during the most critical times.

I also want to thank members of the headquarters staff who got the word out about the situation and who organized the help.

I especially want to thank the Silva lecturers who came to Austin: Rosa Rivas flew in from Portugal, while Alicia Curtis and Janie Dolechek drove down from Oklahoma. They worked in shifts, along with other Silva Lecturers, using the holistic faith healing techniques on my body every four hours.

It has been quite an experience for me. It reminds me of a couple of things:

It reminds me that we must use all of the tools that we have available—objective as well as subjective—to correct problems.

And it reminds me in a very personal way, how many very wonderful people there are in this world.

I hope I get to personally thank every one who helped.

For now, let me just say: Thank you, and may God bless you.

Note: While in the hospital José Silva got a message when he had a vision of a nun coming to him and telling him he couldn't leave yet, he had one more job to do. As he left the hospital he saw a large portrait of the Sister who founded the hospital—it was the same nun who was in the vision. He worked hard the next five years, and when the idea for the MentalVideo Technique and the Silva UltraMind ESP Systems came to him, he knew that was his ultimate life mission. He lived two more years, long enough to travel and teach the new Systems and get them established before he moved on to his next assignment. You can start learning and using the MentalVideo and other techniques right now in the appendix of this book.

75 Let's Work Together to Turn Things Around *(1994)*

If people continue to take a left-brain approach to problem solving, we face a bleak future.

Let me take you on a tour of planet earth.

We will visit the last of the rain forests, the last black rhinoceros lying dead and de-tusked in the mud, the once pristine lakes alive with fish now dead poisoned ponds.

We will visit schools and see how students abuse their teachers and stab themselves.

We will visit city streets where gang warfare fills the gutters with blood.

We will sit in on jury trials where people sit in judgment of each other and award seven figure judgments and interminable prison terms.

We will visit those prisons and see how the guilt of inhumanity on the outside is continued on the inside.

I'll spare you areas of famine and warfare.

We will visit lawmakers taking lobbyists' gifts and enacting preferential laws, diplomats taking favors and siding with the bad guys, enforcement officers breaking the laws they were hired to enforce.

This is the world that left-brainers have created.

This is the world that they would have our infants, babies, and children fit into and perpetuate. This is a world even further deteriorated than the world that Jesus and other greats came to save.

Help Bring Peace

You and I cannot survive in a left brain world. So not only must we activate our right brain and our child's right brain, we must encourage others to do it too.

We have more than five hundred people around the world who are full time encouragers. They are the certified Silva lecturers who constantly set up four-day training sessions that turn left-brainers into centered thinkers and therefore geniuses.

The millions we have trained need to do likewise: encourage others to connect to higher intelligence, and turn this planet around before it is too late.

As I write this, the evening newspaper is opened before me.

On just one single page l see the following words and phrases in headlines and single column heads:

- Corrupt tax men
- Shelling pounds city
- Crooked leaders
- Eight killed
- Warlord
- Embezzlement
- Arms race
- Abuse of Power

What else is new? Don't answer that question—I don't want to know.

Change the World

If we could all tip the balance with right brainers perhaps we will see those negative headlines changed to:

- Centenarians meet
- Reforestation progress
- Energy from space
- Discovery made at alpha
- Prisons converted
- Housing problem solved
- Armaments dumped
- Hunger obsolete

This can come about—it must come about—when enough people are centered and are using their right brain hemispheres, living as much in the spiritual world as in the material world.

Help the Creator
To those who are still left brained, you who live partly in the subjective world appear as geniuses.

In reality, you are merely as your Creator intended you to be.

We all have comforts in this material world that our forefathers did not have the benefit of.

Are we happier for them?

No.

Most of us come home after a hard day's work, plop into a stuffed chair, watch television, have a hot dinner, go to bed and do it all over again tomorrow.

Is that the definition of happiness? Hardly. But these people do not complain because they look around and see everybody doing the same thing. They think that this must be happiness.

By contrast, let's take a look at a centered family, that functions in both the spiritual and physical worlds.

A Better Way
You are coming home after a day's work that was not hard.

Perhaps you went to level two or three times to ward off stress, heighten energy, or solve a problem.

Because you have been functioning throughout the day with both brain hemispheres and because you have been helping to make this a better world by extending God's work, you don't need a stuffed chair; any chair is fine.

You don't need to turn on the television set; you are each company enough for the other.

You are happy.

To magnify this happiness, your health is fine. Your finances are sufficient to take care of your needs. Your marital relationship is fulfilling.

Your parent-child relationship is one of mutual respect and admiration. You are happy.

People are attracted to you because of your serenity and peace of mind. They come to you for advice and guidance—not on such minor matters as whether tomorrow will be all right for a picnic, but rather such matters as which car is a better buy, which book is a better read, and which job offers a better future.

They rely on your opinion on health, finances, and careers.

There is no sign on your front door that reads GENIUS INSIDE, but there might just as well be.

Work for God and God Works for You

You can have no better ally. God will be in your consciousness and you will live normally at a high level of elation.

You will be an example to others who have lost God or have banished Him, through left brain dominance, from their consciousness. While they languish, you will prosper.

Remember always that geniuses use more of their mind and use them in a special manner and since that is exactly what you do, therefore that is exactly who you are.

Thanks to this assistance, you will be able to guess dependably.

Your guess will be more times right than wrong. People will say you are lucky.

What is a "lucky person"? It is one who is more times right than wrong, because that person is helped by God; the person is God-connected, divinely inspired, and prophetic.

This person is more times right than wrong because the person is being constructive and creative and helping God perfect creation on this planet.

Such a person will continue to be "lucky" as long as they continue to use most of the material gains to help God solve problems that hinder constructive progress, and also to correct the problems that cause human suffering.

I know that you are such a person. You are a genius, but you are also a humanitarian, a philanthropist, a prophet, and a clairvoyant.

Congratulations. I won't keep you. You have work to do.

76 Are You Meeting Your Responsibility?
(1990)

Your Biggest Profits Come From Doing What Is Right.

Sometimes it seems like people think that maximizing profits is more important than doing what's right.

We see this in many different areas:

Corporations that make decisions based on "bottom line" profits rather than social responsibility. Where are the industrialists like Henry Ford who raised workers' wages because he thought they needed more money?

Politicians who base policies on public opinion polls rather than their own convictions. Where are leaders like Harry Truman who pushed for financial aid to help our former enemies rebuild after World War II although the polls showed that only 14 percent of Americans supported that?

Television preachers who spend almost half of their air time asking for money from their followers. When did we start putting the money changers on pedestals instead of driving them out of the temples?

Entertainers who say in interviews that "I will go wherever the most money is, and do whatever makes me the most money."

World champion athletes who say that if they find that they have to take drugs to keep winning, then they will take the drugs.

Or athletes like the champion bodybuilder who said during a primetime interview recently, "I'm a marketing guy" in explaining why he said that working out with weights is better than sex.

"Of course it isn't," he admitted many years later. But how many young minds were influenced by his earlier statements, then felt like failures, gave up and stopped training when they found that bodybuilding is hard, hard work and nothing at all like sex? Those statements may have helped make him a valuable celebrity, but what effect did they have on the self-image of those young people?

Does anybody feel a sense of responsibility any more?

Does anybody care?

Profit At Whose Expense?

Many people come to us and tell us that we have to change the Silva Method to make it more acceptable to people.

Teachers have told us that they just want to teach techniques from the first part of the program, starting with Memory Pegs and the Mental Screen. They say that children learn more quickly than adults so we can change the course.

I answer that my research was with children, and the course is structured the way that works best.

Athletes ask us to give them a one day program that shows them how to enter the alpha level and visualize with both the left and the right brain hemispheres.

I explain that they need the creative mental exercises in the third segment of the Basic Lecture Series (and in the newer Silva UltraMind ESP System), and the case working in the fourth segment, that will exercise their right brain hemisphere and bring its strength up to that of the left brain hemisphere.

Managers and executives ask us to teach them how to beat out their competition, but they don't want to get into the techniques that give them the experience of oneness with all life. Many of them rather win at any cost than to work for what's best for all concerned.

Sometimes our lecturers spin off so that they can teach shorter programs that are easier to sell. Why don't they take the course that I developed, a proven program that works, and find ways to present it to specialists in different fields? Why not make the effort to find new applications for our training, instead of taking the easy road of changing and diluting it for the sake of a quick and easy profit?

Business people tell me I should not talk about politics or religion because those are very emotional subjects that can make people angry, and that this can hurt our business and cost us money.

To me, some things are more important than profits. When I feel something strongly, I have to act on it.

Others before me have felt that way. A famous Texan, Sam Houston, said to do right and risk consequences. The Bible tells us that Christ asked if we are willing to give away all we own to follow Him. What does it profit a man if he gains worldly things and loses his soul? Christ was willing to back up His beliefs with action.

I believe we were sent to this planet on a temporary mission to help improve conditions here.

After a short stay, we go back to the other side, where we came from. That is where the higher intelligence that we call God resides. That's the way I see it, my own personal opinion.

When we get back over there, I believe, we are asked to report on our accomplishments.

What will you report?

What have you done?

It is later than you think.

PART 4
WHAT MOTIVATED
MY FATHER

by José Silva Jr.

My father talked a lot about motivation—when you have enough desire, and function as a clairvoyant, you will find a way to get results.

Sometimes he was motivated by his desire to improve living conditions for others, and sometimes he was motivated when he saw an opportunity to earn more money.

Here is an example of each:

Motivated To Serve Humanity

My father used to own Billy Goat Hill, the highest piece of land in Laredo. He bought it before the first television station was built in Laredo, when the only stations were in San Antonio and Corpus Christi, each 150 miles (241 kilometers) away.

Sometimes he used to go sit on top of Billy Goat Hill all alone, looking out over the city of Laredo and the sister city of Nuevo Laredo, Mexico, just across the Rio Grande, and wonder what he could do to help the residents.

He was beginning to develop techniques that helped his own children, and his hope was that some day he could turn all of his research over to someone better equipped to take it to large numbers of people. He offered it to schools, to churches, even to the United States Government—for free. They all turned him down.

It wasn't that he didn't like to earn money—he did. And he was good at it.

Doing What Experts Said Was Impossible

Here is an example involving those two television stations. Each was 150 miles away—in different directions—and both transmitted on the same channel.

The result was that residents of Laredo got two—different—television programs at the same time. Sometimes their television screen would switch back and forth from one to the other. Sometimes the two images would overlap, and the sound was garbled. It was very frustrating.

He saw an opportunity to provide a new service and earn some money, so he analyzed the problem and found a solution. Television engineers were skeptical. Laredo was on the "fringe area" and shouldn't be getting any reception at all.

To show them what he could do, he invited engineers from both cities to come see for themselves.

Fooling the Experts

He set up a demonstration: A television set with the scrambled pictures and sound from the two different stations.

There was a small box on top of the television set, a "project box" with a rotary switch on the front.

The rotary switch was in the center, the "off" position.

When he had everyone's attention he walked over to the box and turned the switch to one side and the screen cleared up and he had the picture and sound from the San Antonio station.

Everyone was impressed . . . or puzzled.

Then he turned the switch to the other side, and the screen now had picture and sound from the Corpus Christi station.

He could switch back and forth at will, and show either station or the scrambled mess he had started with.

Naturally all of the television engineers wanted to know what was in the box.

But he had a surprise for them:

The box wasn't just snapped together, and it wasn't held together with screws.

He had soldered it shut so you would have to heat up a soldering iron and de-solder it if you wanted to see what was inside.

The engineers left and returned home without learning his secret.

His ruse had worked:

Where He Hid the Secret

There was nothing inside the box. It was just a switch. The secret was on the roof, "hidden" in plain sight.

Everyone who is familiar with electronics is familiar with phase-reversal.

Radio waves pulse back and forth or up and down. If two radio waves are pulsing the same direction at the same time, they reinforce each other.

If one of them is reversed so that the pulses are in opposite directions, they cancel each other out.

He had mounted two antennas on the roof, and he used the switch to determine if they would be in-phase or out-of-phase. Thus he could bring up either station.

His plan was to get a patent, but before he did a new television station was built in Laredo, so there was no more need for his magic switch.

Now here are some more of his articles, including more of his problem-solving strategies.

77 The Silva Way to Program for World Peace *(1991)*

Many people, including ourselves, desire to program for "world peace," but that is not a very effective way. It is too vague.

Imagining light around the world has not proven very effective in bringing about world peace.

Programming specific individuals to desire peace seems to work much better.

That means that it will take some time to achieve world peace.

But the more people who are programming, the sooner we will accomplish our goal.

Throughout the Silva training, we instruct you to first identify the problem, then the goal. You need to be specific.

For instance:

The 3-Scenes Technique begins with visualizing the problem in the first scene, then you get to work and correct it.

Awake Control starts with the statement, "I am drowsy and sleepy. . . ."

Headache Control begins, "I have a headache, I feel a headache."

When working health cases, you first scan the body to detect the problem mentally. It is important to know exactly what we need to change. Then you can get to work correcting it.

It is important to know exactly what we want to change. Programming "for peace in the entire world" is a little too vague to be very successful.

Prepare Yourself

It is important to review a recent successful case you have worked. When you obtained correct information mentally, information you did not have before, then you know that you were at the correct level of mind and were using your right brain hemisphere to obtain the information.

Reviewing this success, and how it felt, will help your mind adjust to the same level again so you will be successful on the present project.

Do this at the alpha level, the way you learned in your Silva training or with the Free Introductory Lessons in the appendix.

Identify the Problem

Visualize or imagine a person or persons who are responsible for causing a problem.

For instance, visualize or imagine the person or persons who took over a country, or an embassy, or an airplane by force or hurtful means, and whose actions cause human suffering.

It is important to visualize or imagine the information rather than to verbalize it.

Pictures are the universal language, so make mental pictures of the people involved, and how they caused the problem.

Remember: visualization is memory—remembering what something looks like.

Imagination is the creative process of thinking about what something would look like that you have never seen or imagined before.

You can transmit these mental pictures to the other side, to higher intelligence.

For that, we use the MentalVideo Technique.

The MentalVideo will work even if you don't know how to use the alpha brainwave level. As long as you go to sleep without sleeping pills or other drugs, it works.

Here's how to proceed:

MentalVideo

Before getting into bed to go to sleep, do the following:

At beta with your eyes open, mentally create, with visualization, a MentalVideo of a problem.

Include everything that belongs to the animate matter kingdom. Animate matter means everything that contains life. The MentalVideo must include everything animate that concerns the problem.

After you complete the MentalVideo of the problem, use visualization to review it at beta, with your eyes closed.

When you are ready to go to sleep, do this:

Enter level 1 with the 3 to 1 method when you are in bed and ready to go to sleep. Once you are at your level, review the MentalVideo that you created of the problem previously when you were at beta.

After you have reviewed the problem, mentally convert the problem into a project. Then create, with imagination, a MentalVideo of the solution.

The MentalVideo of the solution should contain a step-by-step procedure of how you desire the project to be resolved.

After both of the MentalVideos have been completed, go to sleep with the intention of delivering the MentalVideo to your mental tutor while you sleep. Take for granted that the delivery will be made.

During the next three days, look for indications that point to the solution. Every time you think of the project, think of the solution that you created in the MentalVideo in a past tense sense.

Coordinated Effort

Many Silva graduates like to go to ten cycles alpha at 10 o'clock at night. That way, a lot of graduates will be programming the same project at the same time. And if graduates all around the world do that, people from every time zone, then we will be programming the project every hour of the day and night.

The more graduates who do this, the better the chances are that the problem situation will be corrected in the best possible manner.

Of course you can also program that the people responsible for causing the problem will have a desire to find a better, more peaceful way to resolve their grievances; that they will desire to use negotiation and other non-violent methods.

Remember that a human is not one who looks like one; a human is one who acts like one by taking part in humanitarian acts.

78 Inside Information Helps You Be More Successful *(1994)*

Would you like some inside information from a high level source that will make you a lot of money?

Would you like inside information to help you get well and stay healthy?

Would you like to know more about the people you are involved with in your personal life and your business life, to help you negotiate with them, and relate to them, more effectively?

For Silva ESP graduates it is easy.

First find a quiet place where you can sit down and relax and not be disturbed by anyone, and I'll give you that inside information.

Actually I'll do even better: I'll remind you how *you* can get that inside information.

Here's a special number you can call mentally any time you need the inside scoop: 3-3-3, 2-2-2, 1-1-1. (Hint: This works after you have conditioned yourself to relax physically with the number 3, relax mentally with the number 2, and expect to be at the alpha brainwave level when you mentally repeat and visualize the number 1, as you can learn in the appendix.)

Then you want extension 10-9-8-7-6-5-4-3-2-1.

That's your clairvoyant level where you can project your mind to get your inside information (after you have completed the ESP training).

There are geniuses waiting there for you, to give you all of the information you need to correct problems and reach your goals.

Of course, we are speaking of the "kingdom within," the one you enter through the alpha dimension.

Learning a New Way to Communicate

The information is available, but since it is in the subjective dimension, we cannot make any sense of it in the objective dimension.

So you need a method to translate the information and put it into a form that you can understand objectively.

You do that by using your imagination.

You start learning this in the Silva ESP training when you project yourself mentally into metals and plants, and study the anatomy of your pet and of a human being. This is how you begin to learn the characteristics of things in the mental dimension.

Then you practice and develop proficiency in your new skill by using your ESP to detect information about health problems of people you don't know.

Imagine what the problems might be. Create mental pictures, imagine hearing the answer. Use your mind—your imagination—to try out different possibilities, and when you get the right one, you'll know. It is all the same thing—a method for getting information from a non-physical dimension, and translating that information so you can use it in the physical dimension.

Many Sources of Information

There are many ways people can get inside information: Dreams, hunches, intuition, deja-vu, insight, creativity, prayer, and so forth. All of these are methods for getting help from the other side.

In the Silva courses, we have developed several specific techniques for getting inside information: Dream Control, awakening automatically during the night to communicate subjectively with another person, the third cycle of the test taking technique, and the MentalVideo Technique are some examples.

All of these methods can help you get information. Sometimes in the beginning, one method will work better for you than another.

But it is good to develop all of these methods.

In the Silva UltraMind ESP System, we teach you how to use the MentalVideo to get an indication from higher intelligence of how to proceed.

This is used only after you have attempted to get the answer yourself, not as a substitute for you doing the work.

All of the inside information you will ever need is available to you. All you need to do is to go within (to the alpha level), and function lawfully (use your talents and abilities to help correct problems and make our world a better place to live).

When you do this, all else will be added unto you: good health, prosperity and abundance, and a fulfilled, happy life.

79 We Are Connected to a Universal Intelligence *(1989)*

All information seen (with your eyes) leaves an impression on your left brain hemisphere. The detection of this information by your mind (remembering) is called visualizing.

Information impressed on your left brain hemisphere is transferred and impressed on your right brain hemisphere.

There is also information impressed directly on your right brain hemisphere. This information comes by subjective (non-physical) means.

The information impressed on the right brain hemisphere is not transferred and impressed on the left brain hemisphere.

The Silva Method calls the left and right brain hemispheres the "mental screen."

Higher Communication

It is believed that high intelligence (God) can know about us through the impressions made on the right brain hemisphere.

High intelligence cannot see or hear on this plane of existence because of their different fundamental atomic structure on their plane of existence. High intelligence is spiritual, and has no eyes or ears. They detect the information that has made an impression on our brain (our mental screen), the right brain hemisphere.

We Are All Connected

The left brain hemispheres of humans are individual and separated from one another physically.

The right brain hemispheres of humans are connected to one another through subjective (invisible) means.

The right brain hemisphere functions as if it were one cell of a giant brain made up of all right brain hemispheres of all humans on planet earth.

Information impressed on any right brain hemisphere can be detected by high intelligence through visualization, and can be detected through visualization by any human who is interested in solving problems.

All a person needs to do is to have a desire to solve problems and know how to function on ten cycles alpha, the connection to the right brain hemisphere.

A Universal Language

Transmission of mental pictures is the universal language for all intelligence on planet earth and throughout the universe.

Communication between us and intelligence on the other side is done by detecting (visualizing) mental impressions made on our mental screen (the right brain hemisphere).

The right brain hemisphere also contains and controls the energy fields that influence, through imagination, animate matter.

Human intelligence, through imaginative picturing, influences the abnormal back into the normal.

The right brain hemisphere (the mental screen) serves as a receiver-transmitter of mental pictures.

This serves as communication between us and others on this side, and between us and those on the other side (the spiritual plane).

80 Overcome Programming Resistance *(1987)*

In the subjective dimension, hard work creates resistance.

Someone recently commented that the realization of desired things or circumstances often seems to be inversely related to how hard she tries to reach them.

She commented that when she desperately wanted a creative solution to a problem, she seemed to be like a tuning fork sending out repellent vibrations. Yet that same tuning fork seems to be irresistibly silent when she ignores her wants.

She went on to suggest that a possible cause is that there is much more potential for disappointment when we have a very great desire.

Two Dimensional Answer

A number of Silva graduates have noted the same phenomenon with their programming, and they wonder why.

They tell us that as they try harder and harder, they seem to have less success.

The answer does not lie so much with our fear of failure, but involves the idea that we do not function on only one dimension, but in two dimensions.

One thing works in one dimension, while another works in the other dimension.

In the physical dimension, we use force, we "try hard" to reach our goals.

"Hard" is a physical tool, a tool we use in the objective dimension.

In the subjective dimension, we do not try hard, but we proceed correctly, and often.

Many people are accustomed to using force in the objective (physical) dimension, and when they first learn to enter the alpha level and function within the subjective (mental) dimension, they try to use the same tools they have used in the physical dimension.

What Is the Correct Way to Program?

You already know the best programming techniques available. Just consult your student manual or your local Silva lecturer and follow the specific instructions for each Silva technique.

To make the techniques work most efficiently, you must learn to program with the correct attitude.

If you are trying desperately to make your programming work, you are defeating yourself. You are using objective tools.

In the subjective dimension, you program properly and expect to reach your goal. You use the subjective tools of desire, belief and expectancy to attract the solution to conform to your mental image.

It is good to reinforce the programming often, by visualizing (recalling) what you have created with your mind in the subjective dimension.

It is not good to program in a fearful way. If you program over and over again because you are unsure of whether you have programmed properly, this is not beneficial.

Remove All Doubt

If you have any doubts about what to program for, then use the appropriate techniques (such as Dream Control Step 3 or the Elimination Technique from the Ultra Seminar) to remove all doubt.

If you are not sure whether you are at the proper level, then take steps to remove that doubt.

Practice the long relaxation exercise (Silva Centering Exercise) for several days until you are getting very relaxed physically and mentally.

Programming is much like ordering merchandise from a catalog: Once you have decided what you want and are sure of it (desire), then you place your order (program) with a company you trust (belief) and get ready for its arrival (expectancy).

If you order items you really want and need (desire), if you are dealing with a reputable firm (using techniques you believe in), then you do not need to keep placing new orders, but simply get ready for your merchandise to be delivered (expectancy).

Of course you also have to pay for it (do the appropriate work in the physical dimension).

For instance, a student can program for good grades, but still must study.

A person can program for more money, but still must offer goods or services in exchange.

A shortcut would be to program to learn, or to program to provide goods or services that people want and need, and to be fairly compensated for this.

And if you program to sell your house, you'd better start packing, to let your mind know you are serious about it.

Observing Feedback

You should set goals that will allow you to monitor your progress. That is, you should be able to get some kind of feedback within three days, to show that you are at least moving towards your goal.

If you do not get any such feedback within three days, then acknowledge this (at your level), and then try another concept for another three days.

If you still do not get any positive feedback, then once again acknowledge the situation, and try a third concept.

If you do not get any positive feedback after this, then program once again and release it to higher intelligence.

Good Technique

There are a few things to keep in mind about programming:

For important projects, program twice a day, for several days at a time as indicated above.

Enter your clairvoyant level for programming. It is best to be in a seated position, with your head lowered (bowed) about 20 degrees, and your eyes turned upwards (in relation to your head) about 20 degrees.

My latest research indicates that this is quite important, because it aligns us with higher intelligence.

When you need additional help, use the MentalVideo Technique, which you can learn in appendix D.

Use My Original Work

Just make sure you get the original Silva products, the ones I created that haven't been changed or altered by somebody else.

We are here to serve you. Take advantage of it.

Note: The techniques in the appendix of this book are the original version exactly the way José Silva wrote them based on his twenty-two years of scientific research. For best results be sure you are using his original scientifically researched and proven techniques.

81 Increase Awareness to Get Better and Better *(1986)*

We are walking brains.

It is sometimes easy for us to think that the body has a brain, but in reality it is just the opposite: the brain has a body.

The brain needs to have information, so it has biological senses to bring it this information.

When the brain needs to see, it uses eyes.

When the brain needs to hear, it uses ears.

When the brain needs to know what something feels like, it uses nerves.

The brain needs nourishment, so it uses the senses of smell and taste to help it find the proper substances.

By doing all of this, the brain is able to function in the physical world.

But that is not all that the brain does.

The Secret Life of Your Brain

The brain also has a connection with the subjective world.

The brain can detect information with subjective senses.

When the brain needs information from the subjective world, it gets this information by using the mind.

The mind is the sensing faculty of human intelligence.

What is human intelligence? It is what is called the soul or spirit in religion, consciousness in metaphysics.

So there are biological senses of the body that send information to the brain, and spiritual senses of human intelligence which send information to the brain.

The biological senses of the body are called sight, hearing, smell, taste and touch.

The subjective senses of human intelligence are referred to as the mind.

We perceive the subjective information as visualization and imagination.

All of the information from both dimensions is transmitted to the brain. It is the brain that transfers information from one dimension to the other. It is the brain that makes it possible to conceive something in the subjective dimension and manifest it in the physical dimension.

When you are centered, with the electrical energy of your brain pulsing at ten cycles per second, this transfer can take place.

Objective information comes through the left brain hemisphere.

Subjective information comes through the right brain hemisphere.

Double Your Ability

At ten cycles per second brain frequency, you can have awareness in both dimensions, and you can synchronize information between them.

Practice developing all your senses, the mental and the physical.

Exercise your brain by using your Silva techniques. This will help you correct more problems.

We have recently created a new audio recording to help you increase your awareness and develop your biological and your subjective senses.

Increased awareness will help you become more aware of information that you can use to solve problems, and this will help reduce the amount of stress in your life.

To do it on your own, with the recording, follow these instructions. You can memorize these instructions, or record them and use the recording to guide you through this exercise.

Silva Enhanced Awareness Mental Exercise

Find a comfortable position, close your eyes, and enter your level. If you haven't yet learned how, you can follow the instructions in the appendix of this book.

We will now practice using imagination to help you improve your sensitivity and develop greater awareness of your environment. Greater awareness and knowledge will help you find more alternatives, so that you can devise better strategies for correcting problems. Having more ways to correct problems, reduces pressure and tension.

Now project yourself mentally to a garden, a natural setting with vegetation such as flowers and trees. You are now in a garden with flowers, trees, and other vegetation.

Look around you and observe this garden. (pause) Now reach out objectively, use your hand, and pick one flower. (pause) Now hold this flower at arm's length, notice how it feels (pause) and observe its appearance: Its size and shape and color. (pause) Bring your hand towards your face now, and observe this flower from just a few inches away. (pause) Now bring your hand to your nose and smell this flower. Recall how a flower smells, and imagine that you can smell this flower now. (pause) Now touch your forehead and mentally project yourself into this flower. (pause)

You are now within the flower, at any depth of this level that you desire. Now test for light, (pause) temperature, (pause) odor, (pause) and solidity of material by reflected sound. Use your hand to make a fist and knock on the inside of the flower. (pause) Now touch your forehead and come out of the flower. (pause) You are now out of the flower. Place the flower off to the side, out of your way.

Now relax, and listen. What sounds do you hear in your garden. (pause) In our environment, there are many sounds that we are not usually aware of. What is the softest sound you hear in your garden? (pause) Is it the breeze blowing, or a cricket, or a bird or other small animal? (pause) What is the loudest sound that you hear? (pause) Does it come from your garden, or from the surrounding neighborhood? (pause) Is it a sound from nature, or a sound from civilization? (pause)

What do you feel in your garden? (pause) What is the temperature? (pause) Do you feel a breeze, or the sunshine? (pause) What does the ground feel like as you stand or sit in your garden? (pause) Is the ground smooth or rough, level or hilly? (pause) What kind of clothing are you wearing in your garden? Feel your clothing in contact with your body. (pause)

Now let's taste some fruit from your garden. What fruit do you have in your garden? Do you have bushes with berries? Vines with grapes? Are there melons on the ground? Are there trees with a favorite fruit? Pick some fruit and taste this fruit. (pause) Is it sweet or tart? (pause) What is the texture as you bite into it? (pause) How juicy is it? (pause) What does it smell like as you eat it? (pause)

As you finish the fruit, again become aware of the other sensations you have of your garden. What do you see? What are the colors? (pause) What do you hear? Where are the sounds coming from? (pause) What do you feel? (pause)

Now at the count of 3, you will project yourself to be in a room where you spend a lot of time. This could be an office, or a room in your home. (pause) You are now in a room that you are familiar with. Look around this room, and notice details. Notice what is in front of you, (pause) observe what is to your left, (pause) what is to your right, (pause) and what is behind you. (pause)

Now select any small object, and pick it up. (pause) Use your hand now, and hold this object at arm's length and observe its color, (pause) its shape, (pause) its weight and texture. (pause) Now bring this object closer and observe it from just a few inches away. (pause) Now touch your forehead and mentally project yourself into this object. You are now within the object.

At this time, test for light, (pause) temperature, (pause) odor, (pause) and solidity of material by reflected sound. (pause) Now touch your forehead and come out of the object. (pause) You are now out of the object. You may place it back where it belongs.

Now relax and make yourself comfortable, and listen to the sounds in this room. What is the softest sound you hear? (pause) What is the loudest sound you hear? (pause) Do you hear any sounds coming from outside of this room? (pause)

What odors do you detect in this room? (pause) Are the odors agreeable or disagreeable? (pause) Notice how you are dressed as you relax in this room. Feel your clothing in contact with your body. (pause) Feel your body in contact with the floor or furniture that you are touching. (pause)

You have been practicing an exercise to enhance your imagination and to increase your awareness of your environment. This will help you to develop and learn to use your biological senses even more, so that you will become and even better problem solver.

In your next session you will again enter level 1, and you will enter a deeper, healthier level of mind faster and easier than this time.

Now count yourself out of your level, so that you are wide awake, feeling fine and in perfect health.

82 Can Knowing the Future Help Us Now? *(1985)*

Q: Have you researched predicting the future, and influencing it? How can I use this to help me?

A: Here Is Our Concept of Time In the Subjective Dimension

Our concept is that the past is composed of materialized thoughts. The present is the process of materializing thoughts. The future is composed of conceived thoughts, not yet materialized.

Once thoughts have been established, to be materialized later, we can get information about them. But they are always subject to change if people make different decisions before the thoughts are materialized.

So we cannot be certain what will happen in the future.

We can say that if these people continue to think this way, and materialize their thoughts, this is what will happen.

During our research, we have gotten information about future events, and confirmed our findings.

Predicting Lottery Numbers

As a research project, we had subjects project ahead to learn what numbers would be selected in the Mexican lottery.

They were able to give us the winning numbers from time to time, but we had a problem with time correlation. We couldn't correlate the time between the objective and subjective dimensions. They could be right on target number, but wrong on target time.

We were doing this only as a research project, not to make money. We believe that we should earn our money by providing services, by helping to correct problems on the planet.

We do not recommend that anyone should go out and try to win a lottery just to make a lot of money.

If you are fulfilling your responsibility and helping to correct problems on the planet, then you will receive all that you need and more besides.

A Practical Approach

One practical application of this ability to predict the future is to project yourself ahead in the future.

For instance, one person was considering accepting a new job in a different city. He wanted to know if the increase in salary would be worth moving, selling his house and buying another one, starting over again, leaving his friends behind and so forth, or whether he should bypass the opportunity.

So he projected himself ahead to find out.

To develop your ability to explore the future, enter your clairvoyant level and practice. You can use your time mechanism device—which you learn in our ESP training—to move forward and back in time.

You must seek specific information when you do this: to learn about your health, your work, or about your loved ones for instance. If you just ask, What will happen in the future, this is too general, too broad.

You need something to lock in on.

Of course, you can always just program for what you want in the future. However, if you can sense what is coming, then if you like it, reinforce it. If you do not like it, cancel it and program what you want.

Why We Face the South Wall

Q: Why do we imagine facing the south wall during the ESP training and when programming for solutions? Why is the future to the left?

A: During our research, we found that you can deal more easily with time if you imagine facing south while functioning in the subjective dimension.

Here is an analogy:

We are moving, mentally, from the physical (objective) dimension to the mental (subjective) dimension.

This could be likened to getting off of the planet (representing the physical) and going out into space (representing the mental). Then you could turn and look back at earth.

If, when you looked back, you saw that the earth was turning towards the left (which means the future is towards your left), and you know that the earth revolves towards the east, then you would know that you are facing south.

Actually, that illustration came after-the-fact.

During the research, subjects reported that when they were moving forward and backward in time, images of the future came from their left, and images of the past came from their right.

After experimenting with different concepts, we found that the concept that worked best was to face south when working in the subjective dimension.

It makes no difference how you face physically. It is the alignment in the subjective dimension that is important.

When you move the mirror towards your left before creating your solution, or goal, in the white framed mirror in the Mirror of the Mind Technique, you are taking advantage of the movement of time in the subjective dimension. The same with having the solution scene to your left in the 3-Scenes Technique.

83 How To Develop Clairvoyance
(1984)

What is ESP? The original definition meant "extra sensory perception," but scientific research has proven that definition to be inaccurate.

Subjective communication is not an extra sense; it is a prior sense, something everyone has but not everyone develops and uses consciously.

Subjective communication takes place during alpha brain wave activity.

During alpha dream time, many people have "precognitive" dreams—they dream of something, and then it happens shortly afterwards.

Since your brain dips into alpha for very brief periods—just microseconds—approximately thirty times every minute, it is possible to have flashes of insight, intuition, creative thought, perception, awareness, while in a waking state.

When you stop and think about it, there is a very good chance that you have had moments when subjective communication was working for you even though you had no training at all to develop this faculty.

So we have retained the familiar initials—E.S.P.—and changed the meaning to Effective Sensory Projection.

In the Silva Method, we begin to develop the ability to use these subjective senses effectively, and in addition to perceiving information, we also project those senses to seek out information to aid us in correcting problems.

Information is available to us if we project to it and obtain it.

This page existed before you became aware of it and projected your sense of eyesight to it to obtain the information it contains.

Similarly, you can project your mind—which is the master sense of human intelligence—to become aware of information if you desire to do so.

Once you have projected your mind to the information, then you need to express this information in a form that is familiar to biological intelligence so that you can use it in the physical world.

You may express this information as images (imagination and visualization) or as words, or as feelings, or even as taste and smell.

In the first half of our ESP training you practice projecting your mind to various places to obtain information, and you practice expressing this information in various ways. You project into metals and into leaves and you sense and describe to yourself the appearance, the amount of light, the temperature, the odor, the sound, and how they feel when you subjectively knock on them.

When you use your physical hand to "make believe" you are knocking on the object, in the subjective dimension you are knocking on the object.

You project to the anatomy of a pet and express what you detect by describing how the anatomy looks and feels as you conduct your subjective investigation.

Later you do the same with human anatomy.

When you create an image to express what you are sensing, this image aids you in focusing your mind on the subject so you can sense even more information, and sense it more accurately.

In the Silva ESP training, you go through all levels and kingdoms in the subjective dimension. You condense the evolutionary process as you project to the inanimate kingdom, the animate (plant and animal) kingdom, and to the human kingdom.

Once you are familiar with all kingdoms, you can function at any level and correct problems wherever they exist.

The more you practice projecting your mind to gather information, the more accurate you become.

However, it is best to practice projecting to real problem areas and correcting those problems. When there are real problems to correct, you will be more accurate. If you are just playing and there is no real purpose, eventually you will probably lose what ability you have.

What Are We Projecting?

Some people ask just how the projection takes place. Are we projecting ourselves by projecting some kind of "astral body"?

Our research indicates this is not the case.

You can project your sense of eyesight across the room to perceive something. So, too, you can project your mind wherever you need to so you can perceive information to help you correct problems.

You can also create with your mind. We demonstrated this in an experiment with two young research subjects.

We had one subject enter his level and create something with his mind. When he had done this, we had another subject, in another location, enter his level and project mentally to the first subject and tell us what the first subject was doing.

The second subject described accurately a little toy truck—"green with red wheels"—that the first subject had created with his mind.

In other words, the first subject created something in the subjective dimension that could be detected by another subject who was functioning in the same dimension.

We believe that subjects who think they are projecting their astral body to a distant location may actually be having a very vivid mental projection, creating with their imagination an image of their body that can be perceived by others who are functioning at the same mental level.

We know that we can prove that mental projection is possible, although at this time astral projection cannot be proven or disproven.

Previously, you may have used your imagination/visualization faculty only for "making up" things with the left brain hemisphere.

Now, however, your imagination/visualization faculty can be a means of real communication, a subjective means of communication with your right brain hemisphere. And imagination at the subjective dimension is the first step in creation.

This is a powerful combination of skills you have for helping to correct problems no matter where they are, and thereby helping to convert our world into a paradise.

Through practice, you can develop great skill at doing this.

Using your ability to project to any place and any dimension, and to correct problems and create what you desire, you can create a paradise in the portion of the world that you inhabit.

84 Current Research on Brain Frequencies *(1986)*

People who work in this and related fields have long known of the phenomenon of brain frequency when the eyes are rolled up.

The amount varies with different people. The amount that the frequency lowers does not seem to be related to the angle of the eyes.

We recommend raising the eyes approximately 20 degrees because this is sufficient to trigger the response, yet it is still a comfortable position.

A higher position, like the 45 degree angle we used to use when we first started teaching the Silva Mind Control course, tires the eyes. We wanted this to happen because tired eyelids are associated with sleep which is associated with lower brain frequencies. But now, this is no longer necessary.

In fact, maintaining such an uncomfortable position would create stress which would make it more difficult to relax and to remain at alpha.

How Do You Function?

When reviewing research on brain frequencies, please keep one thing in mind:

Achieving alpha brain wave functioning is not the end result we are seeking. It is a means to an end.

What's important is that you are able to use your mind to correct problems and help make our world a better place to live.

Your brain is always active and is always emitting a full range of frequencies. When it is producing primarily alpha frequencies—more alpha frequencies than other frequencies—this indicates to us that your mind is focused on an area where you can achieve more things.

It means that your mind is focused in a manner that allows you to use your subjective senses as well as your objective senses, with controlled awareness.

When we speak of alpha functioning, and when we speak of using the right brain hemisphere, you might say that we are creating models to help you improve your functioning.

By using these models, you can more easily grasp the concepts involved.

Since there is no physical measurement of subjective functioning, because there is no physical energy or matter involved in pure subjective functioning, it is rather difficult to comprehend it directly.

So we create models using physical items—such as the brain and the electrical energy produced by the brain (which is a physical energy)—to help you better understand what you need to do to function subjectively and to continue to improve your subjective functioning.

These models—alpha functioning and using the right brain hemisphere—are tools we use to help us achieve our goals.

Silva graduates who have practiced for a few weeks can have alpha functioning even when biofeedback instruments indicate that the brain is emitting predominately beta brain wave frequencies.

Here's how it happens:

Alpha Functioning While In Beta

Your brain automatically dips into alpha approximately 30 times every minute. This is true for everyone.

But the time spent there is only fractions of a second.

However, if a person has not learned to enter alpha consciously and has not established points of reference in the subjective dimension, then these brief trips to alpha will not be productive. In order to have alpha functioning during these micro-second trips to alpha, you must first have stored memories on the right brain hemisphere.

When you practice projecting into various items in the Silva ESP training while you are at your level, you are impressing subjective information on both brain hemispheres. As a result, you now have memories of these subjective impressions of these points of reference that you can use later.

A Silva graduate who has been practicing will "get the picture" during that micro-second trip to alpha. The graduate will sense the information; the graduate will be able to program effectively, even though it feels like he is still at beta.

Rather than get too caught up in the physiology involved, concentrate instead on the functioning and what you can accomplish.

It would be nice to have all the answers to all the questions, but right now we are more interested in getting more people to use what we already know about.

Very few graduates are taking full advantage of what they've learned thus far.

The important thing is to correct problems. We understand enough now to do this.

More understanding will come as we need it.

85 How To Help Find Runaway Children
(1985)

Using your psychic ability to locate missing children is the kind of project where you need many people involved. You need 12 people who have completed our ESP training and who live close enough to each other to meet regularly.

You want five teams of two people each and two supervisors (or overseers or directors).

The people who work on the project must be Silva ESP graduates with the most experience.

They must practice working health cases regularly to keep their intuitive skills sharp.

They Must Be Doers, Not Just Talkers

Look for people who come to graduate meetings and want to work health cases, the people who are called when there is a project to work on.

These people should be highly motivated, and have a strong desire to see the project succeed.

You must be careful to select the right people, and to make sure they stay motivated and keep their desire, belief and expectancy high, especially desire.

The ten psychics will work the case, in teams of two, and correlate their results. After each team member has worked the case, they will discuss it and agree on a team report.

To avoid the chances of the psychics picking up information from each other, each team should work at a different time and a different place from the other teams.

Each team will submit a report.

Correlate Information to Improve Accuracy

The supervisors will then correlate the information from the five teams to determine what information they all can agree on.

We have not found any psychics who are right all the time, so this helps to eliminate the error factor.

To begin with, you will have many possibilities. The psychics will come up with many ideas, many factors. They will say everything that comes to mind.

All of these ideas are then given to each team, and the psychics, at level, determine which factors do not relate to the project, do not belong there, and can be eliminated.

Once again, each team submits a report of all of the factors and ideas that both team members agree can be eliminated, and the supervisors correlate the five reports to determine which factors all five teams agree can be eliminated.

By having ten psychics work the case and correlating the information in this manner, you will be able to reduce the possibilities a certain amount.

Keep on working the project over and over, reducing it each time.

Finally, you will reach a point where you have eliminated all but a few clues and it is time to follow up the information and look into it to see if the person is there or not.

There are experiences reported on finding missing persons in the book *I Have a Hunch, the Autobiography of* José *Silva.*

If anyone gets a group together for such a project, we can offer additional specific guidelines.

More Tips You Can Use

In addition to looking for missing persons, at the same time program them to call home.

It would be difficult to program them to be at a certain place at a certain time because then you are forcing them to move in a certain direction, and it is very difficult to program other people unless they desire to be programmed.

You can, however, program yourself to go to the right places at the right time to find them wherever they are and let your intuitive factor guide you.

You can also do some creative programming to gain more information and insight into the reasons that the person is acting this way.

Why did the person run away?

If there is something about the home environment that causes the person distress, for instance, then you might need to program to correct the problem at home and then communicate subjectively with the runaway to let them know that you have corrected the cause.

Of course, an even better approach is prevention: If they become Silva graduates, then they will be centered, and will be able to cope with whatever causes distress so that problems can be corrected in a more satisfactory manner.

86 Follow This Formula to Greater Prosperity *(1984)*

You can learn to have alpha functioning and be certain that most of your decisions will be correct ones if you will follow a simple formula.

Let me explain why, and give you the formula.

During the day, your brain dips into the alpha level an average of about thirty times per minute. This happens naturally, and it seems to happen for everybody. But the time in alpha is very short, only microseconds. In all, your brain may be in alpha five seconds out of every minute.

It is during these times that people are able to be certain of making good decisions, decisions that will help to correct problems that hurt our planet and the people who inhabit it.

Maybe that is why the average person, who does not know how to function at alpha consciously when desired, is correct only twenty percent of the time.

As you discover when you learn our system, at the alpha level you can be correct more often, probably four times out of five.

But it is not always convenient to find a quiet place where you can relax mentally and physically and enter your level.

Fortunately, you can increase your ability to use the alpha level. When you have had experience functioning at alpha consciously while you are mentally and physically relaxed, then you will also increase your ability to function correctly during the day when your brain is primarily at beta.

With practice, you learn to stay at alpha for longer periods of time. You get acquainted with alpha and get a feeling for alpha.

Then later on, you can simply evoke the feeling and you will have alpha functioning regardless of what level the brain is functioning at. The mental level will be the equivalent of being at ten cycles brain frequency.

In other words, you are functioning in the subjective world, as though the brain were on ten cycles, and because you have found the door and practiced using it consciously, you get the benefits now of ten cycles functioning even if your brain is functioning at beta fifty-five seconds out of each minute.

An untrained person will receive very little benefit from those thirty brief trips to alpha, but a trained person, one who is accustomed to functioning at alpha, will get greater benefit by perceiving more of the message.

When an untrained person gets a flash of insight, they might remember a quarter of it, get only a fraction of the picture.

A trained person, accustomed to functioning at alpha consciously, will get more of the picture.

You can stay at alpha consciously for long periods whenever you need to, to spend time analyzing problems from various perspectives, and programming solutions.

But often it is not necessary to spend a great deal of time at alpha. When you are talking with someone, you can simply desire to be more sensitive to that person, and you will be—provided you have practiced and developed your ability.

Formula for Natural Alpha Functioning

Here is a simple formula for developing this ability: First learn to find the alpha dimension and function there consciously.

Second, use your abilities to help correct problems on the planet, to help make our planet a better place to live. When you do these two things, you will enjoy prosperity in all areas of your life.

You can use the Three Fingers Trigger Mechanism to assist you in developing your alpha functioning in this manner.

At night, before going to sleep, program yourself to awaken automatically at the ideal time to program. Stay at your level and go to sleep.

When you awaken during the night or in the morning, enter your level again and bring together the tips of the first two fingers and thumb of both hands.

Then program that whenever you bring together the tips of the first two fingers and thumb of either hand, or both hands, you will have superior alpha functioning and be aware of information from the subjective dimension that will help you correct problems.

The more you practice entering level, the more effective this will be. And the more you apply it, the more you attempt to correct problems and experience success in your endeavors, the more confidence you will gain, the more faith you will have, and the more successful you will become. It is important to have faith.

The Formula for Faith

Remember that faith is composed of desire, belief, and expectancy.

Desire stems from need. When there is a genuine need, you have genuine desire.

This is important because it is a motive force, a pushing force, compelling us towards our goals. There is little desire in luxuries, but great desire when necessities are lacking, so while learning, seek out the problems and help correct them. Then later, when you have more experience, you will be better able to attain the luxuries.

Expectancy is the goal. It grows through repeated successes, so it is important to practice as much as possible to increase your expectancy factor.

Belief is what sustains you. Belief comes from experiences—successful experiences. Belief is demonstrated by persistence. As long as you continue to practice, you are expressing your belief.

Keep practicing. Enter your level and review your successes. With enough experience and faith, you will achieve more than you imagine.

87 Everybody Visualizes
(1985)

Sometimes people tell me they don't visualize, or they visualize poorly. Let's set the record straight:

It is not a question of whether you visualize—everybody visualizes—but a more important question is whether you are visualizing with the left brain hemisphere or with the right brain hemisphere.

You can get some results when you visualize with the left brain hemisphere. You get much greater results when you visualize with the right brain hemisphere.

A person who is not a Silva graduate but who has extremely clear and detailed visualization will get very poor results if all they can do is visualize with the left brain hemisphere.

A Silva graduate who simply thinks about what things look like can get excellent results, if the graduate thinks about what things look like at the alpha level, using the right brain hemisphere.

What do we mean by visualization?

Visualization is memory. When you recall what something looks like, you are visualizing. If you can describe something to me in full detail, if you can tell me its shape and color, you are visualizing.

Some people tell me they can think about what something looks like and describe it to me, but they do not visualize it. They say that they are just thinking about it.

When they tell me that, I know that they are visualizing.

Remember that you *see* with your eyes, and you *visualize* with your mind.

When you visualize with your left brain hemisphere, you are bringing back (recalling) information that you have perceived with your biological senses only.

When you visualize with your right brain hemisphere, in addition to recalling information that you have perceived with your biological senses, you also recall information you have perceived with your subjective (psychic) senses.

Dreaming

Dreaming is similar to visualizing, but it is different.

You dream and visualize at various brain frequencies, but there are different levels of brain and mind involved in dreaming and in consciously visualizing.

Actually, there are many different kinds of dreams. The dreams you have when you are going into deeper levels of sleep are different from the dreams you have when you are coming out of deep levels of sleep.

There are many stages of dreams. Each is different, and each produces a different type of imagery. The imagery you have with visualization and imagination differs from these.

Sometimes you dream so clearly that it is almost like seeing. Visualizing will never be like seeing, because you are in different stages of brain and mind. There are only certain dimensions where that degree of clarity can take place, and it does not happen consciously.

It happens unconsciously; it happens naturally.

Some people talk about how clearly they visualize, but it is not the same as "seeing."

Imagination

Imagination is thinking about what something may look like when you have never seen it or imagined it before. (If you have imagined it before, and then you recall it, you are visualizing what you previously imagined.)

The Memory Pegs offer excellent practice in both visualization and imagination. Even though you may be doing them at beta, with only the left brain hemisphere, it is still excellent practice for you.

Right-Brain Thinking

To learn to use your right brain hemisphere when you are visualizing and imagining, practice at your level.

The best kind of practice is to work health cases, as you learned to do in the final portion of the ESP training.

To help you get the idea of what we are doing, we use. a model of left-brain/right-brain functioning, as follows:

When you are at your level and visualizing and imagining (thinking about what things look like), you are impressing those experiences on both your left and your right brain hemispheres.

Notice what we do with the Memory Pegs.

First, you peg thirty items at beta, with the left hemisphere. Then at your level, your lecturer guides you to review them so that your experiences are now transferred to and stored on your right brain hemisphere.

This happens because when you are at your level, at the alpha level, there is a connection with the right brain hemisphere. You are synchronizing the two brain hemispheres

Advanced Practice

The first thing you do in the ESP training is to recall experiences already stored on your left brain hemisphere.

You recall these stored experiences at your level, and you transfer them to your right brain hemisphere. Then the next thing you do is use your imagination to sense information with your subjective senses, with your right brain hemisphere, and you store these new experiences on both brain hemispheres.

In the ESP training, when you project into your living room wall, into the metals, into the leaves and to the pet, you are storing experiences on your right brain hemisphere.

When you study human anatomy from a psychic point of view you do the same thing. You recall a relative or friend and, while at your level, transfer these memories—this stored information—to your right brain hemisphere.

Then you sense information subjectively and store this on both brain hemispheres.

Now you have points of reference on your right brain hemisphere that you will use when working health cases of people you do not know.

Psychic Experiences

When you begin working health cases, you begin with information on your right brain hemisphere, using your subjective (psychic) senses, and you transfer it to your left brain hemisphere when you describe to your orientologist the things that you are sensing.

You might have noticed that after doing a mental training exercise, you do not talk about your experiences immediately afterwards.

However, it is all right to talk about those experiences after you have gone through at least one sleep and dream cycle. You want to have this time so that while you are sleeping, your brain can properly file away the new information.

Talking about it before you have had a chance to sleep on it is like digging up a seed. You need time to internalize it.

But working health cases is different.

Since you are reporting on information that comes to you subjectively, experiences that are impressed first on your right brain hemisphere, then the process of reporting these experiences helps transfer the information to the left brain hemisphere also.

This is one of the reasons it is important to tell your orientologist *everything* that you think of or experience while working cases.

Total Functioning

In the beginning, if you desire to use your right brain hemisphere, you must enter your level and call on the experiences you have already stored on your right brain hemisphere as you went through the Silva ESP training.

But as you store more and more experiences on your right brain hemisphere, an interesting phenomenon takes place:

You begin to develop the ability to use both brain hemispheres without closing your eyes (provided your vision is defocused) and without having to use the standard 3 to 1 method to enter your level.

Your brain automatically dips into alpha approximately thirty times every minute. This is true for all people, whether they are Silva graduates or not.

The brain stays at alpha for only a very short period of time, but this time can be very useful if you have points of reference to work with on the right brain hemisphere.

With practice, you can learn to make those brief trips to alpha last longer.

If you have not stored any experiences on your right brain hemisphere, which you do by visualizing and imagining while at the alpha level, then you will be unable to do any right-brain thinking during these brief trips to alpha, because you do not have any points of reference to guide you.

But after you have stored experiences with your right brain hemisphere, you can then begin to develop the ability to use your right brain hemisphere for thinking when your brain dips into alpha for those fractions of a second.

You can sense information with your subjective senses when your brain dips into alpha, but only if you have points of reference (experiences) on your right brain hemisphere to guide you, and you learn to recognize that special feeling of being at alpha and stay longer than that brief instant.

You can program for things you desire with your right brain hemisphere when your brain dips into alpha, but only if you have points of reference (experiences) on your right brain hemisphere to guide you, and you learn to recognize that special feeling of being at alpha and stay longer than that brief instant.

That is why it is important to practice all of the Silva techniques, especially case working. You want to store as many experiences as possible using your right brain hemisphere, not only visualizing and imagining, but sensing information and programming for your desired end results.

Know What Is Important

Now we are back to where we started: visualization and imagination.

When you practice thinking about what things look like while you are at your level and are using your right brain hemisphere, you are doing exactly what is necessary to bring about the results you desire.

A person who is not a Silva graduate can practice visualizing and imagining all day long, can have extremely clear imagery, but still get very poor results if they are using only the left brain hemisphere and they do not know how to enter the alpha level and make points of reference on the right brain hemisphere.

A Silva graduate who practices going to level and thinking about what things look like, who practices the techniques, and practices case working, will develop the ability to achieve any goals because the Silva graduate is using both brain hemispheres.

There are several ways you can take the Silva ESP training and develop your ESP:

- In-person seminars.
- Live webinar.
- Recorded webinar.
- Online Learning
- Downloads
- Some of our new books include the ESP Training.

Note: Check the resources in the appendix of this book to learn where you can obtain ESP training that was authored by José Silva and has not been changed or altered by anybody else after his passing.

88 Success Doesn't Depend On How Smart You Are *(1992)*

We have learned something very interesting since we first started our research back in 1944 into the question of what makes human beings successful.

We learned that you don't have to be real intelligent to be successful; you don't need to be real creative, or have great ideas.

To be successful, just be observant and obedient.

You can know what to do, when and how, and you can be extremely successful if you follow my simple formula, which I'll give to you in a few moments.

Right Attitude

For starters, you must have the right attitude.

What is the right attitude? It is included in the final statements of the conditionings in the Silva training:

"You will continue to strive to take part in constructive and creative activities to make the world a better place to live . . ."

If you want to be close to the Creator, then you must take part in constructive and creative activities.

The Creator does not destroy; the Creator creates.

When you create, you are aligned with the Creator.

Get a Plan

Now the question is, how do you know what to do in order to accomplish all that you should?

Let's assume that you have decided to earn your way by helping to correct problems, and you have selected an occupation that does just that.

How do you know the best way to proceed?

The good news is: You don't have to figure out everything that you are supposed to do. Somebody else already knows.

Who knows?

Somebody on the other side knows. No, not your competitors.

I am referring to those beings in the spiritual dimension who have been assigned to help us.

The great avatars have always understood that we are not alone. We have all the help we need, if we will only enter our level and ask for it. That's why prayers have language like, "thy will be done, on earth as it is in heaven."

That implies that it has already been done in heaven. Now all we need to do is carry out the plan on earth.

Observe and Obey

How do we determine what the plan is, that they have formulated on the other side?

Figuring it out mostly requires observation.

First, go ahead and figure out the best plan you can. There is no need to dwell on this for too long. Come up with a plan, check it out, think it through, and then put it into action.

Once you put it into action, watch to see what kind of results you get.

If you get good results, do even more of what you started.

If you get poor results, then try something different.

I don't mean that you should quit at the first sign of resistance. You need to put a good effort into it.

But we don't batter down doors.

If a door doesn't open for you, then back off and look to see if there is another door that you can use.

You might want to think of it as being similar to putting together a jig saw puzzle. If a piece doesn't fit, turn it around and try again.

If it still doesn't fit, turn it around again, or turn it over and try it that way.

When you've tried a piece every way, and it still won't fit, you don't force it; you put it aside and try another piece.

Find the Right Path

When your plan is not working, enter your level and determine what to do next.

Remember, you don't have to be perfect—you just need a good idea to continue with.

Maybe you can alter your approach. Maybe you can try a different approach.

Sometimes, when nothing seems to work, maybe you have the wrong goal. So ask yourself at level if you should be doing something else.

If you get the feeling that maybe you should be in a different occupation, then take some action in that direction. You don't have to quit your job right away, but you might inquire about opportunities in another field.

If you get a good offer, maybe that is feedback to guide you into what you actually should be doing with your life.

Remember, we don't batter down doors.

We find the right door.

Success Formula

I have a formula for success that works very well for me, and has worked for everyone I know who has applied it. I didn't come up with it; I found it, and have found that it works.

Here is my formula for success:
- First, enter the kingdom of heaven.
- Then function within God's righteousness.
- And all else shall be added unto you.

To put it into Silva language:
- First, enter alpha.

- Then, strive to take part in constructive and creative activities, and let your results tell you whether you are succeeding at this.
- Program to give more service, and keep in mind what your needs are, plus a little bit more.

And all else shall be added unto you.

Note: We have a new technique to help you do this: the MentalVideo. You can learn it right now in appendix D.

89 Can the Body Save the Soul?
(1990)

What do you have to do to "save your soul"? Some religious people tell you that you have to behave in a certain way in order to "save your soul." They say that if you don't behave the way they tell you to that you can "lose your soul."

That brings up an interesting question:

Does your body have a soul, or does your soul have a body?

We know that the body is here for only a short period of time. We are born, we live 70 or 80 or sometimes even 100 years, then the body dies. Ashes to ashes, dust to dust.

And we assume that the soul survives and moves on.

We assume that we had a soul before we had a body.

So which has which:

Does your body have a soul, or does your soul have a body?

If the soul existed first, and exists after the body is gone, then shouldn't we say that the soul has a body?

So when they tell us we have to behave in a certain manner to save our soul, who is talking: the soul, or the body?

Which Dimension Are You Functioning In?

You can easily tell whether a person is functioning in the physical dimension or the spiritual dimension.

If you say, "My clothes, my house," you are functioning in the physical dimension, in the world of the body.

Biological intelligence is speaking.

If you say, "My body," then human intelligence is speaking. You are functioning in the subjective dimension, in the world of the mind.

If you have a tool, you can take care of the tool, but the tool cannot take care of you.

For instance, you can buy a hammer and use it until it wears out. The better care you take of the hammer, the longer it will last.

But the hammer cannot take care of you.

The hammer does not have a person—the person has a hammer.

So back to the original question:

Does your body have a soul, or does your soul have a body?

Rather than the body trying to figure out how to save the soul, shouldn't it be the other way around?

Shouldn't we be spending time functioning in the subjective dimension (at level), figuring out what this tool (the body) is supposed to be used for?

Perhaps your soul has this tool (the body) to use to help correct problems and convert our planet into a paradise.

When we take care of the tool (the body) and use it to help correct problems on our planet, the body will thrive and prosper.

When we use the tool (the body) incorrectly, when we do not use the tool properly, then the tool can be damaged and suffer.

That kind of thinking brings up another interesting question:

Does the body have to make certain decisions and do certain things to save the soul, or should we be making decisions in the subjective dimension about how to use the body correctly to save the body?

As we have said many times, you should do your thinking and make your decisions at alpha, then take action in beta.

The soul (what we call human intelligence) can make decisions for the body, but the body does not have the necessary intelligence to make decisions for the soul. Yet it seems like that's what some religious people are telling us to do.

The carpenter isn't punished if the hammer breaks.

If the carpenter uses the hammer correctly, for its designed purpose, then the hammer will last a long time and do a great deal of good.

As I see it, Jesus came to help humanity by teaching us the way to get help from the other side that can help us on this side.

In other words, Jesus came to help us save the body . . . to save the body from suffering because of ignorance.

Let your human intelligence make your decisions, from the alpha level.

The body is the servant. Use it to do the work that needs to be done.

90 A Place Where You Cannot Hurt Anyone *(1990)*

Despite all of the scientific evidence to the contrary, some people still insist on believing that there is some kind of "mental energy" that can cause harm.

We can only cause physical harm by physical means, in the physical dimension.

Let's look at it this way:

Your body is made up of a collection of atoms (which are composed of protons and neutrons and electrons and quarks and other sub-atomic particles), which function together as molecules, which function together as cells, which function together as organs. . . .

What holds it all together?

What makes the atoms and molecules and cells and organs behave together the way they do?

Some people might say it is a primal force or a spiritual energy, but I prefer not to use terms like "force" and "energy" because those are associated with the physical dimension.

Let's say that there is some kind of intelligence that is behind it all. We can call it human intelligence.

The Soul Mold

Perhaps human intelligence somehow forms a mold that the physical particles fit into, that they conform to. We can call it the soul mold.

The soul is a mold that holds matter together. It is cohesive and adhesive.

The mold can be formed by human intelligence, which is not physical.

A person's body can be damaged by physical force. A person could be punched in the nose for instance. It takes physical force to alter the matter that is in the mold.

But then the matter returns to the original state, to conform to the mold. A doctor can help it come more closely to the original, by using stitches to close the skin and minimize scarring, for instance.

Matter always tries to conform to the mold, to what human intelligence desires. There are no exceptions to this. Human intelligence always seeks perfection.

The mind belongs to human intelligence. It functions in the non-physical—or subjective—dimension.

Therefore, the only thing that the mind can do is to help move matter to conform to the mold, to seek perfection.

You Are the Boss of You

The only way that one person can hurt another physically is by physical means. The mind, at a distance, cannot harm.

Another person's thoughts, at a distance, cannot harm you, any more than something that another person says to you, from a distance, can hurt you physically.

If somebody calls you and threatens to break your arm, your arm will not break just because they say so.

There are two ways they can break it:

They can come and hit you.

Or, you can harm yourself. That's what is known as the psychosomatic effect.

You know about psychosomatic illness. A person may be under so much stress that their heart is damaged, for instance.

Similarly, we can have "accidents." We are drawn in the direction of our dominant thoughts. If a person is so concerned that another person can harm them, that person might dwell on that until they make it happen.

If a "witch doctor" threatens to break a person's arm, that person could be so frightened of that, and think about it so much, that they will eventually stumble and fall and break their own arm.

On the other hand, if that person knows how to enter their level, then they can simply reprogram their mind to dwell only on positive thoughts, and the "curse" will have no effect at all.

We have some statements in the course to help people accomplish this.

We program that negative thoughts and negative suggestions will have no effect on you. This helps you to maintain positive thoughts no matter who says what to you.

There are other statements about not being able to harm anyone in this dimension, and about always remaining in control and having the ability to accept or reject anything.

Your Aura

A person's aura is a physical energy.

The physical part of your aura extends out about 8 meters—about 30 feet—from the body. Anything within the aura range is subject to the physical energy of the aura.

You can decide to bend something with your hands. Some people can decide to distort matter with their aura. That is how they bend spoons.

Just remember that this is a physical energy, and the object must be within the person's aura range.

Beyond that range, nobody can harm you. Especially if you are a Silva graduate, because you have control of your own mind and life.

When you make a habit of spending time at level every day, and you practice the various Silva techniques regularly, your life will continue to get better and better.

91 We Must Learn to Use Our Mind Correctly *(1984)*

What is a prophet, and what does it mean to prophesy?

The dictionary says that to prophesy is to utter, foretell or predict under divine influence, inspiration and direction, a future event.

A prophet is one who can prophesy.

The dictionary also calls prophecy divination, which is the act or art of knowing the future or that which is hidden or unknown. In other words, a clever or correct guess.

The dictionary associates divination with the divine; the divine pertains to God. So if we were able to guess right more times than wrong, we could say that we are divinely inspired.

Divinely inspired means inspired by God, connected with God.

Connected With God

Anyone who desires to develop a connection with God must develop a means to guess right, to prophesy.

Nowhere do we find information on how to develop prophets or learn to prophesy.

What does it mean to guess right or wrong?

When we are Godly inspired, we are correct, or what we call right; then right is what God desires.

Since God is a creator, then "being right" means everything that is creative; wrong will then mean everything that is destructive.

Alleviating suffering, without creating any new suffering, is constructive; causing suffering is destructive.

For humanity to survive on this planet, humanity must have a connection with God. In order for humanity to have a connection with God, humanity must learn to function correctly. For humanity to function correctly, humanity must learn to guess right. For humanity to guess right, humanity must learn to use the mind correctly.

What Is Mind?

Mind is a faculty of human intelligence.

Mind and human intelligence are subjective, non-physical, and function in another dimension, a non-physical dimension.

Since mind and human intelligence function in a non-physical dimension, humans can not detect mind or human intelligence with biological (physical) senses.

It does not mean that since humans cannot detect mind or human intelligence with biological senses that they do not exist.

We humans know that we have a mind and intelligence even though we do not know where they reside or function. Since we can not detect the mind or human intelligence, we must then depend on observing what the mind and human intelligence can do, or have done. In other words, we must be able to detect what effects the mind or human intelligence have caused when they function.

So mind and human intelligence functioning in a spiritual dimension can cause effects in the physical dimension.

How To Create

Everything materialized was first created in the subjective dimension by mind and human intelligence: the clothes you wear, the car you drive, the home you live in. We can then understand that everything humans materialize in this physical dimension has to first take place in the world of the mind, the spiritual world.

We thus realize how important and valuable it is to learn to use our mind in a superior manner.

Learning to use our mind in a superior manner will mean to learn to function mentally in the subjective world of the mind and human intelligence dimension, and to learn to function in a superior manner.

We then understand that to do better in life, we must be connected with God, and to be connected with God we must guess more times right than wrong; and to guess more times right than wrong we must learn to function accurately in a superior manner in the spiritual dimension.

Human intelligence is what others call "soul" or "spirit" and mind is not a thing, mind is a faculty of human intelligence; a faculty such as focusing is a faculty of the eye, and attunement is a faculty of the ear. Mind is used by human intelligence to focus or attune its intentions on the physical from the spiritual so as to cause alterations.

Such alteration are also known as programming.

We must learn how, from the subjective dimension, to program with human intelligence using mind to bring about a change in the physical dimension; meaning, to cause a change in the world of the body dimension from the world of the mind dimension.

Even though we are unable to detect the altering mechanism with our biological senses from the physical dimension, we can detect the altered state that has taken place. By the results we shall know. "By their fruits (or results) they shall be known."

A God-Connected Person

One can be known to produce good results or fruits by being able to be more times right than wrong.

A person who is right more times than wrong is bound to be connected to God, because being right is what solve problems and is constructive, helping God with creation.

It is easy to understand that God created us to help with creation.

We were created first subjectively and then physically.

Human intelligence (the soul) and mind (faculty of the soul) still reside and function in the subjective dimension. Brain and body function in the physical dimension.

The brain is the organ through which human intelligence, using its faculty the mind, causes alterations in the physical dimension. The brain serves as the medium to communicate between spiritual (the invisible world) and the physical (the visible world).

But what is the bridge between the mental and the physical?

It is the brain.

How the Brain Works

The brain is composed of two halves—parts, or hemispheres:

- The left-brain hemisphere
- The right-brain hemisphere.

It is believed that human intelligence (the soul) along with its faculty the mind has existed before a brain was ever conceived. Once a brain is conceived, human intelligence is attuned or assigned to that brain.

Human intelligence uses the right-brain hemisphere to communicate between the spiritual and physical dimensions, and uses the left-brain hemisphere to function in the physical dimension.

It appears as though once human intelligence is assigned a newborn, conceived brain, it concentrates in using the left-brain hemisphere mostly to learn to function in the physical world of the body and to learn to use the biological senses. When this happens, we develop the ability to be conscious of and recall only information that has been impressed on the left-brain hemisphere, and not be able to recall or be conscious of information impressed on the right-brain hemisphere.

The left-brain hemisphere thinks in words, and uses logic.

The right-brain hemisphere thinks in images and mental pictures, and is thus more creative. The left-brain hemisphere is associated with the physical and social aspects of life, while the right-brain hemisphere is associated with the mental and spiritual aspects of life.

Superior Functioning

Persons who are able to use both brain hemispheres to think with are better guessers than people who use only one brain hemisphere. Those who use only one brain hemisphere to think with always use the left one, the one that deals only with the physical dimension, with linear, logical thought.

Therefore, to be better guessers, which means to be right more times than wrong, we must be creative and prophetic using the right-brain hemisphere so we can be connected to God and be Godly inspired in order to correct more problems on this planet.

It has been found that only about ten percent of humanity are prophetic and are more times right than wrong.

God is not getting the proper help by having only ten percent of humanity guessing right and helping to solve problems on this planet.

We must look for and find whatever it is that we must do to be God-connected and help in converting this planet into a paradise.

How To Proceed

In order to use divination, we must be connected to God, and to be connected to God we must first find how to relax mentally, second learn to relax physically, third how to function on the ten cycles per second brain frequency, and finally learn how to become active mentally and physically and remain at the ten cycles per second brain frequency.

In looking for a connection with God, we figured that whatever or wherever it was had to have all kinds of benefits for the human being.

In our research, good things started coming our way when we trained people to function on the ten-cycles frequency.

First, people experienced a feeling of satisfaction, a feeling such as one experiences when having succeeded in "a job well done." Eventually this feeling of satisfaction was interpreted to be happiness.

We further observed that other benefits included being healthier, safer, more spiritual, more human, and more successful.

All these benefits are added unto one who practices functioning at the ten cycles per second alpha dimension, using visualization and imagination to help correct problems on this planet.

If you don't already know how to function this way, you can learn starting right now with the information in the appendix.

92 Imagine Being at Alpha Just by Daydreaming *(1991)*

Imagine what your life would be like if programming became so automatic that you did not need to use the 3 to 1 method to enter your level, and you did not need to use the Mirror of the Mind or the 3-Scenes Technique, but only needed to think about something and it would appear automatically.

That is a big jump from the techniques that you learned in the Basic Lecture Series (BLS).

In the BLS, the average conditioning cycle requires 15 minutes for getting to level, deepening, and programming.

After you complete the BLS, you will probably only need a minute or two to enter level and do some deepening exercises before you are ready to program.

To use the Mirror of the Mind or the 3-Scenes Technique, you need to make a good study of the problem, and then create an image of what you desire in the solution scene.

With practice, you can become very proficient at using these techniques for programming.

In the ESP training you learn to work health cases by using the 3 to 1 method to enter level, then 10 to 1 to enter your clairvoyant level. Then you scan the body, select three areas, scan within the selected areas, to detect problems. Then you correct the problems.

With practice, you can become very proficient at working health cases.

After you have worked 500 health cases, you will find that you are very accurate, and very confident, in your case working.

Are you accurate because you are confident, or are you confident because you are accurate? The answer is: Yes!

With practice, you can learn to get accurate information just by mentally asking the subject.

You can imagine asking them a question, then clear your mind for a moment by thinking of something else. Then start thinking again to figure out the answer; imagine the subject answering "Yes," and imagine them answering "No."

One answer will seem right.

With practice, all of this becomes very natural.

With enough practice, it can become so natural that you will not even need to use all of the rituals in order to get results.

You were given a step-by-step formula in the Human Anatomy conditioning cycle near the end of the ESP training, so that you can learn to function without using the standard rituals:

Magic 50 Health Cases

After you have worked 10 health cases and you are satisfied with the results, you can shorten the ritual to 10 to 1, and you will be at your clairvoyant level.

After you have worked another 10 health cases, and are still satisfied with the results, you can use only the to 1 method to enter your clairvoyant level.

After working another 10 cases satisfactorily, you can just close your eyes and recall being at your clairvoyant level.

Once you are completely satisfied with your results, all you need to do is to defocus your vision and recall your most recent time when you were functioning at your clairvoyant level.

Of course, it is still good to practice with the standard 3 to 1, 10 to 1 ritual when you have time. But when you need to, you can get results automatically by defocusing your vision and visualizing your laboratory.

Defocusing is something like daydreaming. That is the best word I have found to describe it. You have your eyes open and are aware of your surroundings, but you are not focusing your eyesight on anything. Whenever you attempt to focus your eyes, your brain goes to 20 cycles per second beta.

When you daydream, you are aware of your surroundings indirectly, and are daydreaming directly.

Focusing your eyes is like a switch to select beta or alpha. Focus—or attempt to focus your eyesight—when you want beta, defocus when you want alpha.

After you have worked enough health cases, and have spent enough time at level getting information and correcting problems, then you will be at your clairvoyant level when you desire to be there, even though your eyes are open and you are aware of your surroundings but not looking at anything directly.

With enough practice, this becomes so automatic that you may not even be aware it is going on.

Once you have developed this ability, it is then easier for you to get information directly from the subjective dimension, without even thinking about the rituals that you used in the beginning.

When you have completely developed your ability to use both the physical and the mental dimensions, then you will often find yourself getting what you want simply by thinking about it, even without using any specific technique.

How To Develop "Natural" Ability

For the experienced person, "daydreams" will take place at the clairvoyant level. The experienced person has practiced the techniques so many times that it is second nature, and programming is done without giving it conscious thought.

Results seem to come automatically, without worrying about the process that is used to achieve those results.

But please keep in mind that it takes practice, before you can do it automatically in a reliable manner.

We recommend that you enter level every day for 15 minutes.

The more you go to level, the better, but enter level for 15 minutes at least once every day.

Also, practice the Silva Centering Exercise once a week, to make sure you maintain that deep, healthy level.

You should work an average of at least one health case every day. When you obtain information with your mind, that was not available to your physical senses, and you verify that the information is correct, then you know that you are using your right brain hemisphere, and that you are getting information from the subjective dimension.

The more you practice, the more often you will function automatically.

This makes life a lot better.

93 Use the Alpha Level to Create the Life You Desire *(1999)*

We recommend to Silva graduates that you enter your level—the alpha level—at least once a day, for 15 minutes.

How are you going to spend your time there?

Without moving, just using your mind, mental activities, no body movement.

Take an inventory for instance. Review what you did yesterday, that you want to correct today.

Where are you on your progress, on whatever you are trying to accomplish? How far have you gotten towards reaching your goals at this time?

Analyze everything that happened yesterday, and the corrections you want to make. Analyze the mistakes that you made, and what you want for the future.

Always keep your ultimate goals in sight, but break it down into smaller parts, smaller segments.

For instance, break it down into five segments. Work on Segment Number 1 first. When you accomplish this, then go into Segment Number 2, towards your goal.

Important Projects

You can also analyze how you are doing in life: in your health, in family relations, and in business. Always keep in mind those three major areas.

First of all health, because if you're not healthy, you're not going to do anything else. Health comes first.

Better relations, to be the happiest time in your life, comes second.

And then business, to support the others, and to keep them moving. Business is to accomplish the material needs that you need to accomplish, to comply with, because we all have needs for money. Money is the fuel that keeps the machinery going.

If you want to do great things, you must have a lot of money to do it with.

If you have little things to do in life, you don't need too much money to do whatever that is. So it depends on your needs, on what plans you have for the future. That determines what you are going to need to accomplish your goals.

Help One Another

Your goals should be—not just benefits for you and yours—I mean animals do that. Now we want to also help other human beings.

Whenever we say "we," we don't mean just me and my family, we mean humanity in general. All human beings.

Animals take care of themselves and their offspring, but animals don't help other animals of the same species. That's animal reaction.

This is what humans are doing right now. They don't care about anybody else. But we should care about other human beings also. We cannot survive by ourselves.

We need shops to manufacture shoes for us because we don't manufacture shoes, clothing because we don't manufacture clothing, someone to change the oil in my auto. I pay them for the services. We need each other. It is not just about me getting whatever I want, and then forget about everybody else.

All of our plans should be considered as *we*, or *us*, meaning: Humanity is not just me and my immediate family. Animals do that automatically; they don't even have to have intelligence to supply their needs and the needs of their immediate family.

We want to go beyond that. Not just what animals are capable of doing; we want to be able to do what humans are capable of doing with the intelligence that we have, way beyond what animals are capable of doing.

Animals cannot compare with us. We are the highest level of intelligence. We are the gods of this planet. In other words, we are supposed to do on this planet what we believe that the being that we call God can do in the whole universe.

We may not be able to do it in the whole universe, but on this planet: Yes. We are the highest level of intelligence here. There's no other entity with intelligence higher than the human being.

But, you have to know this, and you have to know how to function as a creator. If you are not aware that you can correct problems and improve conditions on planet earth, then you haven't gained anything.

How We Differ From Animals

For instance, we say: Inanimate matter is subjected to environmental influences. Inanimate matter is subjected to variations in temperature, variations in barometric pressure, concept of astrology, and so on.

The vegetable kingdom, which is higher than the inanimate kingdom, is also subjected to temperature changes, changes in barometric pressure, concept of astrology, and biorhythm.

Animals, another kingdom that is higher than the plant kingdom, are also subjected to the environmental influences: changes in barometric pressure, concept of astrology, and biorhythm.

The animal body of a human being is a biological system. It is also subjected to environmental influences: changes of barometric pressure, temperature changes, concepts of astrology, and biorhythm.

Now what about the mind? Animals don't have a human mind.

It is the animal body of a human being that has a human mind.

The animal bodies of animals have animal minds. Animal minds function inductively.

The human mind, after a certain age, starts functioning deductively, which means: The ability—the faculty—of being able to analyze.

The analytical factor is what makes the difference between a human being and an animal.

The human mind can alter, or change, the environment, to be able to counter barometric pressures, changes in temperature, the concept of astrology, and biorhythm.

You need to become aware that you have tremendous power because of the analytical faculty of mind—it is your human power. Nothing else. And other humans have it.

You can function as though you were born under any sign—you don't care about astrology. You can neutralize or change all the effects of biorhythm. The human mind can do it. But you must know how to do it. You must know at what level of brain and mind this is done.

Important Points to Remember

There are two different things that we need to be sure we understand:

1. That we are the kings of this planet, the gods of this planet.
2. That we can change anything we need to change to improve conditions, because of our analytical faculty of mind that we have.

If you do not know that you are the king, or if you know that you are a king but you don't know how to function as one, because you don't know how to use your mind, you might as well be an animal or a plant, because the wind is going to sway you wherever it wants to, you have no control over it. You are out of control because you don't know that you have the power to make these changes. And you have to know how to make these changes.

It is not enough to know that you have the faculty to do it, because if you don't know how to use your faculty to do it, it is as though you didn't know it.

Animals don't have it. Plants don't have it. Inanimate matter doesn't have it. You'll be subjected to environmental influences like inanimate matter, like animals, and like plants if you don't know you have it and how to use it.

Where This Power Resides

You have to know how to function with this power. Not knowing how to use it is like not having it.

Where do we obtain this power? At what level do we have this power? The ultimate power?

Not at beta. Not by using only one brain hemisphere, the left one.

The power comes from using everything God gave us to use: Both brain hemispheres and the alpha part of the brain.

Having both brain hemispheres, we function in two different dimensions.

We can function in one, or we can function in the other.

If you only use one brain hemisphere, you only function in one dimension, using only one set of senses, and that's it.

You need to use both brain hemispheres, not just one. We have two, why is the other one not being used? It is like using one arm, like using only your left hand and not using your right one. You have your right one to also use, why not use it along with the left one—wouldn't it be better than if you just use one hand or arm?

The same here: Instead of using one brain hemisphere, use both brain hemispheres.

Where Problems Are Rooted

Very rarely do you have a problem that's all objective, or all subjective. All problems are partly in each dimension. In order to solve problems, you need to function in both dimensions: in the subjective and the objective.

It is believed that 80 percent of the health problems are rooted in the alpha level, ten percent are rooted in the beta level, and ten percent in the theta level.

Objective medicine corrects problems from the outer to the inner. Beta is objective medicine, using physical means to solve problems.

But medicine cannot reach the subjective dimension where a percentage of problems are rooted.

Psychological medicine, mental medicine, spiritual medicine, immaterial (non physical) medicine is what solves the problems that are rooted in alpha and in theta.

Subjectively we can solve 90 percent of the problems. Objectively, we can solve 10 percent.

Holistic faith healing corrects problems from the inner to the outer.

The basis for the inner, vibration-wise, is ten cycles per second. Ten vibrations per second is the basis for our life, is what produces life in cells and so forth. So we function at two dimensions.

We can perceive an object at alpha and detect the color and shape at alpha without having to see it objectively, only mentally.

Mentally we can project to anywhere. I don't have to be there objectively to sense it. Distance is a barrier when you use only the laws of physics. Walls are a barrier. If it is on the other side of the wall I couldn't see it. But my mind doesn't care if it is on the other side of the wall. Or in China.

Mind, by thinking about it, is going to it.

Every time you think about John Doe, that means that your mind is on John Doe's mind. John Doe doesn't know. You could be implanting information on his brain. If he doesn't alter it, he picks it up then.

Research Shows the Mind Is Real

For instance: An experiment with two children. Two researchers have one child each, and each is in a different location.

Researcher Number 1 takes child Number 1 to alpha, and while the child is at alpha says, "Let us create something here." The child doesn't know what he is talking about.

"What's that?"

"I mean, create something. Like drawing something that was not drawn, you are creating a drawing."

"Oh, that."

The child knows what drawing is. He can draw dogs, cats, birds, whatever. He can create a picture of whatever he wants.

So the researcher says, "What do you want to draw."

"What about a new toy car."

"Okay, go ahead and draw a little toy car."

He draws a little toy car. He draws the front wheels, left wheel, right front wheel, connecting those wheels together. He says, "When I finish it, I want to paint it green with red wheels."

He continues drawing it. Hasn't finished yet.

Researcher Number 1 signals Researcher Number 2. Researcher Number 2 takes Child Number 2 to alpha, to project to where Child Number 1 is, then asks, "What is he doing?"

Child Number 2 is doing what is called remote viewing. Child Number 2 says, "He is drawing a little toy car. And he wants to paint it green with red wheels."

The first child has not painted it yet. The second child detected it up from the child's mind, what he planned to do. He already has plans to paint it. He hasn't gone that far yet, in his drawing. But Child Number 2 picked up not only what the first child had done so far, but what he planned to do in the future.

When he finishes—future—he will paint it green, with red wheels.

Now that's remote viewing.

Anybody can do this at alpha.

These are some of the things that can be done at alpha.

How We Detect the Future

So you see, people who have to do things, they have already done in the subjective world.

- The past is composed of materialized thoughts.
- The present is the process of materializing thoughts.
- The future is composed of conceived thoughts, not yet materialized.

Clairvoyants at alpha can get information from the past if they need it; can get what is taking place and changing from one to the other, what is becoming materialized; and can get information from the minds of whoever has conceived it but not yet materialized it.

This is prophecy, when you say this individual has in mind to do this and that. If they don't change their mind between now and then, this is what's going to happen. That's prophecy.

But after they decide what to do, if something happens on the way and actions do not get far enough to materialize those thoughts, and they change their mind, then prophecy is not right. It didn't happen because they changed their mind.

If they had continued with their plans, this is what is going to happen. Period.

How long would it take? It depends on how fast they go at it. And this cannot be determined.

(This was transcribed from a course José Silva taught in Laredo in 1996 called the Metaphysical Laws of Success Course.)

94 Silva Convention Is an Experience to Remember *(1982)*

You can benefit a lot from being in the presence of people who are achievers, people who have accomplished many things in their lives.

Being around such people can inspire you and motivate you in many ways. Not only do you get benefits objectively, but subjectively as well. These people can transmit their energy to you subjectively, and you can feel it and use it to achieve more things yourself.

That is why each year we assemble in Laredo our top researchers and lecturers and graduates from around the world for our Silva Mind Control International Convention.

This year's convention will be unique. Not only will you have an opportunity to hear many of our top researchers and lecturers present workshops, you will also be able to ask them questions during special "rap sessions" we have scheduled.

Topics will include health, business, education, spiritual growth, personal development and more.

You will be able to talk with some of the subjects from my early research projects—my own children—to find out first hand from them how they developed their abilities. This research, of course, led to the development of the Silva Method of Self-Mind Control.

You can talk with scientists who have supported us through the years, who have conducted many projects on our method.

You can talk with lecturers who have been very successful in business using the Silva techniques, and who teach other business people how to be just as successful using the techniques.

There will be people here who have experienced recovery from serious illness through the use of the Silva Method. There will be healers who have proven their effectiveness with "holistic faith healing."

You can question researchers who have studied the effects of the Silva Method in schools, and find out from them how you can better deal with any specific situations you might be encountering in your experience.

There will be lecturers from around the world who will be glad to share with you their excitement at the growth of the Silva Method in fifty-five countries and fourteen languages.

This year's convention will be held the weekend of Oct. 23 and 24, 1982, at the Laredo Civic Center. Lunch will be included both days, as well as admission to the big awards dance on Saturday night when our top lecturers will be presented awards for outstanding service to humanity.

This awards dance offers still another opportunity to meet and talk with many of the most outstanding people in the Silva Mind Control organization in an informal setting.

Other special features are included at this year's convention, like a tour of Nuevo Laredo, Mexico, and a display of all our electronic biofeedback equipment. You can try out the biofeedback equipment and question our technical staff about it during the convention.

We have designed this convention with you in mind. I want to issue you a special invitation to attend this year's convention. I also urge you to register early, by October 1 if possible. Also, you should make your motel reservations by the first of September. There are a lot of rooms available in Laredo, but they do go rapidly.

You will note that I am presenting the Basic Lecture Series the week before the convention. The Ultra Seminar and Graduate Seminar will follow the convention.

I will look forward to seeing you in Laredo, and will do my best to make this the most worthwhile weekend you can imagine.

Note: José Silva wrote many books over the next 15 years, containing a lot of the information that was only available in person back in 1982, and now José Silva Jr. and others who worked with Mr. Silva are writing even more books. They are available at book sellers worldwide, just be sure you are getting authentic books by José Silva or someone who worked with him.

95 Scientists Help Make Sense of Research *(1992)*

Here are some thoughts from two of the leading researchers in the field of the mind and human potential, José Silva and Dr. William Braud, as they answered questions during the last two days of the two week Ultimate Seminar in Laredo, Texas in 1992.

Making Sense

When trying to figure out how something works, Dr. Braud suggests starting with the simplest explanation, and pushing that as far as you can. Only after that do you look for more complicated explanations.

Dr. Braud On Reincarnation

On the subject of reincarnation—whether we have been here before in a previous lifetime—consider this:

If a subject, at a deep level, gives a story of a previous lifetime, the only way to find out if the story could be true is to check it out. If the person said that they lived in a certain town, you go to that town and check the records to see if someone by that name actually lived there.

If you find a record that verifies the person's story, then that could mean that they actually did live there in a pervious life.

But there could also be another explanation.

In order to check it out, a physical record must exist, Dr. Braud points out. And if a physical record exists, then we know that we can mentally project—while at our level—and find out what that record contains, without being regressed back in time.

"If a record exists," Dr. Braud said, "it is accessible to my psychic abilities. I don't have any way to distinguish between the two," he added, referring to his psychic abilities, and the theory of having lived in a past lifetime.

Mental Projection

José Silva verified the concept of mental projection during his early research that eventually led to the Silva Method as we know it today.

He would have a research subject (in the beginning he worked with children) mentally project to a certain location, while at their level.

He would have them imagine walking down the street to a certain building.

Then he would ask them if there was anything unusual about the building.

In one instance, the child observed a brick with a hole in it. The child even told him which row of bricks it was in, and how far from the corner of the building. Silva went to the site and confirmed the information.

"Did the child project there?" Silva asked. "Or did the child get the information from the mind of someone who had seen it?

"We don't know how the child got it. The important things are:

"Did it happen? Does it solve a problem?

"It did happen. And we can use this ability to help us solve problems."

Pendulums-R-Us

Dr. Braud had an interesting way of expressing the way that he and Silva feel about pendulums, automatic writing, dowsing rods and such:

They are ways of expressing information. They are amplifiers of your thoughts, a readout of your thoughts.

Every Silva graduate has worked health detection cases and knows that it is relatively easy to obtain information with your mind and then verify through objective means that you were accurate.

Pendulums, dowsing rods, Ouija boards, crystal balls, cards, and other items are simply a way of displaying the information that you get psychically.

When one participant in the Ultimate Seminar objected that crystals really have some special power that attracts information,

Silva replied that, "You can use it for your benefit because you believe in it."

Get the Picture

José Silva says that the universal language is visual. That's why he recommends that you use your mental screen regularly. Use words to help you create better mental pictures, he recommends.

If you are programming a child to stop wetting the bed, for instance, create mental images of what you desire.

Dr. Braud's research confirms this. "It is easier for a psychic to detect pictures than numbers or letters," he said.

Someone asked Dr. Braud about how to do this to predict the price of silver.

"Associate an increase or decrease with objects," he suggested. Start with five or six objects, and then project forward in time; how many objects are there at the target time? That will let you know what could happen.

It is easier to predict your own future than somebody else's, according to Dr. Braud. It is easier for a psychic to guess what object will be placed in his own hand the next day, than to guess what will happen to somebody else.

Helping Humanity

Dr. Braud had one cautionary note about programming to get things.

He told a story about someone who invested a lot of money and had made more than $100,000 by following the advice of a psychic.

But when the investor got stingy about paying the psychic, and was demanding more work from the psychic, the psychic became much less accurate, so much so that the investor stopped investing.

If people try to use their psychic ability to win money at gambling, Dr. Braud said, they usually will not be very accurate.

It Depends On Their Motives

If you are using your psychic ability for altruistic motives, to build a children's hospital for instance, you may be very accurate.

But an egotistical motive would be wrong, he added, and you probably would not be very accurate.

José Silva reminds that you are judged more on your record—what you have done in the past—than on your promises of what you might be willing to do in the future.

If you have a record of using your abilities to help correct problems, then you will be much more likely to succeed than if you have not done much along these lines in the past.

A promise to build a children's hospital just doesn't measure up with actually getting to work and laying some bricks.

Join Us

You can get insights like these, and more, when you attend José Silva's two-week Ultimate Seminar in Laredo.

Sometimes Dr. Braud joins him for the last two days, other times it is someone else. It is always interesting.

The idea for the Ultimate Seminar came when a retired doctor said that he wanted to know everything that José Silva had learned in his research. The doctor said he didn't care how much it cost, or how long he needed to be in Laredo.

So Silva developed the two-week program to cover the Basic Lecture Series, Ultra Seminar, Graduate Seminar, and additional topics that Silva encountered in his research but that are not covered in any of the other programs.

The Ultimate Seminar is conducted in English in February and August, and in Spanish in November. It is held in Laredo.

Note: José Silva wrote many books containing a lot of the information that was included in his Ultimate Seminar, and now José Silva Jr. and others who worked with Mr. Silva are writing even more books. They are available at book sellers worldwide, just be sure you are getting authentic books by José Silva or someone who worked with him.

96 José Silva's Tips, Insights on Successes *(1994)*

(The following are thoughts from José Silva, collected from his Ultra Seminars and his two-week Ultimate Seminar)

When you succeed at something, you get a unique feeling of success. Even if you are using only one "talent," you can still solve more than one problem. Every time you solve a problem, every time you correct something that is wrong, you accumulate a feeling of success.

There is a special feeling that comes with success, and the only way to get that feeling is to have a success. However, you can review that success and the special feeling of success at your level, and you will receive almost as much benefit as you do when you have a new success.

When you accumulate enough feelings of success, these serve as a key to discover a second talent.

Then you can use the two talents to accumulate enough experience, enough feelings of success, to discover even more talents.

The successes that you accumulate with the first talent might not be enough to lead to the third talent, even though they can help you discover the second talent. But the successes that you have with the first two talents will be enough to help you find the third talent.

Using those three talents will then give you enough successes to discover a fourth talent.

They used to tell us to learn from our failures. Now we know better:

Success cannot be reached on a ladder of failures; greater success can be reached on a ladder of lesser successes.

It is not enough to put together bits of information. Knowledge is to be used, and to be used correctly.

The correct use of knowledge is problem solving.

The truthful truth and the real reality is anything that, when applied, solves problems. If it creates problems, it goes the other direction.

If we can get enough information, we can solve all problems. We can eliminate suffering. So, it is important that we perfect our information gathering techniques.

Our senses are to detect information. We have biological senses, and we also have subjective—mental—senses.

Most people have been using only animal-type senses, the biological senses.

Now we are learning how to also sense with human intelligence type of senses, the subjective senses.

We feel that the fundamental senses are those of human intelligence, the subjective senses. Biological senses are an extension of these.

Visualization is the fundamental sense of human eyesight.

The physical senses (the extensions of the fundamental senses) are limited. They can be fooled. If you put up a wall, you cannot see beyond the wall with the physical senses.

We can see beyond the wall with human intelligence. You cannot fool or hide from the senses of human intelligence.

We were made in the image of our Creator—not in what we can see with our eyes, but what we can do with our human intelligence. It is an image of the Creator's mind, not of the body.

97 Details of Programming Explained
(1982)

Q: Why does programming sometimes fail to work?
A: Programming works. But we may not always work it properly.

The first step in trouble-shooting your programming is to check your desire, belief and expectancy.

Do you really desire what it is you are programming for, or are you just trying it for the fun of it? Is it important to you? Does it serve a purpose?

Does it solve a problem?

Do you have a strong belief factor?

Do you believe you are worthy of what you are seeking, or that the case merits a solution? Do you have any doubts regarding the case? Is your request fair? Is it best for all concerned?

All the ingredients must be right; then you will get your solution. You will get results as long as you are solving problems and helping the Creator in making this planet a better place to live.

Do you really expect it? That is sometimes a difficult factor to accept.

You must program in the future in a past-tense sense. That is, you must "Pray believing you have already received." You must have the "Take it for granted" feeling. That does not mean to program hoping you will get it; it means to program knowing and feeling that you have already gotten it.

To keep your expectancy factor high, program in this manner: First visualize (which means to recall what something looks like) the existing situation, or problem. Follow the instructions for the technique you are using—the Mirror of the Mind or the 3-Scenes Technique. Both are included in the appendix of this book.

Then create (with your imagination) your desired end result, or solution.

In the future, whenever you think of the project, at level or any other time, then visualize the solution image you created previously.

Remember you have already created and received your solution at your level; now just visualize it (recall what your solution looks like).

It is like ordering something from a catalog (or online). You have ordered it, you know it is on the way, and it will show up in your physical environment soon.

The success of your programming is a result of all of the factors involved.

The right ingredients, lightly programmed, will bring successful results.

The wrong ingredients, strongly programmed, will not bring successful results.

When people have a very strong desire, because of a very strong need (such as the need to correct a life-threatening illness, for example) then it does not require as strong an expectancy to obtain successful results. There is enough energy in the desire portion of the formula to insure success.

But when there is not such a strong desire, then it will take a greater expectancy to get results. For instance, if a person programs to win a contest when they do not really need to win the contest, then the belief and expectancy factors need to be stronger for the programming to be effective.

If a person programs for a $250,000-a-year job, but does not need the money and only wants to put it in the bank, then it will be difficult to achieve successful results. It would be better to work up to the ultimate goal in smaller steps, each step programmed according to your needs.

A careful study of the formula will reveal to you why some people get spectacular results with their programming when they first learn the Silva Method, but then seem to be less successful later. At first, they program for things for which they have a very strong need, thus a very strong desire.

This compensates for a modest expectancy factor.

If the initial success causes the person to develop very strong belief and expectancy factors, then future programming will also be successful.

As the problems become less important, it is more important that you include the right ingredients, applied properly, to your programming. It is more important then that you put more of your positive, expectant, energy into your programming.

As long as one of the three factors (desire, belief, expectancy) is very strong, it will carry the other two along with it. But all three must be present.

This is a "tri-cycle" formula. Practice, and you will succeed.

How To Reinforce Your Programming

Whenever you happen to think of your project during the day, visualize the solution image you created previously. If you don't have time to enter the alpha level, then visualize it at beta, even with your eyes open. Mind guides brain and brain guides body so always think of the solution.

You should go to level to reinforce your programming at least once every 72 hours. On important projects, it would be good to reinforce at level every night. When doing this, be sure to imagine or recall the feeling you would associate with success; have a feeling that you have already received it.

At the beta dimension, you should have a positive expectancy; at the alpha dimension, you should have the attitude that the project has already been successfully completed. You have planted a seed. At the subjective dimension, your project has been completed; physics is like soil and it will take time for the seed to grow through that "soil" and surface where it can be seen in the physical dimension.

Expect your results at beta, accept your results at alpha.

If, after a period of time, you have not seen any results, then add: "May the best thing happen for all concerned."

Adopt the attitude that it has not worked so far, but from this day on the programming will succeed. You are adding another ingredient; you do not need to continue reinforcing your programming. The final result might be a modified result, because your original request was not best for all concerned.

98 Here Is How a Natural Psychic Functions *(1984)*

Q: When I am working health cases, I generally "sense" information rather than perceiving it through mental pictures.

Does this mean I am clairsensient, a sensitive? If so, what is the best way for me to practice?

A: (By José Silva): Terms like clairsensient really do not mean anything at all. You are able to sense information from the subjective dimension, and you sense it exactly the way I do, and the way all of the best psychics do: you simply "know."

To develop accuracy and proficiency, there are certain steps you take as this "knowledge" comes to you.

Let me explain in more detail.

During our research, when subjects started working cases, they would just bring up information, and when we asked them why, they said, "I don't know why I know, I just know."

When people practice working health cases, eventually they get that feeling.

That is why we tell people, in the directives for orientologists, to say anything that enters the mind, because that might be the information they are looking for. It comes to you without even looking for it.

When working cases, we have psychics create a mental image of the body so they will get tuned in to the right person. We establish points of reference with the subject's name and the mental picture, and go from there. First you need to make contact with the correct subject.

After you have a mental picture of the correct body, then notice what idea comes to you.

What part of the body comes to mind? After that, then you go to that part of the body and check it out. If you think the problem might be in the chest, then create a mental picture of the chest and check it out, to verify your information.

After you create a mental picture of the chest, if you think the problem could be the heart, create a mental picture of the heart and check it out.

Once you are attracted to a part of the body, you express in words to the orientologist what you sense, and you express the same thing in mental pictures for yourself to aid you in tuning in to it.

You are not attracted first by a mental picture, but by a feeling, a sense of knowing. Then you create a mental picture so you can better tune in, focus on the specific area.

In other words, first you get an idea, a feeling, about the case, and then you express this feeling in mental pictures and words. The mental pictures are for your benefit, the words are for the benefit of others as well as yourself.

All of this may happen so rapidly that you do not realize that this is what is happening.

You may believe that the mental pictures come first, but at some level, you get the information first, and then create the mental pictures to express what you sense.

Then you observe the mental pictures and describe them with words to other people.

Of course, if you convert the information you receive to words first, instead of pictures, then you might feel that you are clairaudient.

The idea of being clairvoyant, or clairaudient, or clairsensient doesn't mean anything. It is all in one. All the faculties function at the same time. All the faculties come to bear on a problem, but they do not come one at a time, they come together. This creates the "feeling" of "knowing" the desired information, which you then convert to mental pictures, or words, or a feeling in your body.

When sensing information from the subjective dimension, we do so through what is called general ESP. It is a combination of all of the senses. It will only make it more difficult for you if you try to focus on just one means of sensing, for instance to try to "see" the problem, or "hear" the problem, or "feel" the problem.

The information will come to you, and you can make a mental picture, or put it into words or feelings—whatever is easiest for you, to help you focus in on it better and understand it in more depth. But remember the information comes first as a sense of knowing.

To Review:

When working a case, first you are given some information about the subject to help you tune in, so you take this information you hear and, using your hands to help you create a mental picture of the person. One person compared this to desiring to see a certain television program, then turning on the set and switching to the correct channel.

Then you use the mental picture you create, and continue using your hands to tune in and sense additional information about where to look for the problem.

You pick three parts of the body, and create more detailed mental pictures of one of those parts of the body. As ideas come to you, continue to create mental images, imagine what it would look like if you saw those thoughts. This will help you tune in even more.

As it says in the directions to orientologists, the directions used to guide a psychic in effective case working, "Sense it, feel it, visualize it, imagine it, create it, know it is there, take it for granted it is there."

This is general ESP, the way all psychics function, whether they realize it or not.

99 Leave a Legacy to Be Proud of
(1996)

During my 82 years on this planet, I've learned that the only thing that's permanent in life is the legacy that you leave.

The radios that I learned to repair as a teenager are now antiques that are nice to look at but have no practical value today. When is the last time you saw a vacuum tube?

I've traveled all over the world presenting the Silva Method. I've seen the ancient ruins in Rome, that were once part of the greatest empire the world has ever known. They remind me of a story I once heard about a ruler who presided over a great city.

Archaeologists found the ruins of this city that had once been so great, and among the ruins they found a portion of the base of a statue.

The statue had been of the great ruler. All that was left was part of the inscription, which read: "Here lies Ozymandeus, King of Kings. Look on these works, ye mighty, and despair."

The irony was that he had intended that they could never create anything so great as he had, but in reality, he demonstrated that nothing is so great that it will last forever.

Except the legacy that you leave.

Your Legacy

Everybody leaves a legacy:

World leaders who must carefully watch every word that they utter have an obvious impact on the world.

Every child that is born produces a powerful effect on the parents and grandparents and perhaps many others. If you've ever had a child, or a grandchild, or even a great grandchild as I have, then you know that this changes you.

You never know what small action of yours might bring about a big change. The psychiatrist in the Army induction center probably never even remembered that he suggested that I read *The History of Psychiatry*, but that one bit of guidance started me on the path that led to the Silva Method, which has now helped millions of people throughout the world.

What Will You Leave?

Sometimes a tiny kindness has a ripple effect that grows as it goes forward, until it makes a huge difference.

Sometimes a mean gesture also has a ripple effect that winds up hurting many people.

You never know, at the time, what the effect will be.

Think about some of the people in your life: people who gave you a word of encouragement that you still remember; people who were indifferent, or even cruel. They might not even remember it.

But you remember it. And perhaps it influences your life:

- You pass on the kind gesture to others, who in turn pass on that gesture.
- Your hurt and resentment cause you to say or do things you don't really mean, and people learn from your example.

Long after we are all gone, long after the great cities of today have crumbled, long after our modern technology is rendered obsolete, long after our greatest leaders are just names that students read in history books, your legacy will still live.

It will live in the lives of people who follow us. The things that you do spread out, and give you a type of immortality.

Superior Human Being

Here is a formula that I included in the Silva Method, that will help insure that you leave a positive legacy:

"You will continue to strive to take part in constructive and creative activities to make this a better world to live in, so that when we move on, we shall have left behind a better world for those who follow."

"You will consider the whole of humanity, depending on their ages, as fathers or mothers, brothers or sisters, sons or daughters."

"You are a superior human being; you have greater understanding, compassion, and patience with others."

What kind of legacy do you want to leave?

Someone once suggested that you do every act as if it would be your last. How do you want to be remembered?

Go to level. Think about your life at the alpha level, the ideal level to think on. Plan what you are going to do with your life, so as to leave a legacy that you can be proud of.

100 Principles of a Global Ethic
(1997)

(The From the Founder column consisted of the complete "Principles of a Global Ethic" that came from the Parliament of the World's Religions, September 4, 1993, in Chicago, Illinois, which was signed by 143 respected leaders from all of the world's major faiths.)

The Principles

Our world is experiencing a fundamental crisis: A crisis in global economy, global ecology, and global politics. The lack of a grand vision, the tangle of unresolved problems, political paralysis, mediocre political leadership with little insight or foresight, and in general too little sense for the commonweal are seen everywhere: Too many old answers to new challenges.

Hundreds of millions of human beings on our planet increasingly suffer from unemployment, poverty, hunger, and the destruction of their families. Hope for a lasting peace among nations slips away from us. There are tensions between the sexes and generations. Children die, kill, and are killed. More and more countries are shaken by corruption in politics and business. It is increasingly difficult to live together peacefully in our cities because of social, racial, and ethnic conflicts, the abuse of drugs, organized crime, and even anarchy. Even neighbors often live in fear of one another. Our planet continues to be ruthlessly plundered. A collapse of the ecosystem threatens us.

Time and again we see leaders and members of religions incite aggression, fanaticism, hate, and xenophobia-even inspire and legitimize violent and bloody conflicts. Religion often is misused for purely power-political goals, including war. We are filled with disgust.

We condemn these blights and declare that they need not be. An ethic already exists within the religious teachings of the world which can counter the global distress. Of course this ethic provides no direct solution for all the immense problems of the world, but it does supply the moral foundation for a better individual and global order: A vision which can lead women and men away from despair, and society away from chaos.

We are persons who have committed ourselves to the precepts and practices of the world's religions. We confirm that there is already a consensus among the religions which can be the basis for a global ethic—a minimal fundamental consensus concerning binding values, irrevocable standards, and fundamental moral attitudes.

I. No New Global Order Without a New Global Ethic!

We women and men of various religions and regions of Earth therefore address all people, religious and non-religious. We wish to express the following convictions which we hold in common:

- We all have a responsibility for a better global order.
- Our involvement for the sake of human rights, freedom, justice, peace, and the preservation of Earth is absolutely necessary.
- Our different religious and cultural traditions must not prevent our common involvement in opposing all forms of inhumanity and working for greater humaneness.
- The principles expressed in this Global Ethic can be affirmed by all persons with ethical convictions, whether religiously grounded or not.
- As religious and spiritual persons we base our lives on an Ultimate Reality, and draw spiritual power and hope therefrom, in trust, in prayer or meditation, in word or silence. We have a special responsibility for the welfare of all humanity and care for the planet Earth. We do not consider ourselves better than other women and men, but we trust that the ancient wisdom of our religions can point the way for the future.

After two world wars and the end of the cold war, the collapse of fascism and nazism, the shaking to the foundations of communism and colonialism, humanity has entered a new phase of its history. Today we possess sufficient economic, cultural, and spiritual resources to introduce a better global order. But old and new ethnic, national, social, economic, and religious tensions threaten the peaceful building of a better world. We have experienced greater technological progress than ever before, yet we see that worldwide poverty, hunger, death of children, unemployment, misery, and the destruction of nature have not diminished but rather have increased. Many people are threatened with economic ruin, social disarray, political marginalization, ecological catastrophe, and national collapse.

In such a dramatic global situation humanity needs a vision of people living peacefully together, of ethnic and ethical groupings and of religions sharing responsibility for the care of Earth. A vision rests on hopes, goals, ideals, standards. But all over the world these have slipped from our hands. Yet we are convinced that, despite their frequent abuses and failures, it is the communities of faith who bear a responsibility to demonstrate that such hopes, ideals, and standards can be guarded, grounded, and lived. This is especially true in the modern state. Guarantees of freedom of conscience and religion are necessary but they do not substitute for binding values, convictions, and norms which are valid for all humans regardless of their social origin, sex, skin color, language, or religion.

We are convinced of the fundamental unity of the human family on Earth. We recall the 1948 Universal Declaration of Human Rights of the United Nations. What it formally proclaimed on the level of rights we wish to confirm and deepen here from the perspective of an ethic: The full realization of the intrinsic dignity of the human person, the inalienable freedom and equality in principle of all humans, and the necessary solidarity and interdependence of all humans with each other.

On the basis of personal experiences and the burdensome history of our planet we have learned

- that a better global order cannot be created or enforced by laws, prescriptions, and conventions alone;

- that the realization of peace, justice, and the protection of Earth depends on the insight and readiness of men and women to act justly;
- that action in favor of rights and freedoms presumes a consciousness of responsibility and duty, and that therefore both the minds and hearts of women and men must be addressed;
- that rights without morality cannot long endure, and that there will be no better global order without a global ethic.

By a global ethic we do not mean a global ideology or a single unified religion beyond all existing religions, and certainly not the domination of one religion over all others. By a global ethic we mean a fundamental consensus on binding values, irrevocable standards, and personal attitudes. Without such a fundamental consensus on an ethic, sooner or later every community will be threatened by chaos or dictatorship, and individuals will despair.

II. A fundamental demand: Every human being must be treated humanely

We all are fallible, imperfect men and women with limitations and defects. We know the reality of evil. Precisely because of this, we feel compelled for the sake of global welfare to express what the fundamental elements of a global ethic should be-for individuals as well as for communities and organizations, for states as well as for the religions themselves. We trust that our often millennia-old religious and ethical traditions provide an ethic which is convincing and practicable for all women and men of good will, religious and non-religious.

At the same time we know that our various religious and ethical traditions often offer very different bases for what is helpful and what is unhelpful for men and women, what is right and what is wrong, what is good and what is evil. We do not wish to gloss over or ignore the serious differences among the individual religions. However, they should not hinder us from proclaiming publicly those things which we already hold in common and which we jointly affirm, each on the basis of our own religious or ethical grounds.

We know that religions cannot solve the environmental, economic, political, and social problems of Earth. However they can provide what obviously cannot be attained by economic plans, political programs, or legal regulations alone: A change in the inner orientation, the whole mentality, the "hearts" of people, and a conversion from a false path to a new orientation for life. Humankind urgently needs social and ecological reforms, but it needs spiritual renewal just as urgently. As religious or spiritual persons we commit ourselves to this task. The spiritual powers of the religions can offer a fundamental sense of trust, a ground of meaning, ultimate standards, and a spiritual home. Of course religions are credible only when they eliminate those conflicts which spring from the religions themselves, dismantling mutual arrogance, mistrust, prejudice, and even hostile images, and thus demonstrate respect for the traditions, holy places, feasts, and rituals of people who believe differently.

Now as before, women and men are treated inhumanely all over the world. They are robbed of their opportunities and their freedom; their human rights are trampled underfoot; their dignity is disregarded. But might does not make right! In the face of all inhumanity our religious and ethical convictions demand that every human being must be treated humanely!

This means that every human being without distinction of age, sex, race, skin color, physical or mental ability, language, religion, political view, or national or social origin possesses an inalienable and untouchable dignity, and everyone, the individual as well as the state, is therefore obliged to honor this dignity and protect it. Humans must always be the subjects of rights, must be ends, never mere means, never objects of commercialization and industrialization in economics, politics and media, in research institutes, and industrial corporations. No one stands "above good and evil"-no human being, no social class, no influential interest group, no cartel, no police apparatus, no army, and no state. On the contrary: Possessed of reason and conscience, every human is obliged to behave in a genuinely human fashion, to do good and avoid evil!

III. Irrevocable Directives
1. COMMITMENT TO A CULTURE OF NON-VIOLENCE AND RESPECT FOR LIFE

Numberless women and men of all regions and religions strive to lead lives not determined by egoism but by commitment to their fellow humans and to the world around them. Nevertheless, all over the world we find endless hatred, envy, jealousy, and violence, not only between individuals but also between social and ethnic groups, between classes, races, nations, and religions. The use of violence, drug trafficking and organized crime, often equipped with new technical possibilities, has reached global proportions. Many places still are ruled by terror "from above;" dictators oppress their own people, and institutional violence is widespread. Even in some countries where laws exist to protect individual freedoms, prisoners are tortured, men and women are mutilated, hostages are killed.

a) In the great ancient religious and ethical traditions of human-kind we find the directive: You shall not kill! Or in positive terms: Have respect for life! Let us reflect anew on the consequences of this ancient directive: All people have a right to life, safety, and the free development of personality insofar as they do not injure the rights of others. No one has the right physically or psychically to tor-ture, injure, much less kill, any other human being. And no people, no state, no race, no religion has the right to hate, to discriminate against, to "cleanse," to exile, much less to liquidate a "foreign" minority which is different in behavior or holds different beliefs.

b) Of course, wherever there are humans there will be con-flicts. Such conflicts, however, should be resolved without violence within a framework of justice. This is true for states as well as for individuals. Persons who hold political power must work within the framework of a just order and commit themselves to the most non-violent, peaceful solutions possible. And they should work for this within an international order of peace which itself has need of pro-tection and defense against perpetrators of violence. Armament is a mistaken path; disarmament is the commandment of the times. Let no one be deceived: There is no survival for humanity without global peace!

c) Young people must learn at home and in school that violence may not be a means of settling differences with others. Only thus can a culture of non-violence be created.

d) A human person is infinitely precious and must be uncondi- tionally protected. But likewise the lives of animals and plants which inhabit this planet with us deserve protection, preservation, and care. Limitless exploitation of the natural foundations of life, ruth- less destruction of the biosphere, and militarization of the cosmos are all outrages. As human beings we have a special responsibility- especially with a view to future generations-for Earth and the cosmos, for the air, water, and soil. We are all intertwined together in this cosmos and we are all dependent on each other. Each one of us depends on the welfare of all. Therefore the dominance of humanity over nature and the cosmos must not be encouraged. Instead we must cultivate living in harmony with nature and the cosmos.

e) To be authentically human in the spirit of our great religious and ethical traditions means that in public as well as in private life we must be concerned for others and ready to help. We must never be ruthless and brutal. Every people, every race, every reli- gion must show tolerance and respect-indeed high appreciation-for every other. Minorities need protection and support, whether they be racial, ethnic, or religious.

2. COMMITMENT TO A CULTURE OF SOLIDARITY AND A JUST ECONOMIC ORDER

Numberless men and women of all regions and religions strive to live their lives in solidarity with one another and to work for authen- tic fulfillment of their vocations. Nevertheless, all over the world we find endless hunger, deficiency, and need. Not only individuals, but especially unjust institutions and structures are responsible for these tragedies. Millions of people are without work; millions are exploited by poor wages, forced to the edges of society, with their possibilities for the future destroyed. In many lands the gap between the poor and the rich, between the powerful and the powerless is immense. We live in a world in which totalitarian state socialism as well as unbridled capitalism have hollowed out and destroyed many ethical and spiritual values. A materialistic mentality breeds greed for unlimited profit and a grasping for endless plunder. These demands claim more and more of the community's resources without obliging the individual to contribute more. The cancerous social evil of corruption thrives in the developing countries and in the developed countries alike.

a) In the great ancient religious and ethical traditions of humankind we find the directive: You shall not steal! Or in positive terms: Deal honestly and fairly! Let us reflect anew on the consequences of this ancient directive: No one has the right to rob or dispossess in any way whatsoever any other person or the commonweal. Further, no one has the right to use her or his possessions without concern for the needs of society and Earth.

b) Where extreme poverty reigns, helplessness and despair spread, and theft occurs again and again for the sake of survival. Where power and wealth are accumulated ruthlessly, feelings of envy, resentment, and deadly hatred and rebellion inevitably well up in the disadvantaged and marginalized. This leads to a vicious circle of violence and counter-violence. Let no one be deceived: There is no global peace without global justice!

c) Young people must learn at home and in school that property, limited though it may be, carries with it an obligation, and that its uses should at the same time serve the common good. Only thus can a just economic order be built up.

d) If the plight of the poorest billions of humans on this planet, particularly women and children, is to be improved, the world economy must be structured more justly. Individual good deeds, and assistance projects, indispensable though they be, are insufficient. The participation of all states and the authority of international organizations are needed to build just economic institutions.

A solution which can be supported by all sides must be sought for the debt crisis and the poverty of the dissolving second world, and even more the third world. Of course conflicts of interest are unavoidable. In the developed countries, a distinction must be made between necessary and limitless consumption, between socially beneficial and non-beneficial uses of property, between justified and unjustified uses of natural resources, and between a profit-only and a socially beneficial and ecologically oriented market economy. Even the developing nations must search their national consciences. Wherever those ruling threaten to repress those ruled, wherever institutions threaten persons, and wherever might oppresses right, we are obligated to resist-whenever possible non-violently.

e) To be authentically human in the spirit of our great religious and ethical traditions means the following:

- We must utilize economic and political power for service to humanity instead of misusing it in ruthless battles for domination. We must develop a spirit of compassion with those who suffer, with special care for the children, the aged, the poor, the disabled, the refugees, and the lonely.
- We must cultivate mutual respect and consideration, so as to reach a reasonable balance of interests, instead of thinking only of unlimited power and unavoidable competitive struggles.
- We must value a sense of moderation and modesty instead of an unquenchable greed for money, prestige, and consumption. In greed humans lose their "souls," their freedom, their composure, their inner peace, and thus that which makes them human.

3. COMMITMENT TO A CULTURE OF TOLERANCE AND A LIFE OF TRUTHFULNESS

Numberless women and men of all regions and religions strive to lead lives of honesty and truthfulness. Nevertheless, all over the world we find endless lies and deceit, swindling and hypocrisy, ideology and demagoguery:

- Politicians and business people who use lies as a means to success;
- Mass media which spread ideological propaganda instead of accurate reporting, misinformation instead of information, cynical commercial interest instead of loyalty to the truth;
- Scientists and researchers who give themselves over to morally questionable ideological or political programs or to economic interest groups, or who justify research which violates fundamental ethical values;
- Representatives of religions who dismiss other religions as of little value and who preach fanaticism and intolerance instead of respect and understanding.

a) In the great ancient religious and ethical traditions of humankind we find the directive: You shall not lie! Or in positive terms: Speak and act truthfully! Let us reflect anew on the consequences of this ancient directive: No woman or man, no institution, no state or church or religious community has the right to speak lies to other humans.

b) This is especially true
- for those who work in the mass media, to whom we entrust the freedom to report for the sake of truth and to whom we thus grant the office of guardian. They do not stand above morality but have the obligation to respect human dignity, human rights, and fundamental values. They are duty-bound to objectivity, fairness, and the preservation of human dignity. They have no right to intrude into individuals' private spheres, to manipulate public opinion, or to distort reality;
- for artists, writers, and scientists, to whom we entrust artistic and academic freedom. They are not exempt from general ethical standards and must serve the truth;
- for the leaders of countries, politicians, and political parties, to whom we entrust our own freedoms. When they lie in the faces of their people, when they manipulate the truth, or when they are guilty of venality or ruthlessness in domestic

or foreign affairs, they forsake their credibility and deserve to lose their offices and their voters. Conversely, public opinion should support those politicians who dare to speak the truth to the people at all times;

- finally, for representatives of religion. When they stir up prejudice, hatred, and enmity towards those of different belief, or even incite or legitimize religious wars, they deserve the condemnation of humankind and the loss of their adherents.

Let no one be deceived: There is no global justice without truthfulness and humaneness!

4. COMMITMENT TO A CULTURE OF EQUAL RIGHTS AND PARTNERSHIP BETWEEN MEN AND WOMEN

Numberless men and women of all regions and religions strive to live their lives in a spirit of partnership and responsible action in the areas of love, sexuality, and family. Nevertheless, all over the world there are condemnable forms of patriarchy, domination of one sex over the other, exploitation of women, sexual misuse of children, and forced prostitution. Too frequently, social incquities force women and even children into prostitution as a means of survival-particularly in less developed countries.

a) In the great ancient religious and ethical traditions of humankind we find the directive: You shall not commit sexual immorality! Or in positive terms: Respect and love one another! Let us reflect anew on the consequences of this ancient directive: No one has the right to degrade others to mere sex objects, to lead them into or hold them in sexual dependency.

b) We condemn sexual exploitation and sexual discrimination as one of the worst forms of human degradation. We have the duty to resist wherever the domination of one sex over the other is preached-even in the name of religious conviction; wherever sexual exploitation is tolerated, wherever prostitution is fostered or children are misused. Let no one be deceived: There is no authentic humaneness without a living together in partnership!

c) Young people must learn at home and in school that sexuality is not a negative, destructive, or exploitative force, but creative and affirmative. Sexuality as a life-affirming shaper of community can only be effective when partners accept the responsibilities of caring for one another's happiness.

d) The relationship between women and men should be characterized not by patronizing behavior or exploitation, but by love, partnership, and trustworthiness. Human fulfillment is not identical with sexual pleasure. Sexuality should express and reinforce a loving relationship lived by equal partners.

Some religious traditions know the ideal of a voluntary renunciation of the full use of sexuality. Voluntary renunciation also can be an expression of identity and meaningful fulfillment.

e) The social institution of marriage, despite all its cultural and religious variety, is characterized by love, loyalty, and permanence. It aims at and should guarantee security and mutual support to husband, wife, and child. It should secure the rights of all family members. All lands and cultures should develop economic and social relationships which will enable marriage and family life worthy of human beings, especially for older people. Children have a right of access to education. Parents should not exploit children, nor children parents. Their relationships should reflect mutual respect, appreciation, and concern.

f) To be authentically human in the spirit of our great religious and ethical traditions means the following:

- We need mutual respect, partnership, and understanding, instead of patriarchal domination and degradation, which are expressions of violence and engender counter-violence.
- We need mutual concern, tolerance, readiness for reconciliation, and love, instead of any form of possessive lust or sexual misuse.

Only what has already been experienced in personal and familial relationships can be practiced on the level of nations and religions.

IV. A Transformation of Consciousness!

Historical experience demonstrates the following: Earth cannot be changed for the better unless we achieve a transformation in the consciousness of individuals and in public life. The possibilities for transformation have already been glimpsed in areas such as war and peace, economy, and ecology, where in recent decades fundamental changes have taken place. This transformation must also be achieved in the area of ethics and values!

Every individual has intrinsic dignity and inalienable rights, and each also has an inescapable responsibility for what she or he does and does not do. All our decisions and deeds, even our omissions and failures, have consequences.

Keeping this sense of responsibility alive, deepening it and passing it on to future generations, is the special task of religions.

We are realistic about what we have achieved in this consensus, and so we urge that the following be observed:

1. A universal consensus on many disputed ethical questions (from bio- and sexual ethics through mass media and scientific ethics to economic and political ethics) will be difficult to attain. Nevertheless, even for many controversial questions, suitable solutions should be attainable in the spirit of the fundamental principles we have jointly developed here.

2. In many areas of life a new consciousness of ethical responsibility has already arisen. Therefore we would be pleased if as many professions as possible, such as those of physicians, scientists, business people, journalists, and politicians, would develop up-to-date codes of ethics which would provide specific guidelines for the vexing questions of these particular professions.

3. Above all, we urge the various communities of faith to formulate their very specific ethics: What does each faith tradition have to say, for example, about the meaning of

life and death, the enduring of suffering and the forgiveness of guilt, about selfless sacrifice and the necessity of renunciation, about compassion and joy. These will deepen, and make more specific, the already discernible global ethic.

Our Appeal to You

In conclusion, we appeal to all the inhabitants of this planet. Earth cannot be changed for the better unless the consciousness of individuals is changed. We pledge to work for such transformation in individual and collective consciousness, for the awakening of our spiritual powers through reflection, meditation, prayer, or positive thinking, for a conversion of the heart. Together we can move mountains! Without a willingness to take risks and a readiness to sacrifice there can be no fundamental change in our situation! Therefore we commit ourselves to a common global ethic, to better mutual understanding, as well as to socially beneficial, peace-fostering, and Earth-friendly ways of life.

We invite all men and women, whether religious or not, to do the same.

Appendix A

About the Silva Centering Exercise

The Silva Centering Exercise helps you discover an inner dimension, a dimension that you can use to become healthier, luckier, and more successful in achieving your goals.

When you learn to function from this inner dimension, you automatically become more spiritual, more human, healthier, safer from accidents, and a more successful problem-solver.

In order for you to use this inner dimension, you need to hear the Silva Centering Exercise a total of ten hours, and to follow the simple directions in the mind exercise.

4 Ways to Learn

There are 4 ways you can proceed to find the alpha brain wave level with the Silva Centering Exercise, so choose the one that is best for you:

1. The Free Lessons at the SilvaNow.com website
2. Record the script below and listen to the recording
3. Have somebody read the script to you
4. Memorize the script—memorize the steps and follow them

How to Read the Silva Centering Exercise

When reading the Silva Centering Exercise, read in a relaxed, natural voice. Be close enough so that the listener can hear you comfortably. Read loud enough to be heard, and read as though you were reading to a seven year old child. Speak each word clearly and distinctly.

Have the listener assume a comfortable position. A sitting position is preferred, but the most important thing is to make sure the listener is comfortable. If uncomfortable, the listener will not relax as much and will not get as much benefit from the exercise.

Avoid distractions, such as loud outside noises. There should be enough light so you can read comfortably, but not extremely bright lights.

If the person shows any signs of nervousness or appears to be uncomfortable, stop reading, tell them to relax and make themselves comfortable. When they are comfortable and ready, then go back to the beginning and start again.

Take your time when you read; there is no need to rush.

Note: Do not read the titles out loud, they are for your benefit.

The Silva Centering Exercise Script
DEEPENING (PHYSICAL RELAXATION AT LEVEL 3)

Find a comfortable position, close your eyes, take a deep breath and while exhaling, mentally repeat and visualize number 3 three times. (pause)

To help you learn to relax physically at level 3, I am going to direct your attention to different parts of your body.

Concentrate your sense of awareness on your scalp, the skin that covers your head; you will detect a fine vibration, a tingling sensation, a feeling of warmth caused by circulation. (pause) Now release and completely relax all tensions and ligament pressures from this part of your head and place it in a deep state of relaxation that will grow deeper as we continue. (pause)

Concentrate your sense of awareness on your forehead, the skin that covers your forehead; you will detect a fine vibration, a tingling sensation, a feeling of warmth caused by circulation. (pause) Now release and completely relax all tensions and ligament pressures from this part of your head and place it in a deep state of relaxation that will grow deeper as we continue. (pause)

Concentrate your sense of awareness on your eyelids and the tissue surrounding your eyes; you will detect a fine vibration, a tingling sensation, a feeling of warmth caused by circulation. (pause) Now release and completely relax all tensions and ligament pressures from this part of your head and place it in a deep state of relaxation that will grow deeper as we continue. (pause)

Concentrate your sense of awareness on your face, the skin covering your cheeks; you will detect a fine vibration, a tingling sensation, a feeling of warmth caused by circulation. (pause) Now release and completely relax all tensions and ligament pressures from this part of your head and place it in a deep state of relaxation that will grow deeper as we continue. (pause)

Concentrate on the outer portion of your throat, the skin covering your throat area; you will detect a fine vibration, a tingling sensation, a feeling of warmth caused by circulation. (pause) Now release and completely relax all tensions and ligament pressures from this part of your body and place it in a deep state of relaxation that will grow deeper as we continue. (pause)

Concentrate within the throat area and relax all tensions and ligament pressures from this part of your body and place it in a deep state of relaxation going deeper and deeper every time. (pause)

Concentrate on your shoulders; feel your clothing in contact with your body. (pause) Feel the skin and the vibration of the skin covering this part of your body. (pause) Relax all tensions and ligament pressures and place your shoulders in a deep state of relaxation going deeper and deeper every time. (pause)

Concentrate on your chest; feel your clothing in contact with this part of your body. (pause) Feel the skin and the vibration of your skin covering your chest. (pause) Relax all tensions and ligament pressures and place your chest in a deep state of relaxation going deeper and deeper every time. (pause)

Concentrate within the chest area; relax all organs; relax all glands; relax all tissues, including the cells themselves and cause them to function in a rhythmic, healthy manner. (pause)

Concentrate on your abdomen; feel the clothing in contact with this part of your body. (pause) Feel the skin and the vibration of your skin covering your abdomen. (pause) Relax all tensions and ligament pressures and place your abdomen in a deep state of relaxation going deeper and deeper every time. (pause)

Concentrate within the abdominal area; relax all organs; relax all glands; relax all tissues, including the cells themselves and cause them to function in a rhythmic, healthy manner. (pause)

Concentrate on your thighs; feel your clothing in contact with this part of your body. (pause) Feel the skin and the vibration of your skin covering your thighs. (pause) Relax all tensions and ligament pressures and place your thighs in a deep state of relaxation going deeper and deeper every time. (pause)

Sense the vibrations at the bones within the thighs; by now these vibrations should be easily detectable. (pause)

Concentrate on your knees; feel the skin and the vibration of your skin covering the knees. (pause) Relax all tensions and ligament pressures and place your knees in a deep state of relaxation going deeper and deeper every time (pause)

Concentrate on your calves; feel the skin and the vibration of the skin covering your calves. (pause) Relax all tensions and ligament pressures and place these parts of your body in a deep state of relaxation, going deeper and deeper every time. (pause)

To enter a deeper, healthier level of mind, concentrate on your toes. (pause) Enter a deeper, healthier level of mind.

To enter a deeper, healthier level of mind, concentrate on the soles of your feet. (pause) Enter a deeper, healthier level of mind. (pause)

To enter a deeper, healthier level of mind, concentrate on the heels of your feet. (pause) Enter a deeper, healthier level of mind. (pause)

Now cause your feet to feel as though they do not belong to your body. (pause)

Feel your feet as though they do not belong to your body. (pause)

Your feet feel as though they do not belong to your body. (pause)

Your feet, ankles, calves, and knees feel as though they do not belong to your body. (pause)

Your feet, ankles, calves, knees, thighs, waist, shoulders, arms, and hands feel as though they do not belong to your body. (pause)

You are now at a deeper, healthier level of mind, deeper than before.

This is your physical relaxation level 3. Whenever you mentally repeat and visualize the number 3, your body will relax as completely as you are now, and more so every time you practice.

DEEPENING (MENTAL RELAXATION AT LEVEL 2)

To enter the mental relaxation level 2, mentally repeat and visualize the number 2 several times, and you are at level 2, a deeper level than 3. (pause) Level 2 is for mental relaxation, where noises will not distract you. Instead, noises will help you to relax mentally more and more.

To help you learn to relax mentally at level 2, I am going to call your attention to different passive scenes. Visualizing any scene that makes you tranquil and passive, will help you relax mentally.

Your being at the beach on a nice summer day may be a tranquil and passive scene for you. (pause)

A day out fishing may be a tranquil and passive scene for you. (pause) A tranquil and passive scene for you may be a walk through the woods on a beautiful summer day, when the breeze is just right, where there are tall shade trees, beautiful flowers, a very blue sky, an occasional white cloud, birds singing in the distance, even squirrels playing on the tree limbs. Hear birds singing in the distance. (pause) This is mental relaxation level 2, where noises will not distract you.

To enhance mental relaxation at level 2, practice visualizing tranquil and passive scenes.

TO ENTER YOUR CENTER

To enter level 1, mentally repeat and visualize the number 1 several times. (pause)

You are now at level 1, the basic level where you can function from your center.

DEEPENING EXERCISES

To enter deeper, healthier levels of mind, practice with the count-down deepening exercises.

To deepen, count downward from 25 to 1, or from 50 to 1, or from 100 to 1. When you reach the count of 1, you will have reached a deeper, healthier level of mind, deeper than before.

You will always have full control and complete dominion over your faculties and senses at all levels of the mind including the outer conscious level.

WHEN TO PRACTICE

The best time to practice the count-down deepening exercises is in the morning when you wake up. Remain in bed at least five minutes practicing the count-down deepening exercises.

The second best time to practice is at night, when you are ready to retire.

The third best time to practice is at noon after lunch.

5 minutes of practice is good; 10 minutes is very good; 15 minutes is excellent.

To practice once a day is good; 2 times a day is very good; and 3 times a day is excellent.

If you have a health problem, practice for 15 minutes 3 times a day.

TO COME OUT OF LEVELS

To come out of any level of the mind, count to yourself mentally from 1 to 5 and tell yourself that at the count of 5 you will open your eyes, be wide awake, feeling fine and in perfect health, feeling better than before.

Then proceed to count slowly from 1 to 2, then to 3, and at the count of 3 mentally remind yourself that at the count of 5 you will open your eyes, be wide awake, feeling fine and in prefect health, feeling better than before.

Proceed to count slowly to 4, then to 5. At the count of 5 and with your eyes open, mentally tell yourself, "I am wide awake, feeling fine, and in perfect health, feeling better than before. And this is so."

DEEPENING (ROUTINE CYCLE)

To help you enter a deeper, healthier level of mind, I am going to count from 10 to 1. On each descending number, you will feel yourself going deeper and you will enter a deeper, healthier level of mind.

10 - 9 - Feel going deeper,

8 - 7 - 6 - deeper and deeper,

5 - 4 - 3 - deeper and deeper,

2 - 1

You are now at a deeper, healthier level of mind, deeper than before.

You may enter a deeper, healthier level of mind by simply relaxing your eyelids. Relax your eyelids. (pause) Feel how relaxed they are. (pause) Allow this feeling of relaxation to flow slowly downward throughout your body, all the way down to your toes. (pause)

It is a wonderful feeling to be deeply relaxed, a very healthy state of being.

To help you enter a deeper, healthier level of mind, I am going to count from 1 to 3. At that moment, you will project yourself mentally to your ideal place of relaxation. I will then stop talking to you, and when you next hear my voice, one hour of time will have elapsed at this level of mind. My voice will not startle you; you will take a deep breath, relax, and go deeper.

1 - (pause) - 2 - (pause) - 3. Project yourself mentally to your ideal place of relaxation until you hear my voice again. Relax. (Reader: remain silent for about 30 seconds.) Relax. (pause) Take a deep breath and as you exhale, relax and go deeper. (pause)

RAPPORT

You will continue to listen to my voice; you will continue to follow the instructions at this level of the mind and any other level, including the outer conscious level. This is for your benefit; you desire it, and it is so.

Whenever you hear me mention the word, "Relax," all unnecessary movements and activities of your body, brain, and mind will cease immediately, and you will become completely passive and relaxed physically and mentally.

I may bring you out of this level or a deeper level than this by counting to you from 1 to 5. At the count of 5, your eyes will open; you will be wide awake, feeling fine and in perfect health.

I may bring you out of this level or a deeper level than this by touching your left shoulder three times. When you feel my hand touch your left shoulder for the third time, your eyes will open; you will be wide awake, feeling fine and in perfect health. And this is so.

GENIUS STATEMENTS

The difference between genius mentality and lay mentality is that geniuses use more of their minds and use them in a special manner.

You are now learning to use more of your mind and to use it in a special manner.

BENEFICIAL STATEMENTS

The following are beneficial statements that you may occasionally repeat while at these levels of the mind. Repeat mentally after me. (Reader: Read slowly.)

My increasing mental faculties are for serving humanity better.

Every day, in every way, I am getting better, better, and better.

Positive thoughts bring me benefits and advantages I desire.

I have full control and complete dominion over my sensing faculties at this level of the mind and any other level, including the outer conscious level. And this is so.

I will always maintain a perfectly healthy body and mind.

EFFECTIVE SENSORY PROJECTION STATEMENTS
Effective Sensory Projection statements for success.

I am now learning to attune my intelligence by developing my sensing faculties and to project them to any problem area so as to be aware of any actions taking place, if this is necessary and beneficial for humanity.

I an now learning to correct any problems I detect.

Negative thoughts and negative suggestions have no influence over me at any level of the mind.

POST EFFECTS—PREVIEW OF NEXT SESSION
You have practiced entering deep, healthy levels of mind. In your next session, you will enter a deeper, healthier level of mind, faster and easier than this time.

POST EFFECTS—STANDARD
Every time you function at these levels of the mind, you will receive beneficial effects physically and mentally.

You may use these levels of the mind to help yourself physically and mentally.

You may use these levels of the mind to help your loved ones, physically and mentally.

You may use these levels of the mind to help any human being who needs help, physically and mentally.

You will never use these levels of the mind to harm any human being; if this be your intention, you will not be able to function within these levels of the mind.

You will always use these levels of the mind in a constructive, creative manner for all that is good, honest, pure, clean, and positive. And this is so.

You will continue to strive to take part in constructive and creative activities to make this a better world to live in, so that when we move on, we shall have left behind a better world for those who follow. You will consider the whole of humanity, depending on their ages, as fathers or mothers, brothers or sisters, sons or daughters. You are a superior human being; you have greater understanding, compassion, and patience with others.

BRING OUT

In a moment, I am going to count from 1 to 5. At that moment, you will open your eyes, be wide awake, feeling fine and in perfect health, feeling better than before. You will have no ill effects whatsoever in your head, no headache; no ill effects whatsoever in your hearing, no buzzing in your ears; no ill effects whatsoever in your vision and eyesight; vision, eyesight, and hearing improve every time you function at these levels of mind.

1 - 2 - coming out slowly now.

3 - at the count of 5, you will open your eyes, be wide awake, feeling fine and in perfect health, feeling better than before, feeling the way you feel when you have slept the right amount of revitalizing, refreshing, relaxing, healthy sleep.

4—5 - eyes open, wide awake, feeling fine and in perfect health, feeling better than before.

Reader: Be sure to observe whether or not the person is wide awake. If in doubt, touch the person's left shoulder three times and while doing so say: "Wide awake, feeling fine and in perfect health. And this is so."

It is recommended that you practice staying at your Center for fifteen minutes a day to normalize all abnormal conditions of the body and mind.

Appendix B
40-Day Countdown System for Finding the Alpha Level

If you do not have someone to read the Silva Centering Exercise to you, or you don't want to record it yourself or memorize the steps and do it on your own, here is an alternative. It is not necessary to do this if you are using the Silva Centering Exercise.

This alternative method gives you a simple way to relax, and you will do better and better at this as you practice.

I will also give you a beneficial statement to help you.

This is how you train your mind:

You relax, lower your brain frequency to the alpha level, and practice using imagination and visualization.

Because you cannot read this book and relax simultaneously, it is necessary that you read the instructions first, so that you can put the book down, close your eyes, and follow them.

HERE ARE YOUR INSTRUCTIONS

1. Sit comfortably in a chair and close your eyes. Any position that is comfortable is a good position.
2. Take a deep breath, and as you exhale, relax your body.

3. Count backward slowly from 50 to 1.
4. Daydream about some peaceful place you know.
5. Say to yourself mentally, "Every day, in every way, I am getting better, better, and better."
6. Remind yourself mentally that when you open your eyes at the count of five, you will feel wide awake, better than before. When you reach the count of three, repeat this, and when you open your eyes, repeat it ("I am wide awake, feeling better than before").

You already know steps one and two. You do them daily when you get home in the evening. Add a countdown, a peaceful scene, and a beneficial statement to help you become better and better, and you are ready for a final count-out.

Read the instructions once more. Then put the book down and do it.

Learning to Function Consciously at the Alpha Level

As stated previously, you learn to enter the alpha level and function there with just one day of training when you attend the Silva UltraMind ESP Systems live training programs. You can use the audio recordings to learn to enter the alpha level within a few days with either a Silva home-study program or the free lessons at the SilvaNow.com web site. You can also record the Silva Centering Exercise in appendix A and listen to it, or have someone read it to you.

If you have already learned to enter the alpha level by one of those methods, you can skip the following instructions for practicing countdown-deepening exercises for the next forty days.

If not, then follow these instructions from José Silva:

When you enter sleep, you enter alpha. But you quickly go right through alpha to the deeper levels of theta and delta.

Throughout the night, your brain moves back and forth through alpha, theta, and delta, like the ebb and flow of the tide. These cycles last about ninety minutes.

In the morning, as you exit sleep, you come out through alpha, back into the faster beta frequencies that are associated with the outer-conscious levels.

Some authors advise that as you go to sleep at night, you think about your goals. That way, you get a little bit of alpha time for programming. The only trouble is, you have a tendency to fall asleep.

For now, I just want you to practice a simple exercise that will help you learn to enter and stay at the alpha level. Then, in 40 days, you will be ready to begin your programming.

In the meantime, I will give you some additional tasks that you can perform at the beta level that will help you prepare yourself so that you will be able to program more effectively at the alpha level when you are ready at the completion of the 40 days.

YOUR FIRST ASSIGNMENT

If you are using the Silva Centering Exercise (also known as the Long Relaxation Exercise) on the SilvaNow.com web site to enter the alpha level, then you can skip the information that follows.

If you do not want to use the recording of the Silva Centering Exercise, and you have not attended a Silva seminar or used one of our home-study courses to learn to enter the alpha level, then you will need to follow the instructions here to learn to enter the alpha level on your own.

Here Is Your Alpha Exercise:

Practice this exercise in the morning when you first wake up. Since your brain is starting to shift from alpha to beta when you first wake up, you will not have a tendency to fall asleep when you enter alpha.

Here are the steps to take:

1. When you awake tomorrow morning, go to the bathroom if you have to, then go back to bed. Set your alarm clock to ring in fifteen minutes, just in case you do fall asleep again.
2. Close your eyes and turn them slightly upward toward your eyebrows (about 20 degrees). Research shows that this produces more alpha brainwave activity.

3. Count backward slowly from 100 to one. Do this silently; that is, do it mentally to yourself. Wait about one second between numbers.

4. When you reach the count of one, hold a mental picture of yourself as a success. An easy way to do this is to recall the most recent time when you were 100 percent successful. Recall the setting, where you were and what the scene looked like; recall what you did; and recall what you felt like.

5. Repeat mentally, "Every day in every way I am getting better, better, and better."

6. Then say to yourself, "I am going to count from one to five; when I reach the count of five, I will open my eyes, feeling fine and in perfect health, feeling better than before."

7. Begin to count. When you reach three, repeat, "When I reach the count of five, I will open my eyes, feeling fine and in perfect health, feeling better than before."

8. Continue your count to four and five. At the count of five, open your eyes and tell yourself mentally, "I am wide awake, feeling fine and in perfect health, feeling better than before. And this is so."

These Eight Steps are Really Only Three

Go over each of these eight steps so that you understand the purpose while at the same time become more familiar with the sequence.

1. The mind cannot relax deeply if the body is not relaxed. It is better to go to the bathroom and permit your body to enjoy full comfort. Also, when you first awake, you may not be fully awake. Going to the bathroom ensures your being fully awake. But, in case you are still not awake enough to stay awake, set your alarm clock to ring in 15 minutes so you do not risk being late on your daily schedule. Sit in a comfortable position.

2. Research has shown that when a person turns the eyes up about 20 degrees, it triggers more alpha rhythm in the brain and also causes more right-brain activity. Later,

when we do our mental picturing, it will be with your eyes turned upward at this angle. Meanwhile, it is a simple way to encourage alpha brainwave activity. You might want to think of the way you look up at the screen in a movie theater, a comfortable upward angle.

3. Counting backward is relaxing. Counting forward is activating. 1-2-3 is like "get ready, get set, go!" 3-2-1 is pacifying. You are going nowhere except deeper within yourself.

4. Imagining yourself the way you want to be—while relaxed—creates the picture. Failures who relax and imagine themselves making mistakes and losing, frequently create a mental picture that brings about failure. You will do the opposite. Your mental picture is one of success, and it will create what you desire: success.

5. Words repeated mentally—while relaxed—create the concepts they stand for. Pictures and words program the mind to make it so.

6–8. These last three steps are simply counting to five to end your session. Counting upward activates you, but it's still good to give yourself "orders" to become activated at the count of five. Do this before you begin to count; do it again along the way; and again as you open your eyes.

Once you wake up tomorrow morning and prepare yourself for this exercise, it all works down to three steps:

Count backward from 100 to 1.

Imagine yourself successful.

Count yourself out 1 to 5, reminding yourself that you are wide awake, feeling fine, and in perfect health.

40 Days That Can Change Your Life for the Better

You know what to do tomorrow morning, but what about after that? Here is your training program:

Count backward from 100 to 1 for 10 mornings.

Count backward from 50 to 1 for 10 mornings.

Count backward from 25 to 1 for 10 mornings.

Count backward from 10 to 1 for 10 mornings.

After these 40 mornings of countdown relaxation practice, count backward only from 5 to 1 and begin to use your alpha level.

People have a tendency to be impatient, to want to move faster. Please resist this temptation and follow the instructions as written.

You must develop and acquire the ability to function consciously at alpha before the mental techniques will work properly for you. You must master the fundamentals first. We've been researching this field since 1944, longer than anyone else, and the techniques we have developed have helped millions of people worldwide to enjoy greater success and happiness, so please follow these simple instructions.

Appendix C
Conditioning Cycle to Use When Impressing Formulas

Reader: Read this Entry to the Alpha Level first, then move ahead to the formula or formulas you want to impress. After reading the formulas move ahead to the Preview, Post Effects, and Bringout.

Remember: Do not read the headings out loud.

Entry to the Alpha Level

We will start this exercise with the 3 to 1 method.

Find a comfortable position, close your eyes, take a deep breath and while exhaling, mentally repeat and visualize the number 3 three times. (pause)

Take another deep breath and while exhaling, mentally repeat and visualize the number 2 three times. (pause)

Take another deep breath and while exhaling, mentally repeat and visualize the number 1 three times. (pause)

You are now at level 1, the basic plane level that you are learning to use for a purpose, any purpose you desire.

Deepening (routine cycle)

To help you enter a deeper, healthier level of mind, I am going to count from 10 to 1. On each descending number, you will feel yourself going deeper and you will enter a deeper, healthier level of mind.

10 - 9 - Feel going deeper,

8 - 7 -

6 - deeper and deeper,

5—4 -

3 - deeper and deeper,

2 - 1

You are now at a deeper, healthier level of mind, deeper than before.

You may enter a deeper, healthier level of mind by simply relaxing your eyelids. Relax your eyelids. (pause) Feel how relaxed they are. (pause) Allow this feeling of relaxation to flow slowly downward throughout your body, all the way down to your toes. (pause)

It is a wonderful feeling to be deeply relaxed, a very healthy state of being.

To help you enter a deeper, healthier level of mind, I am going to count from 1 to 3. At that moment, you will project yourself mentally to your ideal place of relaxation. I will then stop talking to you, and when you next hear my voice, one hour of time will have elapsed at this level of mind. My voice will not startle you; you will take a deep breath, relax, and go deeper.

1 - (pause) - 2 - (pause) - 3. Project yourself mentally to your ideal place of relaxation until you hear my voice again. Relax. (Reader: remain silent for about 30 seconds.)

Relax. (pause) Take a deep breath and as you exhale, relax and go deeper. (pause)

Rapport

You will continue to listen to my voice; you will continue to follow the instructions at this level of the mind and any other level, including the outer conscious level. This is for your benefit; you desire it, and it is so.

Whenever you mentally or verbally mention the word, "Relax," all unnecessary movements and activities of your body, brain, and mind will cease immediately, and you will become completely passive and relaxed physically and mentally.

I may bring you out of this level or a deeper level than this by counting to you from 1 to 5. At the count of 5, your eyes will open; you will be wide awake, feeling fine and in perfect health.

Genius Statements

The difference between genius mentality and lay mentality is that geniuses use more of their minds and use them in a special manner.

You are now learning to use more of your mind and to use it in a special manner.

Beneficial Statements

The following are beneficial statements that you may occasionally repeat while at these levels of the mind. Repeat mentally after me. (Reader: Read slowly.)

My increasing mental faculties are for serving humanity better.

Every day, in every way, I am getting better, better, and better.

Positive thoughts bring me benefits and advantages I desire.

I have full control and complete dominion over my sensing faculties at this level of the mind and any other level, including the outer conscious level. And this is so.

Protective Statements

The following statements are for your protection.

This is MIND CONTROL, your own self-MIND CONTROL. You are always in control. You may accept or reject anything I say, any time, at any level of the mind. You are always in control.

Preventive Statements

The following preventive statements are for your better health. Keep in mind that from now on, I will occasionally be speaking in your place. (Read slowly.)

I will never learn to develop physically or mentally, mental disorders nor psychosomatic or functional ailments or diseases.

I will never learn to develop physically or mentally, a dependence on drugs or alcohol.

Negative thoughts and negative suggestions have no influence over me at any level of the mind.

I will always maintain a perfectly healthy body and mind.

Mental Projection Statements

Mental projection statements for success.

I am now learning to attune my intelligence by developing my sensing faculties, and to project them to any problem area, so as to become aware of any abnormalities, if this is necessary and beneficial for humanity.

I am now learning to apply corrective measures and to correct any abnormality I detect.

Negative thoughts and negative suggestions have no influence over me at any level of the mind.

Reader: At this time move ahead to the formula/s you want to impress and after reading the formula/s move ahead to the Preview/Post Effects/Bringout.

Formula-Type Techniques

(Scroll down the page to the Technique/s you want to program)

TO AWAKE CONTROL

Impression of information for your benefit, programming a formula-type technique.

To Awake Control, a formula-type technique that you can use to practice awakening without an alarm clock. This helps in your development of MIND CONTROL. To use To Awake Control, practice awakening without an alarm clock.

You can also learn to use Awake Control to remain awake longer when necessary.

Enter level 1 with the 3 to 1 method just before going to sleep.

At level 1 visualize a clock. Mentally move the hands of the clock to indicate the time that you want to awaken and tell yourself mentally, "This is the time I want to awaken and this is the time I am going to awaken."

Stay at level 1 and go to sleep from Level 1. You will awaken at your desired time and be wide awake, feeling fine and in perfect health.

AWAKE CONTROL

To use Awake Control for learning to remain awake longer.

Whenever you feel drowsy and sleepy, and don't want to feel drowsy and sleepy, especially when you are driving, pull to the side of the road, stop your motor, and enter level 1 with the 3 to 1 method.

At level 1 mentally tell yourself, "I am drowsy and sleepy; I don't want to be drowsy and sleepy; I want to be wide awake, feeling fine and in perfect health."

Then tell yourself mentally, "I am going to count from 1 to 5. At the count of 5 I will open my eyes, be wide awake, feeling fine and in perfect health. I will not be drowsy and sleepy; I will be wide awake."

Count mentally, slowly: 1, 2, 3; at the count of 3 mentally remind yourself that, at the count of 5, "I will open my eyes, be wide awake, feeling fine and in perfect health."

Then mentally count slowly to 4, then 5; at the count of 5 and with your eyes open, tell yourself mentally, "I am wide awake, feeling fine and in perfect health, feeling better than before."

DREAM CONTROL

Impression of information for your benefit, programming a formula-type technique.

Dream Control, a formula-type technique that you can use to practice remembering dreams. This helps in your development of Mind Control.

Dream Control step 1. To practice remembering a dream, you will enter level 1 with the 3 to 1 method. Once at level 1, you will mentally tell yourself, "I want to remember a dream, and I am going to remember a dream." You will then go to sleep from level 1.

You will awaken during the night or in the morning with a vivid recollection of a dream. Have paper and pencil ready to write it down. When you are satisfied that Dream Control step 1 is responding, then start with Dream Control step 2.

Dream Control step 2. To practice remembering dreams, you will enter level 1 with the 3 to 1 method. Once at level 1, mentally tell yourself, "I want to remember my dreams, and I am going to remember my dreams." You will then go to sleep from level 1.

You will awaken several times during the night and in the morning with vivid recollections of dreams. Have paper and pencil ready to write them down. When you are satisfied that Dream Control step 2 is responding, then start with Dream Control step 3.

Dream Control step 3. To practice generating a dream that you can remember, understand, and use for problem solving. You will enter level 1 with the 3 to 1 method. Once at level 1, mentally tell yourself, "I want to have a dream that will contain information to solve the problem I have in mind." State the problem and add, "I will have such a dream, remember it, and understand it." You will then go to sleep from level 1.

You may awaken during the night with a vivid recollection of the desired dream, or you may awaken in the morning with a vivid recollection of such a dream. You will have this dream, remember it, and understand it.

HEADACHE CONTROL

Impression of information for your benefit, programming a formula-type technique.

Headache Control, a formula-type technique that you can use to practice stopping headaches. Tension type headaches, 1 application; migraine type headaches, 3 applications, 5 minutes apart.

Headache Control, a formula-type technique that you can use to practice stopping tension type headaches. If you have a tension type headache, enter level 1 with the 3 to 1 method. Once at level 1 mentally tell yourself, "I have a headache; I feel a headache; I don't want to have a headache; I don't want to feel a headache.

"I am going to count from 1 to 5 and at the count of 5, I will open my eyes, be wide awake, feeling fine and in perfect health. I will then have no headache. I will then feel no headache."

You will then count slowly from 1 to 2, then to 3, and at the count of 3 you will remind yourself mentally that, "At the count of 5, I will open my eyes, be wide awake, feeling fine and in perfect health; I will then have no discomfort in my head; I will then feel no discomfort in my head."

Notice that we have made a change at level 3, from ache to discomfort. We left the ache behind. You will then proceed to mentally count slowly to 4, then to 5, and at the count of 5, and with your eyes open, you will say to yourself mentally, "I am wide awake, feeling fine and in perfect health. I have no discomfort in my head. I feel no discomfort in my head. And this is so."

Headache Control, a formula-type technique that you can use to practice stopping the migraine type headache. If you have a migraine headache, enter level 1 with the 3 to 1 method. Once at level 1 go through the same procedure as in the tension type headache application, but use 3 applications, 5 minutes apart.

You will note that the first application will have reduced the discomfort by a certain amount. Wait five minutes, then apply the second application. The second application will take care of a greater amount of the discomfort. Wait five more minutes and apply the third application. With the third application all of the discomfort will have disappeared.

From then on, when symptoms appear, one application will take care of the migraine problem. As you continue to take care of this problem in this manner, the symptoms will appear less frequently, until the body forgets how to cause them, bringing to an end the migraine problem without the use of drugs. And this is so.

To correct health problems, controls are applied under a doctor's supervision.

MENTAL SCREEN

We will now impress new information for your benefit, programming the Mental Screen.

To locate your Mental Screen, begin with your eyes closed, turned slightly upward from the horizontal plane of sight, at an angle of approximately 20 degrees.

The area that you perceive with your mind is your mental screen.

Without using your eyelids as screens, sense your Mental Screen to be out, away from your body.

To improve the use of your Mental Screen, project images or mental pictures onto the screen, especially images having color. Concentrate on mentally sensing and visualizing true color.

3-FINGERS TECHNIQUE

We will now impress information for your benefit, programming a formula-type technique, the Three Fingers Technique. At this time, bring together the tips of the first two fingers and thumb of either hand. (pause)

By bringing together the tips of the first two fingers and thumb of either hand, your mind adjusts to a deeper level of awareness for stronger programming.

Stronger programming of information results in easier recall, producing a better memory.

To read a lesson, enter level 1 with the use of the 3 to 1 method. Tell yourself mentally that you are going to count from 1 to 3 and at the count of 3 you will open your eyes and read the lesson. Mention the lesson title, and subject.

Add: "Noises will not distract me, but will help me to concentrate. I will have superior concentration and understanding." Count from 1 to 3, open your eyes and read the lesson.

When you have read the lesson, once again enter level 1 with the 3 to 1 method. Tell yourself mentally, "I will recall the lesson I have just read (mention title and subject) anytime in the future with the use of the Three Fingers Technique."

To hear a lecturer, enter level 1 with the 3 to 1 method, and tell yourself mentally that you are going to hear a lecture and mention the title, subject, and lecturer's name.

Tell yourself that you are going to use the Three Fingers Technique. Keep your eyes open during the lecture.

Tell yourself that noises will not distract you, but will help you to concentrate; that you will have superior concentration and understanding; and that you will recall the lecture (mention title, subject, and lecturer's name) anytime in the future with the use of the Three Fingers Technique.

For test taking with the Three Fingers Technique, follow the 3-cycle method.

First: Read your test questions the way you always do, but do not stay too long on any of them. If you have a ready answer put it down; if not, skip that question and move to the next one.

Second: Use the Three Fingers Technique, and do as in the first cycle, but stay a little longer on the unanswered question. When an answer comes, put it down; if not, skip that question and move to the next one.

Third: Use the Three Fingers Technique, read the unanswered question, and if still no answer comes, close your eyes, turn them slightly upward, visualize or imagine your professor on your mental screen and ask for the answer. Then clear your mind, and start thinking again to figure out the answer. The answer that comes, is your professor's. Write it down. Do not turn in a blank paper.

3-SCENES TECHNIQUE

We will now impress and program the 3-Scenes Technique, a technique that you can use to help you implement your decisions and the guidance that you receive.

When you desire to use the 3 Scenes Technique, go to your center with the 3 to 1 method. Create and project onto your mental screen, directly in front of you, using visualization, an image of the existing situation.

Recall details of what the situation looks like in this first scene. Make a good study of the existing situation so you are completely aware of all aspects of it.

If you have programmed for this project previously, then take into account any changes that have taken place since your most recent programming session.

After making a good study of the existing situation, then shift your awareness to your left, approximately 15 degrees. In a second scene, to the left of the first scene, use imagination to mentally picture yourself taking action and doing something to implement your decisions, and to follow the guidance you have received, and imagine the desired changes beginning to take place.

Now in a third scene, another 15 degrees farther to your left, use your imagination to create and project an image of the situation the way you desire for it to end up. Imagine many people benefiting. The more people who benefit, the better.

Anytime in the future when you think of this project, visualize (recall) the image that you created of the desired end result in the third scene.

DECISION MAKING

Here is how to proceed when you need to analyze a project, and make decisions about it, at the optimal time to obtain the best results:

At night before you go to sleep, enter your level using the 3 to 1 Method. Once at your level, program yourself to awaken automatically at the best time, when all conditions are optimal to obtain the best results on the project you have in mind. Stay at your level and go to sleep from Level 1.

When you awaken automatically, take it for granted that all conditions are optimal. Assume a sitting position, head lowered approximately 20 degrees, and eyes turned upward approximately 20 degrees relative to your face, re-enter your level, and work on your project.

When there are two options and you desire to know which is better, you bring both to mind: Option Number 1 and Option Number 2.

Then clear your mind from thinking about the project, and think of something else that is not relevant to the project at all, such as: I need to buy a new pair of shoes tomorrow.

Then immediately start thinking again about the two options. The one that enters your mind first is usually the right one, and the one you should go for.

When there are more than two options, work two at a time using the same procedure. The one that comes to mind first can be compared to a third option.

Always retain the option that enters your mind first, until you have dismissed all except one option.

That option is the best one.

WEIGHT AND HABIT CONTROL

We will now impress and program Habit Control, formula-type techniques you can use to control the eating and smoking habits.

Formula type techniques for Habit Control, Weight. When you desire to reduce weight, enter level 1 by the use of the 3 to 1 method and analyze your weight problem. At level 1, mentally mark a big red "No" over every item of food considered to be causing the problem.

Program yourself that hunger between meals will vanish by eating a piece of carrot, celery, or apple, or some such helpful foods, or by taking three deep breaths.

Program yourself to leave something on your plate, realizing that you do not need all the food you have taken. Program yourself not to eat dessert.

Visualize yourself in the Mirror of the Mind or the 3-Scenes Technique the way you are now. Then in the solution scene, stamp what you want to weigh on one corner and the size of suit or dress you want to wear on the other corner, and imagine yourself at your ideal weight and size.

Thereafter, when you think of your weight, always visualize the image you have created of yourself the way you want to be in the solution scene.

Whenever you are eating, visualize the image you have created of yourself the way you want to look and visualize your desired weight stamped on one corner and your desired size of clothing stamped on the other corner of the solution screen.

If you desire to gain weight, eat those foods that you sense at level 1 will help you gain; eat slowly, savoring every bite. Learn to improve your taste and smell by concentrating on your food as you eat.

Visualize yourself the way you want to be; do this every time you think of your weight.

Formula-type techniques for Habit Control, Smoking. Whenever you wish to reduce or discontinue cigarette smoking, enter level 1 by the 3 to 1 method, and at level 1 analyze the problem.

Determine when you smoke the first cigarette of the day, then program yourself at level 1 to smoke it one hour later. When that becomes effective, program yourself to smoke the first cigarette still one hour later, and continue to make these changes by programming at level 1, until you smoke only a few cigarettes a day; it will then be a simple matter to stop smoking altogether.

You can also program yourself to smoke only 1 cigarette per hour on the hour; when this has become effective, then program yourself to smoke only on the even hours. After this has taken effect it will be a simple matter to stop smoking completely.

You can also program yourself at level 1 to stop smoking altogether 30 days from the date of your initial programming.

You can mark a date on a calendar, thirty days from the present and tell yourself mentally that on this date you will stop smoking, and never smoke again in your life. Reinforce this programming for this purpose at level 1 daily, and this will be so.

Tips that help in your programming at level 1 to stop smoking:

Change brands frequently.

Do not inhale the cigarette smoke.

Program that 3 deep breaths will stop the immediate desire to smoke.

Stop smoking for the sake of your loved ones.

JOSÉ SILVA'S MENTALVIDEO TECHNIQUE

Whenever you need to solve a problem, make a decision, or obtain guidance with the MentalVideo Technique, proceed in the following manner:

At beta, with your eyes open, mentally create, with visualization, a MentalVideo of a problem, or the existing situation. Include everything that belongs to the animate matter kingdom. Animate matter means everything that contains life.

After you have completed the MentalVideo of the problem, use visualization to review it at beta, with your eyes closed.

Later, when you are in bed and ready to go to sleep, go to your center with the 3 to 1 method. Once you are at your center, review the MentalVideo that you created of the problem, or the existing situation, when you were at the beta level.

After you have reviewed the problem, mentally convert the problem into a project. Then create, with imagination, a MentalVideo of the solution.

The MentalVideo of the solution should contain a step-by-step procedure of how you desire the project to be resolved.

After both of the MentalVideos have been completed, go to sleep with the intention of delivering the MentalVideos to your tutor while you sleep. Take for granted that the delivery will be made.

During the next three days, look for indications that point to the solution. Every time you think of the project, think of the solution that you created in the MentalVideo, in a past tense sense.

Appendix D

How to Develop Your Natural God-Given ESP

ESP is beyond the scope of this book. You can learn and start using your EPS in just a few days time with expert guidance from a Silva ESP Instructor, either in a live seminar or webinar, or in one of our Online Learning Courses. Courses are also available to download.

Visit the SilvaESP.com website for more information. If you want to get started immediately with our recorded courses, when you check out enter the coupon code MM15 for a special discount.

Meanwhile you can use the MentalVideo. It works best if you analyze your problem at the alpha level, but will work even if you don't know how to function at the alpha level.

Appendix E
Resources and Contact Information

FREE INTRODUCTORY LESSONS AND VIDEOS
Visit the SilvaNow.com website.

SPECIAL OFFER
As an owner of this book, you qualify for a special discount on genuine authentic José Silva home study courses and workshops. Visit SilvaESP.com and submit the coupon code MM15 when you check out.

INFORMATION ABOUT SILVA COURSES AND PRODUCTS
Visit the SilvaESP.com website.

HELP FOR HEALTH PROBLEMS
If you have a health problem and want Silva ESP graduates to program for you, or if you are a Silva ESP graduate and want health cases to work, please visit the SilvaHealthCases.com website.

CPSIA information can be obtained
at www.ICGtesting.com
Printed in the USA
JSHW010502300623
43772JS00001B/1

9 781722 506469